COLLECTED WORKS OF HARRY G. JOHNSON

THE ECONOMICS OF EXCHANGE RATES

THE ECONOMICS OF EXCHANGE RATES

Selected Studies

Edited by
JACOB A. FRENKEL
AND
HARRY G. JOHNSON

Volume 8

Routledge
Taylor & Francis Group

LONDON AND NEW YORK

First published in 1978

This edition first published in 2013
by Routledge
2 Park Square, Milton Park, Abingdon, Oxon, OX14 4RN

Simultaneously published in the USA and Canada
by Routledge
711 Third Avenue, New York, NY 10017

Routledge is an imprint of the Taylor & Francis Group, an informa business

British Library Cataloguing in Publication Data
A catalogue record for this book is available from the British Library

ISBN: 978-0-415-82549-8 (Set) (hbk)
ISBN: 978-0-203-49713-5 (Set) (ebk)
ISBN: 978-0-415-83897-9 (Volume 8) (hbk)
ISBN: 978-1-032-05107-9 (Volume 8) (pbk)
ISBN: 978-0-203-77617-9 (Volume 8) (ebk)

Publisher's Note
The publisher has gone to great lengths to ensure the quality of this reprint but
points out that some imperfections in the original copies may be apparent.

Disclaimer
The publisher has made every effort to trace copyright holders and would
welcome correspondence from those they have been unable to trace.

The Economics of Exchange Rates: Selected Studies

Edited by
Jacob A. Frenkel
UNIVERSITY OF CHICAGO
Harry G. Johnson
FORMERLY UNIVERSITY OF CHICAGO

PREFACE

The evolution of the international monetary system into the regime of flexible exchange rates (or more precisely a regime of managed float) has stimulated a renewed interest in the economics of exchange rates. The renewed interest has led to new developments in the economic theory and the empirical analysis of exchange rates. This book contains a series of studies dealing with the modern approach to the analysis of exchange-rate determination as well as with the various characteristics of the foreign-exchange market.

The main theme of the modern view of exchange-rate determination emphasizes that the exchange rate, being a relative price of two national monies, is determined primarily by the relative supplies and demands for these monies. Since the demands for the various national monies depends on expectations, incomes, and rates of return as well as on other considerations that are relevant for portfolio choice, the new approach is being referred to as an asset-market approach to the determination of exchange rates. The implication of this approach is that an analysis of exchange rates should not be conducted in the partial framework of the foreign trade sector; rather, it should be integrated into the general framework of macroeconomics. This is the central theoretical insight that runs through the various chapters of the book.

A second specific feature that is common to most of the chapters is the integration of theoretical developments with sophisticated empirical testing using modern econometric techniques. The methodological emphasis on the combination of theoretical and empirical research departs from much of the literature in the field of international economics and reflects our preference for a research methodology which integrates theory with empirical work.

This book is a logical sequel to *The Monetary Approach to the Balance of Payments* (London: Allen & Unwin, and Toronto: University of Toronto Press, 1976; paperback edition, 1977) which we have edited previously. Basically, the asset-market approach to the analysis of exchange rates may be viewed as the counterpart to the monetary approach to the balance of payments. These approaches emphasize the role of money and other assets in determining the balance of payments when the exchange rate is pegged, and in determining the exchange rate when it is flexible. Like the previous book, the items included have been chosen from the work of economists associated with the Workshop in International Economics at the University of Chicago which has been one of the important centers in which the new approach has been developed. But, as will be documented in the first chapter, the intellectual origins of the new approach can be traced back to the economic writings of the nineteenth and the early part of the twentieth centuries. Furthermore, it is necessary to acknowledge that fundamentally the same analytical approach has been developed contemporaneously by economists associated with other universities and institutions (but with a somewhat lesser emphasis on applying sophisticated empirical methods). Among the other universities and institutions are Columbia University, Massachusetts Institute of Technology, Princeton University, the Graduate Institute for International Studies in Geneva, the Institute for International Economic Studies at the University of Stockholm, the Board of Governors of the Federal Reserve System and the International Monetary Fund, to mention a few. Several of the original contributors to the new approach were presented in the summer of 1975 at a conference on "Flexible Exchange Rates and Stabilization Policy" held at Saltsjöbaden, Stockholm and organized by the Institute for International Economic Studies at the University of Stockholm, and the proceedings of that conference appeared in the *Scandinavian Journal of Economics*, Vol. 78, No. 2, 1976. We wish therefore to emphasize that there is no intention whatsoever to claim exclusivity for economists associated with the University of Chicago in the development of the new approach.

In the first chapter Frenkel develops a monetary view of the determinants of the exchange rate. He first traces some of the doctrinal origins of the approaches to the analysis of exchange-rate determination dealing with the purchasing-power parity doctrine and with the role of expectations, and then outlines a simple version of the new approach emphasizing considerations which relate to the demand for money and to the interest parity theory. The second part of the chapter tests empirically some of the implications of the monetary approach. The empirical work examines the relationship between money and the exchange rate during the period of the German hyperinflation of the 1920s, and explores some aspects of the efficiency of the foreign-exchange market. Frenkel emphasizes the role of expectations and devises a direct observable measure thereof which builds on information contained in data from the forward market for foreign exchange. This measure is incorporated along with the money supply into the empirical study of the determinants of the exchange rate and is shown to be consistent with the central hypotheses of the monetary approach.

In the second chapter Dornbusch presents three perspectives on the determinants of exchange rates and their interaction with macroeconomic equilibrium and aggregate policies. The first perspective is a long-run view which characterizes exchange-rate determination in terms of monetary and real factors. The real factors include an explicit consideration of relative price structure. The second perspective is that of a short-run view of the exchange rate. This perspective emphasizes the role of expectations and asset market equilibrium. In the short run, monetary and price disturbances are not offset by matching changes in the exchange rate and, for that reason, are spread internationally. Dornbusch shows that flexible exchange rates do not provide insulation from foreign price disturbances as long as in the short run, prices or expectations are slow to adjust. Dornbusch distinguishes between commodities that are traded internationally and those that are not. This aggregation departs from the traditional Keynesian model in which all goods are traded and the economies are completely specialized in production. By distinguishing between tradable and nontradable goods he is able to break the identification of the exchange rate with the terms of trade as well as to introduce scope for a monetary interpretation of the exchange rate and to leave room for intersectoral considerations. The third perspective is a policy view wherein Dornbusch analyzes the effectiveness of aggregate macroeconomic policies and points out that, in the short run, nominal disturbances tend to be transmitted internationally. The chapter concludes with an analysis of a dual (a two-tier) exchange-rate system which distinguishes between the official exchange rate that is applicable to current-account transactions, and the free-market rate that applies to capital-account transactions. It is shown that fiscal policies under a dual exchange-rate system exert a stronger effect on interest rates and on the price level, and result in smaller changes in intersectoral relative prices.

In the third chapter Mussa extends the fundamental principles of the monetary approach to the balance of payments to a regime of floating rates in which the authorities intervene to control rate movements. Mussa forcefully makes four central points. First, the exchange rate is the relative price of different national monies rather than national outputs, and is determined principally by the demands and supplies of stocks of the different national monies. Second, exchange rates are strongly influenced by asset holders' expectations of future exchange rates and these expectations are influenced by beliefs concerning the future course of monetary policy. Third, "real" factors as well as monetary factors are important in determining the behavior of exchange rates. Furthermore, changes in exchange rates are frequently induced by real factors operating through monetary channels; and changes in exchange rates usually have real effects which might be of legitimate concern to government policy. Fourth, the problems of policy conflicts which exist under a system of fixed rates are reduced, but not eliminated, under a regime of controlled floating. The relaxation of the commitment to fixed parities allows greater independence in use of monetary and fiscal policies by introducing an additional policy instrument—the exchange rate, but the undesired real effects of exchange-rate changes limit the usefulness of this additional instrument. In an appendix Mussa develops the implications of "rational expectations" for the theory of exchange rates. These expectations reflect asset holders' knowledge of the structure of the economy, in particular, the structure of the stochastic process generating the demand for and the supply of money.

The first three chapters by Frenkel, Dornbusch, and Mussa are reprinted with permission from the *Scandinavian Journal of Economics,* Vol. 78, No. 2, 1976. The remaining eight chapters (which have not been published before) examine in detail (theoretically and empirically) some of the major building blocks and issues central to the new approach. Magee's chapter deals with aspects of efficiency of commodity and money markets by investigating the serial correlations of changes in the relative price of commodities and exchange rates. Magee shows that even when goods markets are just as efficient as foreign-exchange markets, empirical studies may show that changes in commodity prices are serially correlated while changes in exchange rates are not. The basic reason for this phenomenon is that commodity relative prices are frequently set at the time of contract, and thereby yield an implicit exchange rate that differs from the rate prevailing when the goods are later delivered and recorded in the international trade statistics. Magee goes on to simulate explicitly the spurious autocorrelation in the deviations from relative purchasing-power parity as determined by the frequency distribution of each product's order to delivery lags. His main point is that the use of actual transactions prices for many commodities may cause the price series to be spuriously autocorrelated.

The following two chapters by Bilson and by Hodrick apply sophisticated econometric techniques to test the major implications of the monetary approach to exchange-rate determination using data which pertain to the first few years of floating rates. In Bilson's analysis expectations play the crucial role in accounting for the apparent volatile behavior of exchange rates. Bilson constructs a simple model for a frictionless world in which all parity conditions are being met and then derives the interrelationship between the term structure of interest rates and forward exchange rates. He extends the analysis by introducing endogenous variations of real income by relating the deviations of output from its trend to unanticipated changes in the money supply. Hodrick's chapter applies advanced techniques of time-series analysis to test the empirical content of the monetary approach when applied to various series of exchange rates. He first estimates a stock equilibrium model using monthly data, and second, he examines the proportionate rates of change of the exchange rates in a dynamic framework. The dynamic framework enables Hodrick to apply tests of model adequacy regarding the exogeneity of the independent variables as well as regarding the choice of the functional form. Both Bilson's and Hodrick's results are shown to be consistent with the monetary approach.

The assumption underlying the previously described chapters has been the absence of foreign-exchange controls and restrictions. Blejer's chapter extends

the analytical framework of the monetary approach to situations in which
exchange restrictions lead to the development of a black market for foreign
exchange. The black-market exchange rate is taken to be determined freely
by market forces and is assumed to respond, as do the rate of domestic
inflation and the overall balance of payments, to monetary disequilibria. The
extended analytical framework is then tested against data on the black-market
rates for Brazil, Chile, and Colombia, and the results are shown to be consistent with the hypotheses. In particular, the black-market rate appears to be
affected significantly by current and one-year lagged excess supply of money.
Using his estimates, Blejer concludes that almost all *ex ante* excess flow supply
of money is transmitted to and reflected in the black-market exchange rate
within a period of two years.

The following two chapters by Levich and by Stockman apply analytical
and empirical research methods to an examination of various aspects of the
foreign-exchange market by studying the interrelationships between spot and
forward-exchange rates. Levich examines in great detail two hypotheses concerning the efficiency of the foreign-exchange market. The first hypothesis is
that current exchange rates reflect expectations concerning the future values
of these exchange rates. It follows that market prices can be used to generate
accurate and consistent forecasts of the future values of exchange rates. The
second hypothesis is that these forecasts cannot be used to earn unusual profits
since the forecasts are based on information that is publicly available. Levich
tests these two hypotheses using weekly data for the period 1967-75 for nine
industrial countries and the United States. He shows that the data are consistent with both hypotheses and, in this sense, the foreign-exchange market
may be viewed as being efficient. The relationship between spot and forward-
exchange rates is examined further in the chapter by Stockman. It is shown
that, as an analytical matter, the forward-exchange rate can be expressed as
the sum of three components: the expected future spot rate, a risk premium,
and a convexity term. The expected future spot rate depends on the information that is available to the market. The risk premium depends on the
stochastic properties of variables such as money supplies, rates of return on
real investment, as well as on individuals' taste for risk. The convexity term
is shown to depend on these stochastic properties but not on the taste concerning risk. Stockman shows that, as an empirical matter, the convexity term
is negligible and that, for the exchange rates of the six currencies against the
U.S. dollar, only two have had nonzero risk premia. He concludes the chapter
by showing how the market revises its expectations with the availability of
new information and by providing empirical estimates of the speed by which
the market for foreign exchange incorporates new information.

The last two chapters by Ujiie and by Clements extend the monetary approach to the balance of payments in several important directions. Ujiie's
chapter incorporates into the standard framework a "reaction function" of the
monetary authorities. According to Ujiie's formulation, the balance of pay-

ments should be analyzed in terms of both the reactions of the private sector as well as those of the monetary authorities. He constructs a simple framework in which the private sector's behavior is characterized by a stock adjustment model which emphasizes considerations of portfolio equilibrium, while the monetary authority determines its behavior so as to attain the desired level of international reserves. The two behavioral relationships are estimated using data for Japan which provides a good example of monetary policy that has been assigned to external objectives. Clements' chapter departs from previous studies of the monetary approach to the balance of payments by analyzing the effects of a change in the exchange rate on trade flows and on domestic prices within a novel, fully specified, multisector econometric model of the open economy. Clements constructs a general equilibrium model in a framework which distinguishes among three classes of commodities: exportables, importables, and nontraded goods. Clements' model has three fundamental building blocks consisting of (i) a system of demand equations for the three commodities that is derived from utility maximization, (ii) a system of supply equations that is derived from profit maximization, and (iii) the income identity and the absorption equation. Clements uses this model to study the effects of a devaluation by executing a simulation experiment. The results indicate that devaluation does have substantial real effects and that these effects tend to last for a relatively long period.

Harry G. Johnson died on May 8, 1977 just after the manuscript of this book reached its final stage. The contributors to this book who have all been Harry Johnson's students and colleagues dedicate the volume to his memory.

Chicago, Illinois   J. A. F.
April 1978

CONTENTS

Chapter 1
A MONETARY APPROACH TO THE EXCHANGE RATE: DOCTRINAL
ASPECTS AND EMPIRICAL EVIDENCE
by Jacob A. Frenkel

Abstract	1
Introduction	2
I	
A Doctrinal Perspective to Exchange Rate Determination	3
II	
Empirical Evidence: A Reexamination of the German Hyperinflation	6
Appendix: Data Sources	22

Chapter 2
THE THEORY OF FLEXIBLE EXCHANGE RATE REGIMES AND
MACROECONOMIC POLICY
by Rudiger Dornbusch

Abstract	27
I	
A General View of Exchange Rate Determinants	28
II	
Short-Run Determination of Exchange Rates	32

III
Speculation, Macroeconomic Policies, and the Transmission of Disturbances   35

IV
Speculative Disturbances and Dual Exchange Rates   40

Concluding Remarks   43

Appendix   43

Chapter 3
THE EXCHANGE RATE, THE BALANCE OF PAYMENTS, AND
MONETARY AND FISCAL POLICY UNDER A REGIME OF
CONTROLLED FLOATING
by Michael Mussa

Abstract   47

Introduction   47

I
A Monetary Approach to Exchange Rate Theory   48

II
The Exchange Rate as the Relative Price of Two Monies   50

III
Expectations and Exchange Rates   53

IV
Real Causes and Effects   54

V
Policy Conflict and Policy Coordination   56

Appendix   58

Chapter 4
CONTRACTING AND SPURIOUS DEVIATIONS FROM PURCHASING-
POWER PARITY
by Stephen P. Magee

I
The Financial Market   68

II
Efficient Goods Market Behavior   69

III
Spurious Inefficiency in Markets for Internationally Traded Goods   70

Chapter 5
RATIONAL EXPECTATIONS AND THE EXCHANGE RATE
by John F. O. Bilson

I
Introduction   75

II
The Money Supply Process   79

III
The Real Income Process   80

IV
The Final Exchange Rate Equation   82

V
The Stability of the Exchange Rate   82

VI
The Term Structure of the Forward Premium   83

VII
Extensions   84

VIII
Empirical Tests of the Model   84

IX
An Alternative Formulation   89

X
Conclusion   93

Chapter 6
AN EMPIRICAL ANALYSIS OF THE MONETARY APPROACH TO THE
DETERMINATION OF THE EXCHANGE RATE
by Robert J. Hodrick

I
Introduction   97

II
Equilibrium Determination of the Exchange Rate   98

III
Tests with Variables in the Levels of Natural Logarithms   101

IV
Tests using Rates of Change of Variables   105

V
Conclusions   113

Chapter 7
EXCHANGE RESTRICTIONS AND THE MONETARY APPROACH TO THE EXCHANGE RATE
by Mario I. Blejer

I
Introduction 117

II
The Model 118

III
Empirical Results 124

IV
Summary 127

Chapter 8
TESTS OF FORECASTING MODELS AND MARKET EFFICIENCY IN THE INTERNATIONAL MONEY MARKET
by Richard M. Levich

I
Introduction 129

II
Statistical Methods and Exchange-Rate Forecasting 130

III
Statistical Properties of Forecast Errors 134

IV
Forecasts and Risky Investment Opportunities 152

V
Summary and Conclusions 156

Chapter 9
RISK, INFORMATION, AND FORWARD EXCHANGE RATES
by Alan C. Stockman

Introduction 159

I
Theoretical Analysis 160

II
Empirical Results 166

III
New Information in the Foreign Exchange Market 173

IV
Conclusions   176

Chapter 10
A STOCK ADJUSTMENT APPROACH TO MONETARY POLICY AND
THE BALANCE OF PAYMENTS
by Junichi Ujiie

I
Introduction   179
II
The Theoretical Framework   180
III
Empirical Results   185
IV
Conclusions   191

Chapter 11
DEVALUATION IN AN EMPIRICAL GENERAL EQUILIBRIUM MODEL
by Kenneth W. Clements

I
Introduction   193
II
Overview of the Model and Its Empirical Implementation   194
III
Devaluation Mechanisms   197
IV
Simulation Results   198
V
Concluding Comments   202
Appendix   203

Author Index   213

A MONETARY APPROACH TO THE EXCHANGE RATE: DOCTRINAL ASPECTS AND EMPIRICAL EVIDENCE

JACOB A. FRENKEL

University of Chicago, Illinois,
USA and Tel-Aviv University, Tel-Aviv, Israel

What, then, has determined and will determine the value of the Franc? First, the quantity, present and prospective, of the francs in circulation. Second, the amount of purchasing power which it suits the public to hold in that shape.

Keynes (Introduction to French edition, 1924, xviii).

ABSTRACT

This paper deals with the determinants of the exchange rate and develops a monetary view (or more generally, an asset view) of exchange rate determination. The first part traces some of the doctrinal origins of approaches to the analysis of equilibrium exchange rates. The second part examines some of the empirical hypotheses of the monetary approach as well as some features of the efficiency of the foreign exchange markets. Special emphasis is given to the role of expectations in exchange rate determination and a direct observable measure of expectations is proposed. The direct measure of expectations builds on the information that is contained in data from the forward market for foreign exchange. The empirical results are shown to be consistent with the hypotheses of the monetary approach.

Reprinted by permission from *Scandinavian Journal of Economics* 78, No. 2 (May, 1976): 200–224.

The author is indebted to John Bilson for comments, suggestions and efficient research assistance. In revising the paper the author has benefited from helpful assistance from R. W. Banz and useful suggestions by W. H. Branson, K. W. Clements, R. Dornbusch, S. Fischer, R. J. Gordon, H. G. Johnson, M. Parkin, D. Patinkin and L. G. Telser. Financial support was provided by a grant from the Ford Foundation.

INTRODUCTION

This paper deals with the determinants of the exchange rate. The approach that is taken reflects the current revival of a monetary view, or more generally an asset view, of the role of the rates of exchange.[1] Basically, the monetary approach to the exchange rate may be viewed as a dual relationship to the monetary approach to the balance of payments. These approaches emphasize the role of money and other assets in determining the balance of payments when the exchange rate is pegged, and in determining the exchange rate when it is flexible.

Being a relative price of two assets (moneys), the equilibrium exchange rate is attained when the existing *stocks* of the two moneys are willingly held. It is reasonable, therefore, that a theory of the determination of the relative price of two moneys could be stated conveniently in terms of the supply of and the demand for these moneys.

The renewed emphasis on the role of the supply of and the demand for moneys and assets as stocks in contrast with the circular flow approach to the determination of the exchange rate (that gained popularity with the domination of the Keynesian revolution), revives the basic discussion of the Bullionist controversy which culminated in the early 1800's and led to the developments of the "Balance of Trade Theory" and the "Inflation Theory" of the determination of the exchange rate (Ricardo, 1811; Haberler, 1936; Viner, 1937). Reminiscence of that controversy can be traced to present times in the various discussions and interpretation of the purchasing power parity doctrine. It may be argued that the long experience with the gold standard and with the gold exchange standard may have led to the retrogression of the theory of flexible exchange rates (Wicksell, 1919, p. 231; Gregory, 1922, p. 80).[2]

The first part of the paper traces some of the doctrinal origins of approaches to exchange rate determination. Its purpose is to provide some perspective into the evolution of the theory.[3] The main emphasis of the paper lies in its second part where we examine some of the empirical hypotheses of the monetary approach. In that part we analyze the role of expectations, we describe a direct measure thereof, examine the efficiency of the foreign exchange market during the German hyperinflation; and provide some evidence which supports the asset view of exchange rate determination.

---

[1] This view has been forcefully emphasized by Dornbusch (1975, 1976, 1976a). See, too, Frenkel and Rodriguez (1975), Johnson (1975), Kouri (1975) and Mussa (1974, 1976). For an early incorporation of monetary considerations in exchange rate determination see Mundell (1968, 1971).

[2] It is of interest to note that the introduction of the "liquidity preference" schedule which emphasizes the role of asset markets and characterizes much of the Keynesian revolution in macroeconomic analysis of the closed economy, did not carry over to the popular versions of the Keynesian theories of the balance of payments. The Keynesian analysis of the balance of payments emphasizes the circular flow of income, the foreign trade multiplier and, in its popular version, ignores to a large extent the role of money and other assets. For a notable exception, see Metzler (1968).

[3] An analogous doctrinal perspective of the evolution of the monetary approach to the balance of payments under fixed exchange rates is contained in Frenkel & Johnson (1976) and Frenkel (1976). For a further analysis see Myhrman (1976).

I. A DOCTRINAL PERSPECTIVE TO EXCHANGE RATE DETERMINATION

I.1. The Purchasing Power Parity Doctrine:
The Nature of Equilibrium

The purchasing power parity doctrine (in its absolute version) states that the equilibrium exchange rate equals the ratio of domestic to foreign prices. The relative version of the theory relates changes in the exchange rate to changes in price ratios. Many of the controversies around that doctrine relate to the question of choice of proper indices to be used in computing the parity.[1] One extreme view argues that the proper price index should pertain to traded goods only (Angell, 1922; Bunting, 1939; Heckscher, 1930; Pigou, 1920; Viner, 1937), while according to the other extreme view the proper price index should cover the broadest range of commodities (Hawtrey, 1919, p. 109; Cassel, 1928, p. 33).[2]

Those who advocate the use of traded goods index emphasize the role of commodity arbitrage while those who advocate the broader price index emphasize the role of asset equilibrium as determining the rate of exchange. If the role of the exchange rate is to clear the money market by equating the purchasing power of the various currencies, then the relevant measure should be a consumer price index.[3] Proponents of this view reject the use of the wholesale price index since it gives an excessive weight to traded goods (Ellis, 1936, pp. 28–9; Haberler, 1945, p. 312 and 1961, pp. 49–50).

The two views differ fundamentally in the interpretation of the equilibrium exchange rate. The commodity arbitrage view goes even further in arguing that no aggregate price index is relevant and only individual commodity prices should be analyzed:

Foreign exchange rates have nothing to do with the wholesale commodity price level as such but only with individual prices (Ohlin, 1967, p. 290).

The equilibrium exchange rate reflects spatial arbitrage from which non-traded goods are excluded:

Patently, I cannot import cheap Italian haircuts nor can Niagara-Falls honeymoons be exported (Samuelson, 1964, p. 148).

The asset view takes it for granted that the operation of commodity arbitrage equates the prices of traded goods and emphasizes that if the doctrine only applies to traded goods, then:

the purchasing power parity doctrine presents but little interest ... (it) simply states that prices in terms of any given currency, of same commodity must be the same

---

[1] See Viner (1937) and Johnson (1968).

[2] It might be of interest to compare these discussions with those concerning the range of transactions and prices that is relevant for the quantity theory of money. The latter ranged from suggestions to include transactions in assets and prices of securities to suggestions to include only what is defined as national product.

[3] On the relevance of the consumer price index as a measure of the purchasing power of money see Marshall (1923, p. 30) and Keynes (1930, p. 54).

everywhere . . . Whereas its essence is the statement that exchange rates are the index of
the monetary conditions in the countries concerned (Bresciani-Turroni, 1934, p. 121).

In fact since the exchange rate links the purchasing power values of moneys in terms
of the broad definition of the price level, one may imagine a situation in which all
traded goods possess the same price, when expressed in common currency, but the
exchange rate is in disequilibrium:

The equilibrium to which the foreign exchange market tends is an equilibrium of the
price level . . . If the currency units of two countries be considered in terms of foreign
trade products only, then the rate of exchange between the two currency units will
approximate closely to the ratio of their purchasing power so calculated . . . But that
is not the condition of equilibrium . . . It is to the price level in general, of home trade
products as well as foreign trade products, that the rate of exchange must adjust
(Hawtrey, 1919, p. 109).

To completely divorce the determination of exchange rates from considerations
of commodity arbitrage, one could even go further in developing an argument for using
price indices of non-traded goods only. Such an argument was advanced by Graham:

Strictly interpreted then, prices of non-internationally traded commodities only
should be included in the indices on which purchasing power pars are based (Graham,
1930, p. 126, n. 44).

Further pursuit of that idea leads to the use of the price of the least traded
commodity—the wage rate parity—advocated by Rueff in 1926 (reproduced in Rueff,
1967), and similar views can also be found in Hawtrey (1919, p. 123) and Cassel
(1930, p. 144). The wage rate approach was extended to the concept of production
cost parities advocated by Hansen (1944, p. 182), Houthakker (1962, pp. 293–4)
and Friedman and Schwartz (1963, p. 62).

Whatever the price index used for computations of parities, the question remains
of distinguishing between an equilibrium relationship and a causal relationship. Most
authors recognized that prices and exchange rates are determined simultaneously. A
minority, however, argued that there exists a causal relationship between prices and
exchange rates. While Cassel (1921) claimed that the causality goes from prices to the
exchange rate, Einzig (1935, p. 40) claimed the opposite.

I.2. The Asset View

Since in general both prices and exchange rates are endogenous variables that are determined simultaneously, discussions of the link between them provide little insights into
the analysis of the determinants of the exchange rate. The original formulation of
Cassel (1916) was stated in terms of the relative quantities of money. The formulation
was then translated into a relationship between prices via an application of the quantity theory of money. Conceptually, however, it seems clear that the role of prices in
Cassel's computation of the equilibrium exchange rate serves only to proxy the underlying monetary conditions. The determination of exchange rates does not seem to rely,
directly or indirectly, on the operation of arbitrage in goods.

In retrospect it seems that the translation of the theory from a relationship between moneys into a relationship between prices—via the quantity theory of money—was counterproductive and led to a lack of emphasis on the fundamental determinants of the exchange rate and to an unnecessary amount of ambiguity and confusion. It is noteworthy that the originators of the theory (although not in its present name)—Wheatley (1803) and Ricardo—stressed the monetary nature of the issues involved as well as the irrelevance of commodity arbitrage as determining the equilibrium rate:

In speaking of the exchange and the comparative value of money in different countries, we must not in the least refer to the value of money estimated in commodities in either country. The exchange is never ascertained by estimating the comparative value of money in corn, cloth or any commodity whatever but by estimating the value of the currency of one country, in the currency of another (Ricardo, 1821, p. 128).

When considering moneys for the purpose of determining the exchange rate, the relevant concept is that of a stock rather than of a flow. These concepts were an integral part of monetary theory:

We may consequently think of the supply (of currency) as we think of the supply of houses, as being a stock rather than the annual produce . . . (and) of the demand for currency as being furnished by the ability and willingness of persons to hold currency (Cannan, 1921, pp. 453–4).

Indeed, as Dornbusch (1976a) puts it "The exchange rate is determined in the stock market". It is this conception of money as a stock that resulted in Keynes' perceptive statement that was quoted at the start of this paper. The asset view of exchange rate determination became the traditional view as witnessed by Joan Robinson:

The traditional view that the exchange value of a country's currency in any given situation depends upon the amount of it in existence is thus seen to be justified, provided that sufficient allowance is made for changes in the internal demand for money (Robinson, 1935–6, p. 229).

I.3. The Role of Expectations
A natural implication of the asset approach is the special role expectations play in determining the exchange rate. The demand for domestic and foreign moneys depends, like the demand for any other asset, on the expected rates of return. Thus it may be expected that current values of exchange rates incorporate the expectations of market participants concerning the future course of events. This notion can account therefore, for large changes in prices resulting from large changes in expectations. This was indeed the logical argument used by Mill (1862, p. 178) in accounting for the sharp change in the price of bills occurring with the news of Bonaparte's landing from Elba.

The specific role of expectations in determining the exchange rate has been also emphasized by Marshall (1888), Wicksell (1919, p. 236), Gregory (1922, p. 90) and Einzig (1935, p. 120). If the foreign exchange market is efficient—as many other asset markets appear to be—then current prices should reflect all available information.

Therefore, an expectation of monetary expansion should be reflected in the current spot exchange rate since asset holders will incorporate the anticipated reduction in the real rate of return on the currency in their pricing of the existing stocks. This notion was clearly stated by Cassel:

A continued inflation ... will naturally be discounted to a certain degree in the present rates of exchange (Cassel, 1928, pp. 25–26).

Similarly:

The international valuation of the currency will, then, generally show a tendency to anticipate events, so to speak, and becomes more an expression of the internal value the currency is expected to possess in a few months, or perhaps in a year's time (Cassel, 1930, pp. 149–150).

The empirical analysis in Section II will be concerned with details of the role of expectations in determining the exchange rate.

Prior to concluding this section it should be emphasized that its purpose has *not* been to argue that "It's all in Marshall". On the contrary, a rereading of the writings of some of the eminent classical and neo-classical economists reveals the great need for supplementing their general conceptions with a detailed analysis of the transmission mechanisms. On the other hand, however, it is important to gain perspective and to recognize that some of the general conceptions and framework of analysis have already been developed by earlier generations of economists. It is appropriate, therefore, to view the recent revival of the monetary approach as a natural evolution rather than a revolutionary change in views.[1]

II. EMPIRICAL EVIDENCE: A REEXAMINATION OF THE GERMAN HYPERINFLATION

The foregoing discussion contained a doctrinal perspective to the assets approach to the determination of exchange rates. In this section we develop further some of the theoretical aspects and reexamine the determinants of the exchange rate during the German hyperinflation in light of these considerations. That episode is of special interest since it provides an opportunity to examine the assets approach to a situation in which it is clear that the source of disturbances is monetary. Furthermore, during

---

[1] There are, of course, fundamental difficulties in defining the nature of the various junctions of intellectual understanding. As noted by H. G. Johnson: "the concept of revolution is difficult to transfer from its origins in politics to other fields of social science. Its essence is unexpected speed of change, and this requires a judgement of speed in the context of a longer perspective of historical change the choice of which is likely to be debatable in the extreme" (Johnson, 1971, p. 1).

A casual reading of many of the popular textbook versions of balance of payments theories suggests, however, that the conditions, outlined by Johnson, for a rapid propagation of a new theory may be satisfied: "the most helpful circumstances for a rapid propagation of a new and revolutionary theory is the existence of an established orthodoxy which is clearly inconsistent with the most salient facts of reality, and yet is sufficiently confident of its intellectual power to attempt to explain those facts, and in its efforts to do so exposes its incompetence in a ludicrous fashion" (Johnson, 1971, p. 3).

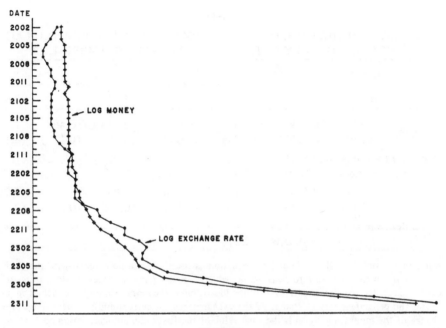

Figure 1

the hyperinflation domestic (German) influences on the exchange rate dominate those occurring in the rest of the world. It is therefore possible to examine the relationship between monetary variables and the exchange rate in isolation from other factors, at home and abroad, which in a more normal period would have to be considered.

II.1. Money and the Exchange Rate

Prior to a more elaborate analysis it may be instructive to examine the association between the German money stock and its relative price in terms of foreign exchange (i.e., the exchange rate). This association is shown in Fig. 1 which describes the time series of the monthly logarithms of the German money supply and the mark/dollar exchange rate for the period February 1920–November 1923 (data sources are outlined in the Appendix). As evident from Fig. 1 the two time series are closely related. A high supply of German marks is associated with its depreciation in terms of foreign exchange.

The relationship can be examined further by estimating a polynomial distributed lag of the effects of the money supply on the exchange rate. The estimates reported in Table 1 pertain to (i) the effects of current and lagged values of the money supply on the current *level* of the exchange rate and (ii) the effects of current and lagged values of the *rates of change* of the money supply on the current *rate of* change of the exchange rate. The estimates of the distributed lags for the equation of the rates of change reveal that the current rate of change of the exchange rate depends only on the current rate of monetary expansion. Furthermore, an acceleration of the rate of monetary expansion induces an equi-proportionate contemporaneous acceleration in

Table 1

MONEY AND THE EXCHANGE RATE: POLYNOMIAL DISTRIBUTED LAG
MODEL. MONTHLY DATA: FEBRUARY 1920–NOVEMBER 1923

Lag structure						
0	1	2	3	4	5	Sum
1.032	− 0.019	− 0.248	− 0.009	0.348	0.468	1.572
(0.140)	(0.099)	(0.127)	(0.082)	(0.107)	(0.125)	(0.177)

Dependent variable: Log Exch.
$R^2 = 0.996$, s.e. $= 0.379$, D.W. $= 2.05$, $\rho = 0.775$, $\sigma_u = 0.617$

0.975	0.114	− 0.186	− 0.136	0.052	0.168	0.987
(0.147)	(0.121)	(0.130)	(0.101)	(0.189)	(0.203)	(0.357)

Dependent variable: Δ Log Exch.
$R^2 = 0.895$, s.e. $= 0.390$, D.W. $= 2.27$

Note: In the polynomial distributed lag equation, a fourth degree polynomial with the sixth lag coefficient constrained to zero, was employed. The first equation relates the logarithm of the exchange rate to current and past levels of the logarithm of the money supply. The second equation relates the percentage rate of change of the exchange rate to current and past percentage rates of change of the money supply. ρ is the final value of the first order autocorrelation coefficient. An iterative Cochran–Orcutt transformation was employed when first order serial correlation in the residuals of the regression equations was evident. σ_u given in the Table is the standard error of the regression equation when the autoregressive component of the error is included. All of the other statistics are for the transformed model. Standard errors are in parentheses below the coefficients.

the rate at which the currency depreciates. None of the lagged variables are statistically significant. The distributed lags on the level of the exchange rate also show a unit elastic contemporaneous effect. In this case, however, some lagged values exert a significant effect on the rate of exchange. The sum of the coefficients is 1.57, i.e., during that period the elasticity of the exchange rate with respect to the money stock exceeded unity.[1] The magnification effect of money on the exchange rate is consistent with the prediction of Dornbusch's model (1976a) as well as with the prediction of the rational expectations models of Black (1973) and Bilson (1975). If the money supply process is generated by an autoregressive scheme, expectations will multiply the influence of current changes in the money stock since these changes are transmitted into the future through the autoregressive scheme.[2]

---

[1] The first equation in Table 1 should be interpreted with some caution since the high first order autocorrelation coefficient may reflect a misspecification. Its purpose is to provide a preliminary description of the relationship between money and the exchange rate. A more detailed analysis follows.

[2] Previous empirical work emphasizing monetary considerations in the analysis of the German exchange rate during the hyperinflation include Graham (1930), Bresciani-Turroni (1937) and more recently, Tsiang (1959–60) and Hodgson (1972).

II.2. The Building Blocks of the Monetary Approach

The foregoing analysis indicated the close association between monetary developments and the exchange rate. In this section we outline the major building blocks of the monetary approach to the exchange rate. Since in what follows we apply the framework to examine data pertaining to the German hyperinflation, the following presentation is simplified considerably by ignoring developments in the rest of the world.

Consider first the demand for real cash balances m^d as a function of the expected rate of inflation π^*:

$$m^d \equiv g(\pi^*); \quad \partial g/\partial \pi^* < 0 \tag{1}$$

The formulation in eq. (1) reflects the assumption that during the hyperinflation, changes in the demand for money were dominated by changes in inflationary expectations so that the effects of changes in output and the real rate of interest may be ignored.

The supply of real balances is M/P where M denotes the nominal money stock and P "the" price level (we bypass for the moment the question of what is the appropriate price level). Equating the supply of money with the demand enables us to express the price level as a function of the nominal money stock and inflationary expectations:

$$P = M/g(\pi^*); \quad \partial P/\partial M > 0, \quad \partial P/\partial \pi^* > 0. \tag{2}$$

The elasticity of the price with respect to π^* should approximate the (absolute value of the) interest elasticity of the demand for money, and in the absence of money illusion the elasticity of the price with respect to the money stock should be unity.

The second building block of the theory links the domestic price level with the foreign price level P^* through the purchasing power parity condition:

$$P = SP^* \tag{3}$$

If the purchasing power parity condition holds we can substitute eq. (3) into (2) to get a relationship between the exchange rate, the money stock, inflationary expectations and the foreign price level. Since during the German hyperinflation it is justifiable to assume that P^* is practically fixed (as compared with P), we can normalize units and define P^* as unity. Thus the exchange rate can be written as

$$S = M/g(\pi^*); \quad \partial S/\partial M > 0; \quad \partial S/\partial \pi^* > 0. \tag{4}$$

It is noteworthy that the implication that $\partial S/\partial \pi^* > 0$ is in conflict with some of the theories of exchange rate determination. It should be possible, therefore, to discriminate among alternative theories by examining the empirical relationship between anticipated inflation and the exchange rate. A popular analysis of this relationship goes as follows: a higher anticipated inflation raises the nominal rate of interest which induces a surplus in the capital account by attracting foreign capital, and thereby induces a *lower* spot exchange rate (i.e., an appreciation of the domestic currency). A variant of this approach would argue that the higher rate of interest lowers spending, and thus induces a surplus in the balance of payments which leads to a lower spot exchange rate. A third variant would reach the same result by emphasizing the implications of the interest parity theory (which is discussed in the next Section).

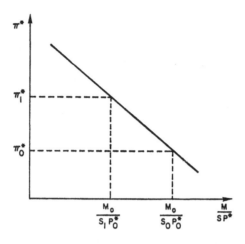

Figure 2

Accordingly, a higher rate of interest implies a higher forward premium on foreign exchange and if the rise in the forward exchange rate is insufficient to induce the required premium on foreign exchange, the spot exchange rate will have to fall (i.e., the domestic currency will have to appreciate). Whatever the route, the above analyses predict a *negative* relationship between the rate of interest and the spot exchange rate while equation (4) predicts a positive relationship.

The alternative theory presented here emphasizes the role of asset equilibrium in determining the exchange rate and its implications are illustrated in Fig. 2. A rise in anticipated inflation from π_0^* to π_1^* lowers the demand for real balances, and given the nominal money stock, asset equilibrium requires a higher price level. Since the domestic price level is tied to the foreign price via the purchasing power parity, and since the foreign price is assumed fixed, the higher price level can only be achieved through a *rise* in the spot exchange rate from S_0 to S_1 (i.e., a depreciation of the domestic currency).

The foregoing analysis did not specify the cause of the rise in the domestic rate of interest. It is necessary to emphasize that the exact analysis of the effects of a change in interest rates depends upon the source of the disturbance. The presumption, however, is that during the hyperinflation the source of disturbances was monetary. The higher interest rate may be thought of as resulting from a rise in the rate of monetary expansion which is immediately incorporated (via the Fisher effect) in inflationary expectations; to complete the experiment, it is possible to imagine (at least analytically) an acceleration in the monetary growth rate which does not instantaneously affect the monetary *stock*.

The result has an intuitive appeal in that easy money induces a depreciation of the currency. It emphasizes again the possible confusion that may arise from viewing the interest rate as an indicator of tight or easy monetary policy. The traditional expectation of a negative relationship between interest rates and the exchange rate may, however, be reconciled with the asset approach if it emphasizes the short run liquidity effect of monetary changes. Thus, in the short run, a higher interest rate is due to tight money which induces an appreciation of the currency (Dornbusch, 1976*a*). During hyperinflation, however, the expectations effect completely dominates the liquidity effect resulting therefore in a predicted *positive* relationship between the rate of interest and the price of foreign exchange.

The previous discussion emphasized the role of expectations about future events in determining the current value of the exchange rate. A major difficulty in incorporating the role of expectations in empirical work has been the lack of an observable variable measuring expectations. Thus, for example, in analyzing the demand for money during the hyperinflation, Cagan (1956) in his classic study constructed a time series of expected inflation using a specific transformation of the time series of the actual rates of inflation. The conceptual difficulty with such an approach stems from the fact that expectations are assumed to be based only on past experience and the choice of the specific transformation used to generate the series of expectations is to a large extent arbitrary. The third building block of the approach involves the choice of the measure of expectations that is appropriate for empirical implementation. In what follows we propose a direct measure of expectations which is then incorporated in the analysis of the determination of the exchange rate.

The fundamental relationship that is used in deriving the market measure of inflationary expectations relies on the interest parity theory. That theory maintains that in equilibrium the premium (or discount) on a forward contract for foreign exchange for a given maturity is (approximately) related to the interest rate differential according to:

$$\frac{F-S}{S} = i - i^* \tag{5}$$

where F and S are the forward and spot exchange rates (the domestic currency price of foreign exchange), respectively, i the domestic rate of interest and i^* the foreign rate of interest on comparable securities for the same maturity. Evidence available for various countries over various time periods suggests that this parity condition holds (Frenkel & Levich (1975, 1977); for an early analysis of the 1920's see Aliber (1962)). Although, due to lack of data, no comparable study has been done on the period of the German hyperinflation, it is assumed that the parity condition has been maintained. Furthermore, it is reasonable to assume that during the hyperinflation most of the variations in the difference between domestic and foreign anticipated rates of inflation were due to anticipated domestic (German) inflation. It follows, therefore, that the variations of the forward premium on foreign exchange $(F-S)/S$, may be viewed as a measure of the variations in the expected rate of inflation (as well as the expected rate of change of the exchange rate).

II.3. The Efficiency of the Foreign Exchange Market
Prior to incorporating the forward premium as a measure of expectations, it is pertinent to explore the efficiency of the foreign exchange market during the turbulent hyperinflation period. Evidence on the efficiency of that market will support the approach of using data from that market as the basis for inference on expectations.

If the foreign exchange market is efficient and if the exchange rate is determined in a similar fashion to other asset prices, we should expect the behavior in that market to display characteristics similar to those displayed in other stock markets. In particular, we should expect that current prices reflect all available information, and that the residuals from the estimated regression should be serially uncorrelated.

To examine the efficiency of the market we first regress the logarithm of the current spot exchange rate, $\log S_t$, on the logarithm of the one-month forward exchange rate prevailing at the previous month, $\log F_{t-1}$.

$$\log S_t = a + b \log F_{t-1} + u \qquad (6)$$

The expectation is that the constant term does not differ significantly from zero, that the slope coefficient does not differ significantly from unity and that the error term is serially uncorrelated. Since data on the German Mark-Pound Sterling (DM/£) forward exchange rate are available only for the period February 1921–August 1923, eq. (6) was estimated over those 31 months. The resulting ordinary-least-squares estimates are reported in eq. (6') with standard errors in parentheses below the coefficients.

$$\log S_t = -0.46 + 1.09 \log F_{t-1} \qquad (6')$$
$$(0.24)\,(0.03)$$

$$\bar{R}^2 = 0.98, \text{s.e.} = 0.45; \text{D.W.} = 1.90$$

As can be seen, the constant term does not differ significantly from zero at the 95 percent confidence level (although it seems to be somewhat negative), the slope coefficient is somewhat above unity (at the 95 percent confidence level) and, most importantly, the Durbin-Watson statistics indicate that the residuals are not serially correlated. The fact that the slope coefficient is slightly above unity may be explained in terms of transaction costs or in terms of the Keynesian concept of normal-backwardation (Keynes, 1930, vol. II, p. 143).[1]

Fig. 3 describes the monthly time series plot of the logarithms of the spot exchange rate and the forward rate prevailing in the previous month. The general pattern reveals that typically, when the spot exchange rate rises, the forward rate lies below it while when the spot exchange rate falls the forward rate exceeds it. This pattern is also suggested by the fact that the elasticity of the spot rate with respect to the previous month's forward rate is somewhat above unity.

To explore further the implications of the efficient market hypothesis we examine whether the forward exchange rate summarizes all relevant information. In an efficient market F_{t-1} summarizes all the information concerning the expected value of S_t that is available at period $t-1$. Specifically, one of the items of information available at $t-1$ is the stock of information available at $t-2$, and if the market is efficient, that information will be contained in F_{t-2}. If, however, F_{t-1} summarizes all available information including that contained in F_{t-2}, we should expect that adding F_{t-2} as an explanatory variable to the right-hand side of (6) will not affect the

---

[1] The joint hypothesis that the constant term is zero *and* that the slope coefficient is unity is rejected at the 95 percent confidence level.

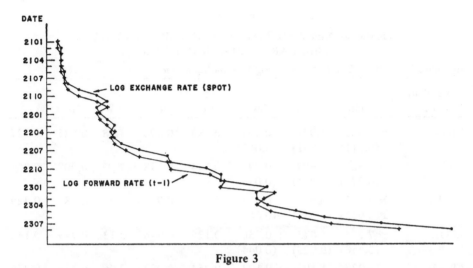

Figure 3

coefficient of determination and will have a coefficient that is not significantly different from zero. Eq. (6″) reports the results of that regression:

$$\log S_t = -0.45 + 1.10 \log F_{t-1} - 0.006 \log F_{t-2} \qquad (6'')$$
$$(0.26) \ (0.08) \qquad\qquad (0.08)$$

$$\bar{R}^2 = 0.98, \text{s.e.} = 0.46; \text{D.W.} = 1.91$$

The results in (6″) support the efficient market hypothesis.

To examine further the stability of the regression coefficients during the various phases of the hyperinflation we divided the sample into two parts: "Moderate" hyperinflation and "severe" hyperinflation, where the latter characterized the last eight months of the sample period. A Chow test was performed on the estimates of equations (6′) and (6″) to test the equality of each and every coefficient of the two sub-period's regressions. This procedure showed that the hypothesis that the regression coefficients do not differ between the two sub-periods cannot be rejected at the 95 percent level.

The results reported in this section provide support to the notion that during the hyperinflation expectations may have behaved "rationally" in the Muth sense. In fact, it should not be surprising that even during the turbulent period of the hyperinflation the efficient market hypothesis cannot be rejected. It stands to reason that the larger variability of exchange rates increases the rate of return from and the amount of resources invested in accurate forecasting.[1]

II.4. Prices, Money and Expectations
In this section we examine the empirical content of the first building block of the monetary approach to the exchange rate by using the market measure of inflationary expectations in estimating eq. (2). Log-linearizing eq. (2) and adding an error term yields:

---

[1] For an application of the "rational" expectations hypothesis to the German hyperinflation see Sargent & Wallace (1973).

Table 2

PRICES, MONEY AND EXPECTATIONS. MONTHLY DATA:
FEBRUARY 1921–AUGUST 1923

Estimated equation: $\log P = a + b_1 \log M + b_2 \log \pi + u$

Dependent variable	Constant	$\log M$	$\log \pi$	s.e.	R^2	D.W.	ρ	σ_u
LWPI	−5.983 (0.611)	1.021 (0.041)	0.497 (0.061)	0.193	0.996	1.88	0.525	0.227
LWIG	−5.423 (0.779)	0.997 (0.041)	0.293 (0.053)	0.144	0.998	1.95	0.909	0.366
LWHG	−4.923 (0.925)	0.983 (0.051)	0.374 (0.069)	0.187	0.996	1.79	0.889	0.429
LCOL	−7.215 (0.450)	1.073 (0.029)	0.236 (0.044)	0.125	0.998	2.13	0.729	0.182
LWAG	−10.027 (0.749)	1.103 (0.051)	0.194 (0.074)	0.254	0.992	2.06	0.373	0.274

Note: LWPI = log wholesale price index, LWIG = log imported-goods price index, LWHG = log home-goods price index, LCOL = log cost of living index, LWAG = log wage index. Standard errors are in parentheses below each coefficient. ρ is the final value of the autocorrelation coefficient. An iterative Cochran–Orcutt transformation was employed to account for first order serial correlation in the residuals. s.e. is the standard error of the equation and σ_u is the standard error of the regression when the autoregressive component of the error is included.

$$\log P = a + b_1 \log M + b_2 \log \pi^* + u \qquad (2')$$

One of the difficulties of using the double-log form is that during some months, early in the sample period, the forward premium on foreign exchange was negative (reaching − 0.8 percent per month in early 1921) reflecting the initial expectation that the price rise was temporary, that the process would reverse itself and prices would return to their previous levels. Since the logarithm of a negative quantity is not defined, the independent variable was transformed from π^* to $(k + \pi^*)$ which henceforth is referred to as π. Thus, the estimated equation was:

$$\log P = a' + b_1' \log M + b_2' \log \pi + u. \qquad (2'')$$

A maximum likelihood estimation of the coefficients in $(2'')$ along with the value of k resulted in a value of k ranging between 0.9 and 1.1 percent per month.[1] For ease of

[1] While the anticipated difference between the domestic and the foreign rates of inflation that is proxied by the forward premium π^* may be negative, the nominal rate of interest may not. In principle, a relevant variable in the demand for money is "the" nominal rate of interest which from (5) is equal to $\pi^* + i^*$. Our estimate of k, therefore, is not unreasonable in proxying "the" foreign nominal rate of interest. Since the purpose of this section is to indicate, in somewhat general terms, the implication of the first building block rather than to provide a precise estimate of the parameters of the demand for money, the procedure that was followed seems justifiable. In a separate paper we apply the market measure of expectations to a more detailed reexamination of the functional form and the estimates of the demand for money during the German hyperinflation (Frenkel, 1977).

exposition, in what follows, we set the value of k at 1 percent per month, and thus the coefficient $b_2 = b_2' \pi^*/(1 + \pi^*)$.

It may be recalled that in postulating eq. (2) we bypassed the question of the appropriate price deflator. To a large extent that question is empirical and depends on the theory that underlies the derivation of the demand for money. The presumption, however, is that if the aggregate demand for money is dominated by household behavior, then the relevant price index should be the consumer price index (the cost of living). Table 2 reports the results of estimating eq. (2″) using alternative price deflators. Judged by the goodness of fit it seems that the cost of living index is the most appropriate deflator although, strictly speaking, such a comparison is insufficient since the various equations in Table 2 differ in the dependent variable.

Judged as a whole it seems that the results in Table 2 are consistent with the first building block of the monetary approach to the exchange rate. In all cases the elasticity of the price level with respect to the money stock is close to unity and the elasticity with respect to π is positive as predicted from the consideration of the demand for money.

II.5. The Purchasing Power Parity

The second building block of the theory of exchange rate determination is the purchasing power parity. The high statistical correlation between prices and the exchange rate typically observed during periods of monetary disturbances led to the development of the purchasing power parity doctrine. Figs. 4, 5 and 6 show the relationships between (DM/$) exchange rate and the wholesale price index, the cost of living index and the wage rate index, and Figs. 7–8 show the relationships between the percentage change of the exchange rate and prices. These relationships correspond to the various price indices advocated for the computation of purchasing power parities.[1] In view of the observed high correlation among prices and the exchange rate, even the skeptics agreed that the doctrine may possess an element of truth when applied to monetary disturbances (e.g., Keynes (1930, p. 91), Haberler (1936, pp. 37–8), Samuelson (1948, p. 397)).

Table 3 reports the results of estimates of the purchasing power parity for the alternative price indices. The estimated equations are derived from equation (3) by log-linearizing and assuming that during that period P^* could be viewed as being fixed. As can be seen this building block of the theory of exchange rate determination also stands up rather well. In all cases the elasticities of the exchange rate with respect to

---

[1] In addition to pure monetary disturbances some sharp turning points in the path of the exchange rate (and its rate of change) can be attributed to political events which created facts and affected expectations. The following outlines some of the critical events that are reflected in the sharp turning points (based on Tinbergen (1934)). August 29. 1921: Murder of Erzberger; October 20, 1921: League of Nations decision concerning partition of Upper Silesia–renewed disturbances. On that date there was the Wiesbaden agreement between Rathenau and Loucheur concerning deliveries in Rind. April 16, 1922: Rapallo Treaty with Russia. June 24, 1922: Murder of Rathenau leading to a heavy depreciation of the mark. January 11, 1923: Ruhr territory occupied by French. End of February 1923: Beginning action to support the mark. April 18, 1923: Collapse of supporting measures.

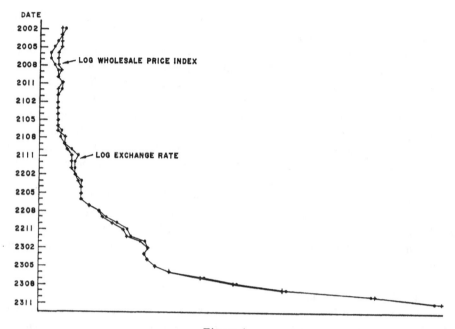

Figure 4

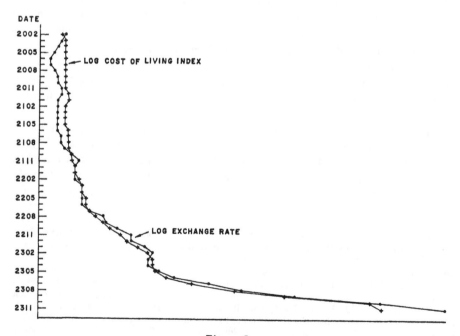

Figure 5

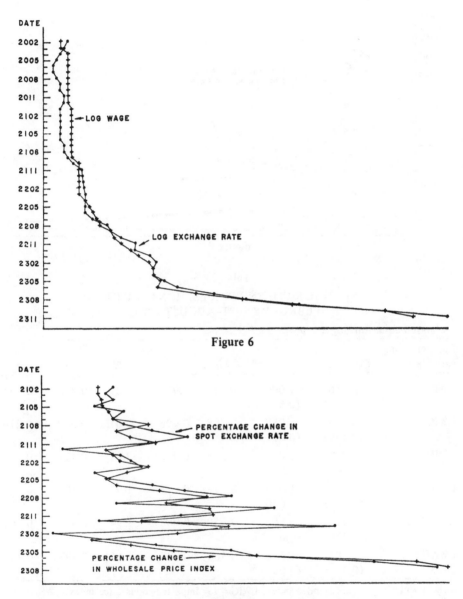

Figure 6

Figure 7

the various price indices are very close to unity. It also seems that while the cost of living index may be the appropriate deflator in estimating money demand functions, the wholesale price index performs best in the purchasing power parity equations.[1]

---

[1] It is of interest to note that during the recent float (1973–74) the percentage deviation of the wholesale price index from purchasing power parity exceeded that of the consumer price index (Aliber (1976)).

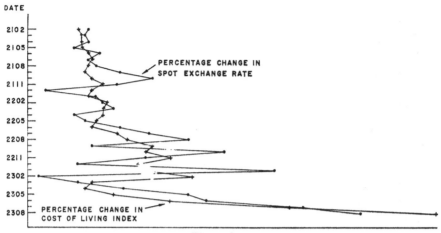

Figure 8

Table 3

EXCHANGE RATE AND PRICES. MONTHLY DATA:
FEBRUARY 1921–AUGUST 1923

Estimated equation: $\log S = a + b \log P + u$

Independent variable	Constant	$\log P$	s.e.	R^2	D.W.	ρ	σ_u
LWPI	0.146 (0.114)	1.006 (0.010)	0.124	0.998	2.01	0.356	0.135
LWIG	−0.219 (0.177)	1.058 (0.017)	0.208	0.996	2.01	0.269	0.216
LWHG	−0.383 (0.244)	1.031 (0.022)	0.215	0.995	2.09	0.471	0.241
LCOL	0.115 (0.311)	1.076 (0.030)	0.273	0.993	1.97	0.499	0.325
LWAG	4.415 (0.788)	0.887 (0.070)	0.350	0.988	1.94	0.889	0.767
LWAG 2SLS	2.682 (0.310)	1.074 (0.038)	0.360	0.987	1.66	0.471	0.414

Note: LWPI = log wholesale price index, LWIG = log imported-goods price index, LWHG = log home-goods price index, LCOL = log cost of living index, LWAG = log wage index. Standard errors are in parentheses below each coefficient. ρ is the final value of the autocorrelation coefficient. An iterative Cochran–Orcutt transformation was employed to account for first order serial correlation in the residuals. s.e. is the standard error of the equation and σ_u is the standard error of the regression when the autoregressive component of the error is included. To allow for a possible simultaneous equation bias due to the endogeneity of the various prices the above equations were also estimated using a two-stage least squares procedure with the percentage change in the money supply and the money-bond ratio as instruments. None of the coefficients was significantly affected except for the equation using LWAG as the independent variable. The 2SLS estimates are reported in the last line of the Table.

There remains, however, a question of interpretation. Does the doctrine specify an equilibrium relationship between prices and exchange rates or does it, in addition, specify causal relationships and channels of transmission? While the high correlation between the various price indices and the exchange rate is of some interest in describing an equilibrium relationship or in manifesting the operation of arbitrage in goods (depending on the price index used), they are of little help in *explaining* and analyzing the *determinants* of the exchange rate.

II.6. The Determinants of the Exchange Rate

The two building blocks analyzed in the previous sections provide the ingredients to the estimation of the determinants of the exchange rate. Given the foreign price level the purchasing power parity determines the ratio P/S. Given the nominal money stock and the state of expectations, the price level is determined so as to clear the money market. These two relationships imply the equilibrium exchange rate. We turn now to the estimation of the empirical counterpart of eq. (4). Log-linearizing and adding an error term yields

$$\log S = a' + b_1' \log M + b_2' \log \pi + u \qquad (4')$$

where as before, $\pi \equiv 1 + \pi^*$. The estimates are reported in eq. (4") with standard errors below the coefficients:

$$\log S = -5.135 + 0.975 \log M + 0.591 \log \pi \qquad (4'')$$
$$\quad\;\;(0.731)\;\;(0.050)\qquad\;\;(0.073)$$

$$R^2 = 0.994; \text{s.e.} = 0.241; \text{D.W.} = 1.91.$$

As is evident these results are fully consistent with the prior expectations. The elasticity of the exchange rate with respect to the money stock does not differ significantly from unity (at the 95 percent confidence level) while the elasticity of the spot exchange rate with respect to the forward premium is positive. The order of magnitude of the latter elasticity is similar (in absolute value) to the interest elasticity of the demand for money.[1] In comparison with the polynomial distributed lag of Table 1 it is seen that the standard error of equation (4") is significantly smaller. It is also noteworthy that the lower elasticity of the exchange rate with respect to the money stock is consistent with the intuitive explanation provided to the high elasticity of Table 1. There it was argued that the magnification effect was due to the role of expectations. Indeed as is shown in eq. (4") when expectations are included as a separate variable, the homogeneity postulate reemerges, the magnification effect of the money stock

---

[1] Recall that due to the transformation on the independent variable the (average) interest elasticity of the exchange rate b_2 is $b_2' \pi^*/(1 + \pi^*)$ where π^* is the average forward premium. Over the sample period the average π^* was about 6.2 percent per month, yielding therefore an estimate of about 1/2 as the interest elasticity. This estimate of the elasticity is consistent with the estimates in Frenkel (1975) as well as with the predictions of the various models of the transactions demand for cash.

disappears and thus indicating that the equations in Table 1 might have been mis-specified.

II.7. Conclusions, Limitations and Extensions

The foregoing analysis examined the empirical relationships among money, prices, expectations and the exchange rate during the German hyperinflation. Concentrating on that period provided the opportunity to isolate empirically some of the key relationships relevant to exchange rate determination. In particular, special attention has been given to simultaneous roles played by expectations and by monetary policy in determining the exchange rate. The empirical results are consistent with the monetary (or the asset) approach to the exchange rate.

It should be emphasized that the monetary approach to the exchange rate *does not* claim that the exchange rate is determined only in the money (or the asset) market and that only stock considerations matter while flow relationships do not. Clearly, the exchange rate (like any other price) is determined in general equilibrium by the inter-action of flow and stock conditions. In this respect the asset market equilibrium relationship that is used in the analysis may be viewed as a reduced form relationship that is chosen as a convenient framework.

Concentration on the period of the hyperinflation has, however, some short-comings. First it does not provide any insight into the exchange rate effects of real disturbances like structural changes (see for example Balassa (1964); Hekman (1975)). Second, and probably more important, the rapid developments occurring during the hyperinflation prevented a detailed analysis of the channels of transmission of distur-bances among the various sectors in the economy. For example, it might be useful to examine the exact pattern and chronological order by which monetary disturbances get transmitted into changes in the various price indices. The monthly data used in the present paper do not permit such a detailed analysis since most of the dynamics of adjustment occur within the month. The extent of this phenomenon is reflected in Table 4—a correlation matrix of the various variables for the monthly data over the entire period (February 1920–November 1923). To gain insight into the more refined details of the adjustment process, it may be necessary to analyze the period using weekly data. A preliminary examination of the weekly data suggests that the various prices do differ in the details of their time paths but at this stage no conclusive evidence can yet be offered.[1]

Although the monthly data do not reveal the details of the adjustment process, they do reveal some systematic relationships among the coefficients of variation of the (logarithms of the) variables as reported in Table 5. As is seen in Table 5, the coef-ficient of variation of the money stock is about 0.15 while the coefficients of variation corresponding to the various price indices are about twice as large—about 0.30. In this respect all price indices (wholesale, imported-goods, home-goods and cost of living) display a common behavior. A third group of variables includes the various exchange

---

[1] An inspection of Figs. 7–8 reveals that changes in the cost of living index lag behind changes in the wholesale price index which are closely related to changes in the exchange rate.

Table 4

CORRELATION MATRIX: PRICES, EXCHANGE RATE AND MONEY.
MONTHLY DATA: FEBRUARY 1920–NOVEMBER 1923

	LWPI	LWIG	LWHG	LCOL	LWAG	LEXC	LMON
LWPI	1.000	0.9986	0.9985	0.9959	0.9969	0.9992	0.9933
LWIG		1.000	0.9956	0.9934	0.9947	0.9968	0.9942
LWHG			1.000	0.9945	0.9949	0.9987	0.9892
LCOL				1.000	0.9984	0.9956	0.9875
LWAG					1.000	0.9960	0.9927
LEXC						1.000	0.9850
LMON							1.000

Note: LWPI = log wholesale price index, LWIG = log imported-goods price index, LWHG = log home-goods price index, LCOL = log cost of living index, LWAG = log wage index, LEXC = log exchange rate index, LMON = log money supply index.

Table 5

SUMMARY STATISTICS: PRICES, EXCHANGE RATE AND MONEY.
MONTHLY DATA: FEBRUARY 1921–AUGUST 1923

Variable	Mean	Variance	Standard deviation	Coef. of variation
LMON	15.3567	5.0948	2.2571	0.1469
LWPI	10.0477	9.5613	3.0921	0.3077
LWIG	9.8978	8.6178	2.9356	0.2965
LWHG	10.3210	9.1950	3.0323	0.2938
LCOL	9.4337	7.9337	2.8166	0.2985
LWAG	7.0522	7.6616	2.7679	0.3924
LEXC	8.6235	10.3370	3.2151	0.3728
LSPO	8.6235	10.3370	3.2151	0.3728
LFOR	8.6853	11.0123	3.3184	0.3820

Note: LMON = log money supply index, LWPI = log wholesale price index, LWIG = log imported-goods price index, LWHG = log home-goods price index, LCOL = log cost of living index, LWAG = log wage index, LEXC = log (DM/$) spot exchange rate index, LSPO = log (DM/£) spot exchange rate index, LFOR = log (DM/£) one month forward exchange rate index.

rates (spot and forward) *and* the wage rate. All of these variables display a similar coefficient of variation—about 0.40. The interesting phenomena are that the extent of variations in the various exchange rates (and in the wage rate) exceeds the extent of variations in the various prices which in turn exceeds the variation in the money stock. Furthermore, in view of the wage rate approach to the exchange rate (some of the doctrinal origins of which were mentioned in Section I), the association among variations in the wage rate and the various exchange rates deserves a special notice. While a detailed analysis of the implications of Table 5 is beyond the scope of the present paper, it is of interest to note the association among the exchange rates and the price of labor services–the commodity which may be most naturally classified as a non-traded good.

APPENDIX: DATA SOURCES

Data on the DM/$ exchange rate (spot) are taken from Graham (1930) and from *International Abstract of Economic Statistics 1919–30*. London: International Conference of Economic Services, London, 1934.

The one-month forward exchange rate (DM/£) as well as the (DM/£) spot rates are from Einzig (1937). The primary source for this data is the weekly circular published by the Anglo-Portuguese Colonial and Overseas Bank, Ltd. (originally the London branch of the Banco Nacional Ultramarino of Lisbon). The rates quoted are those of the Saturday of each week, but in cases where the market was closed, the latest quotation available prior to that Saturday is used.

Data on money supply are from Graham and *Historical Statistics* as well as some interpolations. Prices and wages are from *Historical Statistics* and some interpolations and primary sources.

Outstanding Treasury Bills are from Graham.

REFERENCES

ALIBER, R. Z.: Speculation in the foreign exchanges: The European experience, 1919–1926. *Yale Economic Essays*, Spring 1962.

ALIBER, R. Z.: The firm under fixed and flexible exchange rates. *Scandinavian Journal of Economics 78*, No. 2, pp. 309–322, 1976.

ANGELL, J. W.: International trade under inconvertible paper. *Quarterly Journal of Economics 36*, 309–412, 1922.

BALASSA, B.: The purchasing power parity doctrine: a reappraisal. *Journal of Political Economy 72*, No. 6, 584–96, 1964.

BILSON, J. F.: Rational expectations and flexible exchange rates. 1978. Reproduced in this volume as Chapter 5.

BLACK, S. W.: International money markets and flexible exchange rates. *Princeton Studies in International Finance*, No. 32. Princeton University, 1973.

BRESCIANI-TURRONI, C.: The purchasing power parity doctrine. *Egypte Contemporaire*, 1934. Reprinted in his *Saggi Di Economia*, 1961, Milano, pp. 91–122.

BRESCIANI-TURRONI, C.: *The Economics of Inflation*. Allen & Unwin, London, 1937.

BUNTING, F. H.: Purchasing power parity theory reexamined. *Southern Economic Journal 5*, No. 3, 282–301, 1939.

CAGAN, P.: The monetary dynamics of hyperinflation. In M. Friedman (ed.), *Studies in the Quantity Theory of Money*. University of Chicago Press, Chicago, 1956.

CANNAN, E.: The application of the theoretical apparatus of supply and demand to units of currency. *Economic Journal 31*, No. 124, 453–61, 1921.

CASSEL, G.: The present situation of the foreign exchanges. *Economic Journal 26*, 62–65, 1916.

CASSEL, G.: "Comment", *Economic Journal 30*, No. 117, 44–45, 1920.

CASSEL, G.: *The World's Monetary Problems*. Constable and Co., London, 1921.

CASSEL, G.: *Post-War Monetary Stabilization*. Columbia University Press, New York, 1928.

CASSEL, G.: *Money and Foreign Exchange after 1919*. Macmillan, London, 1930.

DORNBUSCH, R.: "Discussion". *American Economic Review Papers and Proceedings*, 147–151, 1975.

DORNBUSCH, R.: The theory of flexible exchange rate regimes and macroeconomic policy. *Scandinavian Journal of Economics 78*, No. 2, pp. 255–275, 1976. Reprinted in this volume as Chapter 2.

DORNBUSCH, R.: Capital mobility, flexible exchange rates and macroeconomic equilibrium. In E. Claassen and P. Salin (eds.), *Recent Issues in International Monetary Economics*. North-Holland, 1976a.

EINZIG, P.: *World Finance, 1914–1935*. Macmillan & Co., New York, 1935.

EINZIG, P.: *The Theory of Forward Exchange*. Macmillan, London, 1937.

ELLIS, H. S.: The equilibrium rate of exchange. In *Explorations in Economics. Notes and Essays contributed in honor of F. W. Taussig*. McGraw-Hill, New York, 1936.

FRENKEL, J. A.: Adjustment mechanisms and the monetary approach to the balance of payments. In E. Claassen and P. Salin (eds.), *Recent Issues in International Monetary Economics*. North-Holland, 1976.

FRENKEL, J. A.: The forward exchange rate, expectations and the demand for money: the German hyperinflation. *American Economic Review 67*, No. 4 (September, 1977).

FRENKEL, J. A. & JOHNSON, H. G.: The monetary approach to the balance of payments: essential concepts and historical origins. In J. A. Frenkel and H. G. Johnson (eds.), *The Monetary Approach to the Balance of Payments*. Allen & Unwin, London and University of Toronto Press, Toronto, 1976.

FRENKEL, J. A. & LEVICH, R. M.: Covered interest arbitrage: unexploited profits? *Journal of Political Economy 83*, No. 2, 325–338, 1975.

FRENKEL, J. A. & LEVICH, R. M.: Transaction costs and interest arbitrage: tranquil versus turbulent periods, *Journal of Political Economy 85*, No. 6 (December, 1977): 1209–1226.

FRENKEL, J. A. & RODRIGUEZ, C. A.: Portfolio equilibrium and the balance of payments: a monetary approach. *American Economic Review 65*, No. 4, 674–88, 1975.

FRIEDMAN, M. & SCHWARTZ, A.: *A Monetary History of the United States, 1867–1960*. Princeton University Press, Princeton, 1963.

GOSCHEN, G. J.: *The Theory of the Foreign Exchanges*. 1st ed. London, 1861; 2nd ed. London, 1863; 4th ed. reprinted, 1932.

GRAHAM, F.: *Exchange Prices and Production in Hyper-Inflation: Germany, 1920–23*. Princeton University Press, Princeton, N.J., 1930.

GREGORY, T. E.: *Foreign Exchange before, during and after the War*. Oxford University Press, London, 1922.

HABERLER, G.: *The Theory of International Trade*. William Hodge and Co., London, 1936.

HABERLER, G.: The choice of exchange rates after the war. *American Economic Review 35*, No. 3, 308–318, 1945.

HABERLER, G.: *A Survey of International Trade Theory*. Special Papers in International Economics 1 (July 1961). International Finance Section, Princeton University.

HANSEN, A. H.: A brief note on fundamental disequilibrium. *Review of Economics and Statistics 26*, No. **4**, 182–84, 1944.

HAWTREY, R. G.: *Currency and Credit*. Longmans, Green and Co., 1st ed. 1919, 4th ed. 1950, London.

HECKSCHER, E. F., et al.: *Sweden, Norway, Denmark and Iceland in the World War*. New Haven, 1930.

HEKMAN, C. R.: Structural change and the exchange rate: an empirical test. Unpublished manuscript, University of Chicago, 1975.

HODGSON, J. S.: An analysis of floating exchange rates: The dollar sterling rate, 1919–1925. *Southern Economic Journal 39*, No. 2, 249–257, 1972.

HOUTHAKKER, H. S.: Exchange rate adjustment. *Factors Affecting the U.S. Balance of Payments*. Joint Economic Committee, 87th Congress, 2nd Session, December 14, 1962, pp. 289–304.

JOHNSON, H. G.: The Keynesian revolution and the monetarist counterrevolution. *American Economic Review 61*, No. 2, 1–14, 1971. Reprinted as Ch. 7 in H. G. Johnson, *Economics and Society*. University of Chicago Press, Chicago, 1975.

JOHNSON, H. G.: Theory of international trade. In *International Encyclopedia of the Social Sciences*. The Macmillan Company and Free Press, 1968.

JOHNSON, H. G.: World inflation and the international monetary system. *The Three Banks Review*, No. **107**, 3–22, 1975.

KEYNES, J. M.: A tract on monetary reform. 1st ed. 1923, French Edition, 1924; vol. IV in *The Collected Writings of J. M. Keynes*. Macmillan, London, 1971.

KEYNES, J. M.: *A Treatise on Money*. Vol. II. Macmillan, London, 1930.

KOURI, P. J. K.: Exchange rate expectations, and the short run and the long run effects of fiscal and monetary policies under flexible exchange rates. Presented at the Conference on The Monetary Mechanism in Open Economies, Helsinki, Finland, August 1975.

LURSEN, K. & PEDERSEN, J.: *The German Inflation 1918–1923*. North-Holland, Amsterdam, 1964.

MARSHALL, A.: *Memorandum to the Effects which Differences between the Currencies of Different Nations have on International Trade*, 1888.

MARSHALL, A.: *Money, Credit and Commerce*. London, 1923.

METZLER, L. A.: The process of international adjustment under conditions of full employment: a Keynesian view. In R. E. Caves and H. G. Johnson (eds.), *Readings in International Economics*, pp. 465–86. Irwin, Homewood, Ill., 1968.

MILL, J. S.: *Principles of Political Economy*. 5th ed. Parker & Co., London, 1862.

MUNDELL, R. A.: *Monetary Theory*. Pacific Palisades, Goodyear, 1971.

MUNDELL, R. A.: *International Economics*. Macmillan, New York, 1968.

MUSSA, M. L.: A monetary approach to balance of payments analysis. *Journal of Money, Credit and Banking 6*, No. 3, 333–351, 1974.

MUSSA, M. L.: The exchange rate, the balance of payments and monetary and fiscal policy under a regime of controlled floating. *Scandinavian Journal of Economics 78*, No. 2, pp. 229–248, 1976. Reprinted in this volume as Chapter 3.

MYHRMAN, J.: Experiences of flexible exchange rates in earlier periods: theories, evidence and a new view. *Scandinavian Journal of Economics 78*, No. 2, pp. 169–196, 1976.

OHLIN, B.: *Interregional and International Trade*. Revised ed., Harvard University Press, Cambridge, Mass., 1967; 1st ed. 1933.

PIGOU, A. C.: Some problems of foreign exchanges. *Economic Journal 30*, No. **120**, 460–472, 1920.

RICARDO, D.: The high price of bullion. London, 1811. In *Economic Essays by David Ricardo*. Edited by E. C. Conner. Kelley, New York, 1970.

RICARDO, D.: *Reply to Mr. Bosaquet's practical observations on the report of the Bullion Committee*. London, 1811. In *Economic Essays by David Ricardo*. Edited by E. C. Connor. Kelley, New York, 1970.

RICARDO, D.: *Principles of Political Economy and Taxation*. London, 1821. Edited by E. C. Connor. G. Bell and Sons, 1911.

RINGER, F. K. (ed.): *The German Inflation of 1923*. Oxford Press, New York, 1969.

ROBINSON, J.: Banking policy and the exchanges. *Review of Economic Studies 3*, 226–29, 1935–36.

RUEFF, J.: *Balance of Payments*. Macmillan, New York, 1967.

RUEFF, J.: *Les fondements philosophiques des systèmes economiques*. Payol, 1967.

SAMUELSON, P. A.: Disparity in postwar exchange rates. In S. Harris (ed.), *Foreign Economic Policy for the United States*, pp. 397–412. Harvard University Press, Cambridge, 1948.

SAMUELSON, P. A.: Theoretical notes on trade problems. *Review of Economics and Statistics 46*, No. 2, 145–154, 1964.

SARGENT, T. J. & WALLACE, N.: Rational expectations and the dynamics of hyperinflation. *International Economic Review 14*, No. 2, 328–50, 1973.

TAUSSIG, F. W.: *International Trade*. Macmillan, New York, 1927.

TINBERGEN, J. (ed.): *International Abstract of Economic Statistics 1919–30*. International Conference of Economic Services, London, 1934.

TSIANG, S. C.: Fluctuating exchange rates in countries with relatively stable economies *IMF Staff Papers 7*, 244–273, 1959–60.

VINER, J.: *Studies in the Theory of International Trade*. Harper and Bros., New York, 1937.

WHEATLEY, J.: *Remarks on Currency and Commerce*. Burton, London, 1803.

WICKSELL, K.: The riddle of foreign exchanges. 1919. In his *Selected Papers on Economic Theory*. Kelley, New York, 1969.

CHAPTER 2

THE THEORY OF FLEXIBLE EXCHANGE RATE REGIMES AND MACROECONOMIC POLICY

RUDIGER DORNBUSCH
*Massachusetts Institute of Technology,
Cambridge, Mass., USA*

ABSTRACT

This paper develops three perspectives on the determination of exchange rates and their interaction with macroeconomic equilibrium and aggregate policies. A long-run view characterizes exchange rate determination in terms of monetary and real factors where the real aspects include an explicit consideration of relative price structures. A short-run or "liquidity" view of the exchange rate emphasizes the role of asset market equilibrium and expectations. A policy view, finally, analyzes the effectiveness of aggregate policies and points out that in the short-run nominal disturbances will tend to be transmitted internationally. The paper concludes with an analysis of dual exchange rate systems as a stabilizing policy in the presence of speculative disturbances.

This paper is concerned with some issues in the theory of flexible exchange rates. Specifically, we study the determinants of the exchange rate, both in the short and long run, the role of capital mobility and speculation in that context, and the scope for the international transmission of disturbances. In discussing the transmission of disturbances particular emphasis is given to the idea that in the short run monetary and price disturbances are not offset by matching exchange rate changes and, for that reason, are spread internationally.

The issues raised in this paper have been, to a large extent, discussed in the literature. We note here, in particular, Mundell (1964, 1968) and Fleming (1962) in their discussion of stabilization policy under flexible exchange rates as well as the subsequent work by Argy & Porter (1972) that formalizes the role of expectations in this context. Work by Black (1973, 1975) has emphasized the role of asset markets in exchange rate determination and a paper by Niehans (1975) has explored the

Reprinted by permission from *Scandinavian Journal of Economics*, 78, No. 2 (May, 1976); pp. 255–275.

The author wishes to acknowledge helpful comments on an earlier draft from Stanley Black, Stanley Fischer, Jacob Frenkel and Dwight Jaffee. Financial support was provided by a grant from the Ford Foundation.

interaction of exchange rate expectations and relative price responses to question the effectiveness of monetary policy under flexible rates.

The present paper adds to that strand of literature in that it distinguishes short-run effects of policies, sustained in part by price rigidities and expectational errors, from the longer run effects where relative prices and homogeneity are given emphasis. The aggregation departs from the standard Keynesian model of complete specialization and two traded goods in distinguishing traded goods as a composite commodity and nontraded goods. Such an aggregation is preferred since it breaks the identification of the exchange rate with the terms of trade, introduces scope for a monetary interpretation of the exchange rate and leaves room at the same time for intersectoral considerations.

In Section I we lay out a general equilibrium framework for the discussion of exchange rates from a long-run perspective. The critical assumptions of that theory are purchasing power parity for traded goods and monetary equilibrium. In Section II the assumption of purchasing power parity is relaxed to yield a short-run or "money-market" theory of the exchange rate. In Section III we return to purchasing power parity and investigate the role of speculation in affecting the scope for the international transmission of monetary disturbances and for the operation of monetary and fiscal policy. In Section IV the discussion is extended to a dual exchange rate system.

I. A GENERAL VIEW OF EXCHANGE RATE DETERMINANTS

In this section we outline a fairly general and eclectic view of the determinants of exchange rates. Such a view links monetary and real variables as jointly influencing the equilibrium level of the exchange rate. The view is appropriate to full equilibrium or the "long run" and is a benchmark from which to judge departures and alternatives.

A critical ingredient of this approach is purchasing power parity, in the narrow sense of goods arbitrage for internationally traded goods, so that the exchange rate equates the prices of traded goods in alternative currencies:[1]

$$P_T = eP_T^*. \tag{1}$$

where P_T and P_T^* represent the domestic and foreign currency prices of traded goods and where e is the domestic currency price of foreign exchange.[2]

The prices of traded goods can be related to the price levels, P and P^*, respectively. The appropriate relationship is given by the equilibrium *relative* price of traded goods in terms of the price levels, θ and θ^*:

$$P_T = \theta P; P_T^* = \theta^* P^*. \tag{2}$$

The determinants of the equilibrium relative price structure, denoted here by θ and θ^*,

---

[1] We abstract here from tariffs and transport costs that introduce obvious modifications in (1).
[2] All starred variables refer to the foreign country.
[3] See pp.35–36 below.

will be discussed below.[3] For the present it suffices to note that an increase in the equilibrium price of traded goods by x percent raises their relative price θ by $(1 - \gamma)x$ percent where γ and $(1 - \gamma)$, respectively, denote the shares of traded goods and non-traded goods in the price index.

Using (2) in eq. (1), we can express the exchange rate in terms of price levels and relative prices:

$$e = (P/P^*)(\theta/\theta^*). \tag{3}$$

The next step is to link up the discussion with the monetary sector. This is achieved by multiplying and dividing (3) by the domestic and foreign nominal quantity of money, M and M^*.[1] Furthermore, imposing the conditions of monetary equilibrium:

$$M/P = L(\ );M^*/P^* = L^*(\ ), \tag{4}$$

where L and L^* represent the domestic and foreign demand for real balances, we arrive at (5):[2]

$$e = (M/M^*)(L^*/L)(\theta/\theta^*). \tag{5}$$

Eq. (5) collects the principal determinants of exchange rates. These are, respectively, the nominal quantities of monies, the real money demands, and the relative price structure. It can be viewed as an *equilibrium* exchange rate since in its derivation we have used the conditions of goods arbitrage, money market equilibrium and, implicitly in using (2), home goods market equilibrium. The usefulness of (5) is enhanced by considering the logarithmic differential denoting a percentage change by a "^":

$$\hat{e} = (\hat{M} - \hat{M}^*) + (\hat{L}^* - \hat{L}) + (\hat{\theta} - \hat{\theta}^*). \tag{6}$$

The first term in (6) captures the effects of monetary changes on the exchange rate. Other things equal, the country with the higher monetary growth will have a depreciating exchange rate. This particular term captures the effect of differences in long-run inflation rates between countries and their reflection in exchange rates.

The effect of changes in real money demand is captured in the second term in (6). The country that experiences a (relative) increase in real money demand will have an appreciation in the exchange rate. Among the factors that exert an influence on real money demand, we note here, in particular, interest rates, expected inflation, and real income growth. The real money demand term in (6) constitutes one of the links between the exchange rate, the monetary sector and the real sector. This term helps explain how changes in productivity, for example, get reflected in exchange rate changes.

The last term in (6) collects the effect of changes in the relative price structure on the exchange rate. This term arises entirely from real considerations and, in fact, has

---

[1] The choice of monetary aggregate in (4) is presumably that for which real money demand is most stable. Furthermore, we do not require that in (4) the same monetary aggregate for both countries be used.

[2] For a similar equation that concentrates on traded goods, see Collery (1971).

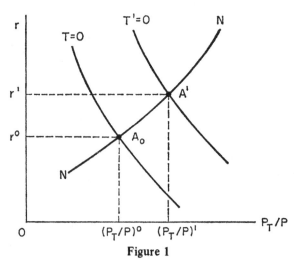

Figure 1

been identified in some literature as the "real exchange rate".[1] Given the nominal quantity of money and the demand for real balances, and therefore the price level, an increase in the equilibrium relative price of traded goods will be reflected in a depreciation in the exchange rate. Changes in absorption, shifts in demand, or biased output growth, *given* a monetary policy that sustains the price level, will therefore directly affect the exchange rate.

An example will show how eq. (6) can be applied. Assume that in the home country we have an increase in spending that falls entirely on traded goods, while abroad everything remains unchanged. Assume further that because of the absence of capital mobility the exchange rate adjusts to maintain trade balance equilibrium. In Fig. 1 we show the equilibrium in the home goods market along the NN schedule. At higher interest rates, and hence lower real spending, we require a higher relative price of traded goods to clear the home goods market. An increase in interest rates has an expenditure reducing effect that has to be offset by the expenditure and production switching effects of a relative price change. Along the $T = 0$ schedule, we have trade balance equilibrium. At lower interest rates and hence higher aggregate real spending, we require a higher relative price of traded goods to maintain trade balance. The initial equilibrium is at point A_0.

An increase in spending that falls on traded goods creates at the initial equilibrium an excess demand for traded goods and therefore requires higher interest rates and/or a higher relative price of traded goods to maintain trade balance. The $T = 0$ schedule accordingly shifts to $T' = 0$, and our new equilibrium is at point A' with an increase in both interest rates and the relative price of traded goods. The higher interest rate is required to restore balance between income and spending. At that higher

---

[1] See, for example, Corden (1971, Chapter 5) and Dornbusch (1974*b*). Much of the partial equilibrium literature concerned with real trade questions uses implicitly (3) together with the assumption that monetary or fiscal policies maintain constant the level of prices, P and P^*. Under these assumptions the exchange rate can be identified with the relative price structure.

interest rate, spending on home goods has declined and we accordingly require a reduction in their relative price.

Consider next the implications of this disturbance for the exchange rate. The higher equilibrium interest rate lowers the demand for real balances and therefore contributes, via an increase in the price level, to a depreciation of the exchange rate. This effect is further enhanced by the required increase in the relative price of traded goods so that the net result is an unambiguous depreciation of the exchange rate.[1]

The example features several aspects of the exchange rate determination that are worth spelling out in more detail. First, and perhaps foremost, the exchange rate is determined in a general equilibrium framework by the interaction of all markets (and countries). A particularly important feature is that the equilibrium obtains in *both* the flow and stock markets so that the exchange rate is in no manner determined by the current flow demands and supplies of foreign exchange.[2]

Next we give emphasis to the role of *monetary* considerations in the context of exchange rate determinations. As has been emphasized by J. Robinson (1935), the exchange rate is proximately determined by the balance between money supply and real money demand. The fact that the approach taken here is "monetary" in no manner precludes the role of "real" factors since these must be expected to enter as determinants of the demand for real balances and thus exert an effect on the exchange rate. Mussa (1974) has emphasized this point for the analysis of the balance of payments and has noted the obvious extension to a flexible rate regime.

Since the exchange rate is determined as part of the general, real and monetary equilibrium of the system, there is no relevant sense in which one would want to assert that the exchange rate is an exclusively monetary phenomenon. Indeed, the equilibrium exchange rate can change without any accompanying change in the money supply, or the real money demand. Such would, for example, be the case if there were a change in the composition of production between home goods and traded goods. Having noted the role of real considerations in this context, it is important, however, to recognize that organizing thought about the exchange rate around the monetary sector is likely to be a direct and informative approach. To appreciate this point, consider the alternative of a "wage approach".

A wage approach can be formulated by using in (3) the definition of real wages, $w = W/P$ and $w^* = W^*/P^*$, to obtain an equation similar to (6):

$$\hat{e} = (\hat{W} - \hat{W}^*) + (\hat{w}^* - \hat{w}) + (\hat{\theta} - \hat{\theta}^*). \qquad (6)'$$

---

[1] If the increased spending had fallen entirely on home goods, the required relative price adjustment would have been a fall in the relative price of traded goods and therefore ambiguity in the net effect of the disturbance on the exchange rate.

[2] There is a peculiar tradition in the discussion of the markets for both bonds and foreign exchange, and unlike in the discussion of equity prices, that associates price formation with the rate at which funds flow, rather than with the conditions required for the existing stocks to be held. The "tradeable funds" approach in the foreign exchange market has a "loanable funds" equivalent in the bond market. This issue is not new. See, for example, Polak (1944) and Laursen (1955). The latter raises the issue quite explicitly and opts for a stock approach. See, also, Dornbusch (1974a, 1975), Johnson (1975), and, in particular, Black (1973).

Provided the general equilibrium structure is used to fill in the details of (6)', we arrive at the same answer as we would obtain from (6). The choice then must lie in an assumption about the stability of the relevant behavioral equations and, perhaps, an assumption about the dominant source of disturbances.

A third feature of this approach is the *long-run* or *equilibrium* nature of exchange rate determination. This view is implicit in the fact that we allow all markets to clear and that we explicitly impose the condition of monetary stock equilibrium, goods market equilibrium and purchasing power parity for traded goods. Either of these conditions may not hold in the short run, and, therefore, exchange rates can depart from the prediction in (6)'.

For short-run purposes, we will assume that the exchange rate is altogether dominated by the asset markets and more specifically by capital mobility and money market equilibrium. Arbitrage of traded goods prices and goods market equilibrium is attained only over time.[1] Within such a perspective, we could assume that the price level and real income, at a point in time, are given and that the interest rate is determined by the quantity of money along with elements that shift the demand for real balances. Interest arbitrage for given expected future spot rates, determined by speculators, will then set the spot rates. Such a view is explored in the next section.

II. SHORT-RUN DETERMINATION OF EXCHANGE RATES

In the short run, the scope for goods arbitrage may be limited, and accordingly purchasing power parity as in (1) may only obtain for a limited set of commodities. Under these conditions, it is useful to abstract altogether from the detail of goods markets and rather view exchange rates as being determined entirely in the asset market. Such a view will assume capital mobility and indeed assign a critical role to it. Exchange rates in this perspective are determined by interest arbitrage together with speculation about future spot rates. To provide an example of this approach, we consider the effects of an increase in the nominal quantity of money in a "small country".

Given real income and other determinants of the demand for real balances, the equilibrium interest rate, at which the existing quantity of money is willingly held, will be a function of the real quantity of money.[2]

$$r = r(M/P, \ldots). \qquad (7)$$

Interest arbitrage, assuming that on a covered basis domestic and foreign assets are perfect substitutes, requires that the domestic interest rate, less the forward premium on foreign exchange, λ, be equal to the foreign interest rate, r^*:[3]

$$r - \lambda = r^*, \qquad (8)$$

---

[1] Magee (1974) has presented information on the adjustment time for purchasing power parity, or arbitrage, to be achieved. The evidence suggests a significant lag and a substantial dispersion across commodities.

[2] Eq. (7) is obtained by solving the money market equilibrium condition, $M/P = L(r, \ldots)$.

[3] For recent evidence on covered interest arbitrage, see Frenkel & Levich (1977).

where the forward premium is defined as the percentage excess of the forward rate, $\bar{e}$, over the current spot rate:

$$\lambda \equiv (\bar{e} - e)/e.$$

Substituting (7) and λ in (8) we have a relationship between the real money supply, the spot rate and the forward rate:

$$r(M/P, \ldots) = r^* + \bar{e}/e - 1 \tag{8}'$$

Differentiating (8)$'$ and denoting the interest responsiveness of money demand by σ we obtain:[1]

$$\hat{e} = \hat{\bar{e}} + (1/\sigma)\hat{M} \tag{9}$$

where by assumption the foreign interest rate and the price level are held constant. Eq. (9) suggests that a change in the forward rate induces an equiproportionate change in the spot rate, while an increase in the money supply causes a depreciation in the spot rate that is inversely proportional to the interest responsiveness of money demand. Since the interest responsiveness of money demand is of the order of $\sigma = 0.5$, a monetary expansion will be matched by significantly more than proportionate depreciation.

So far we have assumed that the forward rate is exogenous. The next step is therefore to link the forward rate to the analysis. For the point to be made it is sufficient to assume that the forward rate is set by speculators in a perfectly elastic manner at the level of the expected future spot rate and that expectations about the latter are formed in an adaptive manner. With these assumptions we have:

$$\bar{e} = \pi e + (1 - \pi)e_{-1}; \quad 0 < \pi < 1 \tag{10}$$

The impact effect of a change in the spot rate is therefore to raise the forward rate but proportionately less, so the price of foreign exchange is at a forward discount. Substituting from (10), the expression $\hat{\bar{e}} = \pi\hat{e}$ in (9) yields the total impact effect of a monetary expansion on the spot rate:

$$\hat{e} = \frac{1}{(1 - \pi)\sigma}\hat{M} \tag{9}'$$

We note that the adaptive expectations serve to increase the impact effect of money on the exchange rate. In fact, the more closely the forward rate is determined by the current spot rate, the closer π is to unity, the larger the exchange rate fluctuations induced by a variation in money.

In interpreting the effect of a monetary expansion on the exchange rate, three considerations stand out: First domestic and foreign assets are assumed perfect substi-

---

[1] From the conditions of money market equilibrium $M/P = L(r, \ldots)$, we have: $dr = \hat{M}(M/P)/L_r \equiv -(1/\sigma)\hat{M}$. The interest responsiveness of money demand, that is, the semilogarithmic derivative $\sigma \equiv -L_r/L$, is for the short run significantly less than unity. Econometric models such as the MPS model estimate a short run elasticity of $-rL_r/L = 0.05$, so that with an interest rate of $r = 0.1$ we obtain a value $\sigma = 0.5$.

tutes on a covered basis as is reflected in (8). This implies that, independently of any particular assumptions about expectations, a reduction in domestic interest rates has to be matched by a forward discount on foreign exchange in order to equalize the net yields on domestic and foreign assets. The next two considerations are dependent on the particular expectations assumption in (10) and concern, respectively, the direction and magnitude of the change in the spot rate. A reduced domestic interest rate, for asset market equilibrium, has to be matched by an expected appreciation of the exchange rate. The expectations mechanism in (10) implies that a depreciation in the spot rate will give rise to such an expectation, since the elasticity of expectations, π, is less than unity. With an elasticity of expectations less than unity, a depreciation of the spot rate is accompanied by a less than proportionate depreciation of the expected future spot rate, or an anticipated appreciation. Finally, the magnitude of the depreciation in the spot rate that is required depends on both the interest response of money demand, σ, and the elasticity of expectations, π. The smaller the interest responsiveness of money demand, the larger the interest rate change that is brought about by a monetary expansion and therefore, the larger the expected appreciation that has to be brought about by a depreciation in the spot rate. Furthermore, a given depreciation of the spot rate will give rise to an expected appreciation of the future spot rate that is smaller, the larger the elasticity of expectations. Accordingly, large exchange rate changes will arise in circumstances where interest response of money demand is small and the elasticity of expectations is large.

The short run determination of exchange rates is entirely dominated by the conditions of equilibrium in the asset markets and expectations. The *liquidity* effect of money on the interest rate has a counterpart in the immediate depreciation of the spot rate that has to be sufficient to cause the existing stock of domestic assets to be held. It is in this sense that in the short run the exchange rate is determined in the asset markets.

Over time the exchange rate is determined by the interaction between goods markets and asset markets. This is so because the price level will rise to match the expansion in the nominal quantity of money until, in the long run, the monetary expansion is exactly matched by a price increase so that real balances and interest rates are unchanged and the spot and forward rate depreciate in the same proportion as the increase in the nominal quantity of money. The exact dynamics of that adjustment process will depend on the speed with which prices respond as compared to expectations. The response of prices will be due, in part, to the traditional effect of a reduced interest rate on aggregate spending. There will be in the present framework an additional channel that serves to speed up the responsiveness of prices to a monetary expansion. The impact effect of a monetary expansion on the spot rate, as of a given price level, will cause a departure from goods arbitrage. Domestic goods will become relatively cheap as compared to foreign goods and therefore induce a substitution of world demand toward domestic goods. This additional channel implies that even if domestic aggregate spending were unresponsive to the interest rate, or slow to adjust, there remains a subsidiary channel, the arbitrage effect, that serves to drive up domestic prices and causes the real effects of a monetary expansion to be transitory.

III. SPECULATION, MACROECONOMIC POLICIES AND THE TRANSMISSION OF DISTURBANCES

In the present section we go beyond the impact effect of disturbances and consider the behavior over time of the economy in response to policy-induced or speculative disturbances. In particular, we want to show that speculation that is not guided by "rational expectations" allows monetary changes to be transmitted internationally even under circumstances where prices are fully flexible. For the purposes of the present section, we continue to assume that the home country is small and therefore faces given world prices of traded goods and a given world rate of interest. We furthermore assume that goods arbitrage is continuously maintained. In addition to internationally traded commodities, the home country produces and consumes nontraded goods. Price and factor cost flexibility ensure that markets clear all the time and full employment is maintained.

The analysis focuses on the equilibrium conditions in the markets for home goods and in the asset market. Consider first the home goods market. The excess demand for home goods will depend on the relative price of traded goods in terms of the price level, P_T/P, the interest rate that determines absorption for a given level of real income, and the level of government spending on nontraded goods, g:

$$N(P_T/P, r, g) = 0; \quad N_{P_T/P} > 0, N_r < 0, N_g = 1 \tag{11}$$

An increase in the relative price of traded goods creates an excess demand as consumers substitute toward home goods, while productive resources move into the traded goods sector, thus reducing the supply of home goods. An increase in the interest rate reduces absorption, part of which falls on home goods and to that extent creates an excess supply. Finally, an increase in government spending directly adds to home goods demand. We can solve the equilibrium condition in (11) for the equilibrium relative price of traded goods in terms of the interest rate and government spending:

$$P_T/P = \theta(r; g); \quad \theta_r > 0, \theta_g < 0. \tag{11'}$$

Eq. (11)′ is plotted in Fig. 1 as the NN schedule.[1]

Consider next the condition of equilibrium in the money market. With a demand for real balances that depends on interest rates and real income, we can solve the money market equilibrium condition for the equilibrium interest rate as a function of the real money supply and real income.

$$r = r(M/P; y); \quad r_{M/P} < 0, r_y > 0. \tag{12}$$

Next we substitute the equilibrium interest rate in (11), and noting that purchasing power parity obtains with a given price of foreign goods, $P_T = eP_T^*$, we can write the home goods market equilibrium condition as:

$$N(eP_T^*/P, r(M/P), g) = 0 \tag{13}$$

---

[1] The trade balance is given by $T = T(P_T/P, r)$ where the relative price term again reflects substitution between home goods and traded goods and the interest rate term reflects absorption or the level of spending. Accordingly, an increase in the relative price of traded goods worsens the trade balance, while an increase in the interest rate improves the trade balance.

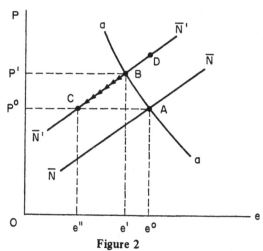

Figure 2

where $\bar{N}$ denotes the reduced form that embodies the condition of money market equilibrium and where the constant level of real income is suppressed as an argument.

In Fig. 2 we show the home goods market equilibrium schedule $\bar{N}\bar{N}$. The schedule is positively sloped and flatter than a ray through the origin. The reason is as follows. At a higher price level, we have lower real balances, higher interest rates, and therefore reduced real spending. Part of the reduction in real spending falls on home goods and creates an excess supply that has to be eliminated by a decline in their *relative* price, that is, by an increase in the exchange rate or the price of traded goods relative to the price level.[1] The $\bar{N}\bar{N}$ schedule is drawn for a given nominal quantity of money and a given foreign currency price of traded goods.

We again assume that covered interest arbitrage ensures that interest rates are linked internationally so that (8) continues to hold. The forward rate is set by speculators, according to the adaptive expectations scheme in (10). Substituting the expression for the forward rate in (8), and using the equilibrium interest rate in (12), we obtain the condition for money market equilibrium together with covered interest arbitrage:

$$r(M/P) - (1 - \pi)(e_{-1}/e - 1) = r^*. \tag{14}$$

A critical property of the speculative behavior is that an increase in the spot rate creates a forward discount, since it will cause the forward rate to rise less than proportionately. To maintain interest parity, a forward discount on foreign exchange has to be accompanied by a reduction in domestic relative to foreign interest rates. Given the nominal quantity of money, such a decline in interest rates would arise if the domestic price level declined. The asset market equilibrium schedule aa in Fig. 2 reflects eq. (14) for a given foreign interest rate, a given nominal quantity of money, and a given past spot rate e_{-1}. The initial equilibrium obtains at point A with all markets clearing and the forward rate at par so that no revision of expectations is required.

---

[1] For a given foreign currency price of traded goods, the ratio e/P represents the domestic relative price of traded goods in terms of the price level.

Consider next the effect of an increase in the foreign price level. We note from (14) that there is no direct effect on the asset market and therefore the *aa* schedule remains unaffected. Consider next the home goods market. At an unchanged exchange rate, the increase in the foreign price level raises the domestic currency price of traded goods and hence their relative price, so that an excess demand for home goods would arise. To eliminate the excess demand, the exchange rate would have to appreciate to fully offset the foreign price increase. This is represented in Fig. 2 by a leftward shift of the $\bar{N}\bar{N}$ schedule to $\bar{N}'\bar{N}'$ in the proportion of the foreign price increase.

The short-run effect of the price increase is to move the economy to point B with an appreciation in the exchange rate that falls short of the foreign price increase and an increase in the domestic price level. Furthermore, the *relative* price of traded goods rises, and the increase in the price level reduces real balances and therefore raises interest rates with a matching premium on forward exchange.

Quite obviously, the foreign price change in the short run exerts real effects in the home country. The flexible exchange rate, in this formulation, fails to isolate the home country from foreign nominal disturbances. The explanation for this non-neutrality lies in the behavior of speculators.

The adjustment process from the initial equilibrium at point A to the short-run position of equilibrium can be viewed in the following manner: The increase in the foreign currency price of traded goods, at the initial exchange rate, raises the domestic currency price of traded goods, the price level and therefore the rate of interest. Such a position is shown at point D where the home goods market clears and the price level has risen, although proportionately less than the price of traded goods. At that point covered interest arbitrage is not satisfied, since the increased interest rate is not compensated by an offsetting forward premium on foreign exchange. Therefore, an *incipient* capital inflow develops that causes the spot rate to appreciate until the appropriate premium has been generated. This is the move from point D to the short run equilibrium at point B.[1]

In the short run the failure of exchange rates to fully offset the foreign price increase implies that the domestic nominal and real equilibrium is affected by a foreign nominal disturbance. The domestic price level rises as do interest rates. Domestic absorption declines and real spending on home goods falls so that a deflationary effect is exerted on that sector. The reduction in absorption and the induced increase in the relative price of traded goods imply an expansion in the production of traded goods and a trade balance surplus. The trade surplus in turn is financed by a capital outflow.

The equilibrium at point B is only transitory, since it is sustained by expectational errors. Speculators underpredict the actual appreciation of the exchange rate and therefore will revise their forecast. That revision causes at each current rate the premium to decline and therefore to create a covered differential in favor of the home

---

[1] The effect of a foreign price increase on the exchange rate at point B is given by $\hat{e} = [-\delta/(\delta + \sigma(1-\pi))]\hat{P}_T^*$ where δ is the elasticity of the price level with respect to the price of traded goods along the $\bar{N}\bar{N}$ schedule. Unless $\pi = 1$, the exchange rate change does not fully offset the increase in foreign prices. See Appendix I.

country that leads to continued appreciation of the exchange rate. That process moves the economy from point B to C over time. The process will continue until the exchange rate has sufficiently appreciated to fully offset the increase in foreign prices. This is true at point C, where the domestic price level and hence interest rates have returned to their initial level.[1]

The lack of homogeneity that the system exhibits in the short run applies similarly to an increase in the domestic money stock. In the short run, price flexibility notwithstanding, the price level and the exchange rate increase proportionately less than the money supply, and accordingly, the interest rate decreases while the forward rate goes to a discount. The change in the spot rate induced by a monetary expansion in the short run is given by:

$$\hat{e} = \frac{\delta}{\delta + \sigma(1 - \pi)}\hat{M}, \quad 0 < \delta < 1 \tag{15}$$

where δ is the elasticity of the price level with respect to the price of traded goods along the $\bar{N}\bar{N}$ schedule. We note that in the present context, and unlike in Section II, the exchange rate changes proportionately less than the nominal quantity of money. This is entirely due to the adjustment in prices that is permitted here and that serves to lower the increase in real balances associated with a given increase in the nominal quantity of money.

Over time, as expectations are revised, the system will converge to neutrality in the sense that the monetary change leaves all real variables unchanged. The short run real effects of a monetary change are again due to expectational errors, or more precisely, to the fact that speculators use irrelevant information and therefore affect the real equilibrium. If instead the equilibrium exchange rate in (5) were used as a basis of prediction, the system would be homogeneous, even in the short run.

The adjustment process to a monetary disturbance is illustrated in Fig. 3. Initial equilibrium obtains at point A, with a relative price structure indicated by the slope of the ray OR. The increase in the nominal quantity of money at the initial equilibrium exchange rate and prices lowers interest rates and therefore creates an excess demand for home goods and a departure from covered interest arbitrage. For home goods equilibrium to obtain, the exchange rate and prices would have to increase in the same proportion as the nominal quantity of money. This is indicated by an upward shift of the $\bar{N}\bar{N}$ schedule in the proportion $AC/OA = \hat{M}$. The asset market equilibrium in the short run does not possess homogeneity properties, since the elasticity of exchange rate expectations is less than unity, which is equivalent to saying that expectations are sticky. Accordingly, the aa schedule shifts upward in a smaller proportion. Short run equilibrium will obtain at point B with an increase in the exchange rate and prices that are proportionately smaller than the increase in money. In that short-run equilibrium, the relative price of home goods will be higher compared to A, which is a reflection of the fact that in the short run the interest rate declines and absorption expands. The adjustment of expectations over time will shift the $a'a'$ schedule up and

---

[1] The dynamics and stability of the adjustment process are studied in Appendix I.

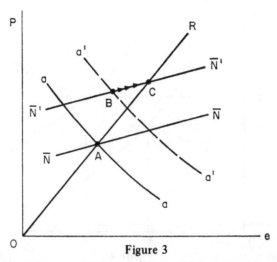

Figure 3

to the right until the long run real equilibrium is restored at point C, where expectational errors have subsided and prices and exchange rates fully reflect the monetary change.

In discussing stabilization policy under flexible exchange rates, Mundell (1964, 1968) notes that with perfect capital mobility monetary policy exerts strong effects on nominal income, while fiscal policy has no effect. The reason is that, in the absence of forward market considerations, the given interest rate in the world determines the domestic interest rate and hence velocity. Given velocity, fiscal policy has no effect on nominal income, while monetary policy becomes most powerful. The present framework, following Mundell (1964) and Wonnacott (1972), notes that the short-run changes in forward premia allow interest rate and hence velocity changes that tend to dampen the effect of monetary policy. In the short run, monetary policy causes a depreciation of the exchange rate accompanied by a premium on forward exchange and a decline in interest rates. The decline in interest rates lowers velocity and therefore dampens in the short run the nominal income expansion. Over time the revision of expectations eliminates the premium and therefore restores interest rates and velocity to their initial level and thus causes monetary changes to be reflected in equiproportionate changes in nominal income.

In concluding this section we return to the transmission of foreign price disturbances and ask what policies the government could pursue to offset the transmission process. Here the choice has to be made between price level stability, or stability of the real equilibrium, that is, of interest rates, absorption and relative prices. If the preference is for stability of the real equilibrium, then the government should peg the interest rate, or the exchange rate, and therefore increase the domestic nominal quantity of money in the same proportion as the foreign price increase. If such a policy is followed, domestic prices move along with foreign prices at constant exchange rates and without any real effects. The alternative of a constant domestic price level will require a reduction in the nominal quantity of money in the short run and will involve larger relative price fluctuations. Noting that a constant price level policy will require

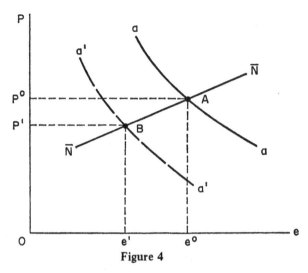

Figure 4

in the adjustment process, first a decline in the nominal price of home goods, and increase in the nominal price of traded goods with a subsequent reversal, any downward rigidity of prices will make such a policy costly. The same argument applies to the automatic adjustment process associated with a constant nominal quantity of money. These remarks accordingly provide a support for a policy of pegging interest rates and exchange rates in the case of foreign nominal disturbances.

IV. SPECULATIVE DISTURBANCES AND DUAL EXCHANGE RATES

In the present section, we will investigate the effects of exogenous speculative disturbances and proceed from there to a discussion of a dual exchange rate system that has been advocated as a remedy against the influence of speculation on the real sector.

To allow for an exogenous change in the expected future spot rate, we modify (10) to:

$$\bar{e} = \pi e + (1 - \pi)e_{-1} - eu, \tag{16}$$

where u denotes a current shift term in expectations. Specifically, an increase in u implies that given the current and past spot rate, we have an expected appreciation in the exchange rate and therefore a forward discount. Using the present form of the forward rate in the asset market equilibrium condition yields:

$$r(M/P) - (1 - \pi)(e_{-1}/e - 1) + u = r^*. \tag{17}$$

Consider now the implication of an anticipated appreciation of the exchange rate. In Fig. 4 we have the initial full equilibrium at point A. An increase in the expected future spot rate will shift the asset market equilibrium schedule down and to the left to $a'a'$. At the initial equilibrium interest rate and prices, the anticipated appreciation creates a covered differential in favor of the home country and therefore causes an incipient capital inflow that appreciates the exchange rate.

Short-run equilibrium obtains at point B. The anticipated increase in the future spot rate is reflected in an appreciation in the current spot rate, a discount on forward exchange, and a decline in the domestic interest rate. More importantly, the decline in traded goods prices that is implied by the appreciation and the decline in the relative price of traded goods imply a deflationary influence in that sector. Traded goods prices decline relative to costs, and for that reason, the speculative attack imposes a real cost on the traded goods sector. This is very much the problem currently experienced by strong currency countries and, in particular, Switzerland.[1]

The short-run equilibrium at B is sustained by expectations that will prove erroneous and, to that extent, will over time give rise to revision of expectations and a return to the initial equilibrium. More likely, however, the sectoral problems caused by the speculative pressure on the exchange rate will give rise to some form of intervention. There would seem to be a case for dual exchange rates that isolate the current account transactions from speculative attacks; alternatively, and this has been a solution favored by the Swiss, to join a strong currency area and thereby share the burden of a speculative attack.

A dual or two-tier exchange market can be readily introduced in the preceding analysis. Under such a regime, we distinguish the official rate, $\tilde{e}$, applicable to current account transactions, from the free rate that applies to capital account transactions.[2] In the following, we will assume that interest earnings can be converted at the free rate, e. The latter assumption implies that the analysis underlying the asset market equilibrium schedule aa in Fig. 5 remains unchanged. Equilibrium in the asset market continues to require that covered interest arbitrage obtains where the forward rate continues to be formed by an adaptive expectations mechanism.[3] The home goods market equilibrium schedule $\bar{N}\bar{N}$ is drawn as a function of the official rate $\tilde{e}$. Initial equilibrium obtains at point A, where the official rate, $\tilde{e}^0$, happens to coincide with the free rate.

To illustrate the working of the system, now consider again in Fig. 5 the problem of a speculative attack in the form of an increase in the expected future spot rate. The incipient capital flow will immediately bid up the free rate to e', where the spot rate has appreciated sufficiently to offset the expected appreciation. There is no effect at all on the equilibrium price level, relative prices, or interest rate because the relevant rate for the determination of relative prices is the fixed official rate $\tilde{e}^0$. Under these circumstances, the economy is entirely shielded from the effects of speculation on the real sector. How does the system differ from a unified free rate? Under the latter, the appreciation of the exchange rate would have put downward pressure on traded goods prices and the price level, while here the international price connection via the official rate remains undisturbed.

---

[1] Under the heading, "Are the Swiss Enjoying Their Strong Currency? No. Not in the Least", the *Wall Street Journal* of February 27, 1975 notes: "And what is it like to be the cynosure of international money markets? It is, the Swiss will tell you, increasingly uncomfortable, if not miserable".

[2] For a discussion of dual exchange rate systems, see Fleming (1971), Swoboda (1974), and Sheen (1974).

[3] What determines the level of the free rate in the long run? The present model is not equipped to answer that question because the adaptive expectations mechanism implies that in the long run the forward rate is equal to the spot rate. In the absence of a difference between spot and forward rates, interest rates will be equated at any level of the free rate. The free rate has no effect on the real system and therefore, in the present model, is indeterminate in the long run.

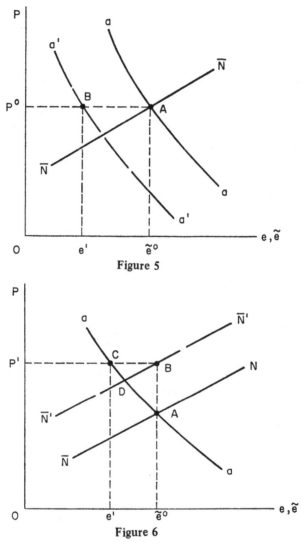

Figure 5

Figure 6

How does a dual exchange rate system affect the scope of domestic policies? Consider an increase in government spending or a cut in taxes that gives rise to an expansion in aggregate real spending. In Fig. 6, we show that, as a consequence of higher real spending, we have an excess demand for home goods and therefore the market equilibrium schedule shifts up to $\bar{N}'\bar{N}'$. With the official rate fixed at $\tilde{e}^0$, the increased spending causes an increase in the domestic price level and in the relative price of home goods, to P'. The increased price level, in turn, implies higher interest rates. To maintain asset market equilibrium in the face of higher domestic interest rates, we experience an appreciation in the spot free rate to e'. At that rate, the spot rate has sufficiently fallen relative to the forward rate to generate a premium that offsets the higher domestic interest rate.

The equilibrium at point B implies that fiscal policy under a dual exchange rate system exerts a stronger effect on interest rates and the price level and that the same increase in spending gives rise to a smaller increase in the relative price of home goods. The latter point can be appreciated by noting that under a unified free rate we would be at point D. The explanation is simply that under a dual system we have larger increases in interest rates and therefore more of a dampening of the increased spending and for that reason require only smaller *relative* price changes. The counterpart of the smaller relative price changes is, however, a larger change in nominal income. To the extent that sectoral considerations are relevant, and they most assuredly are, the question of relative prices and intersectoral resource allocation is important. From that perspective, the dual rate system is more nearly neutral than a system with a free unified rate.

CONCLUDING REMARKS

This paper has developed models of the determination of exchange rates and of the operation of a flexible exchange rate system. Among the conclusions, two deserve emphasis here. First, that the exchange rate, as a first approximation, is determined in the asset markets. This implies that expectations and changes in expectations as much as changes in money supplies dominate the course of the exchange rate in the short run.

The second conclusion that we wish to retain here concerns the lack of homogeneity that a flexible rate system is likely to exhibit in the short run. With prices sticky, or exchange rate expectations sticky, monetary changes as much as foreign price disturbances will be transmitted internationally and thus destroy the argument that a flexible rate system provides isolation from and for monetary disorder.

APPENDIX I

In this appendix we will derive some of the results presented in Section III and discuss the stability of the adjustment process. We start with the equation for the $\bar{N}\bar{N}$ schedule that embodies equilibrium in the home goods market, given monetary equilibrium:

$$\bar{N}(eP_T^*/P, r(M/P), g) = 0. \qquad (1)$$

We can solve that equation for the equilibrium price level, $\bar{P}$, as a function of the money supply, traded goods prices in terms of foreign currency and the exchange rate:

$$P = \bar{P}(eP_T^*, M, g). \qquad (2)$$

Noting that the excess demand in (1) is homogeneous of degree zero in all prices and the quantity of money it follows that the equilibrium price level in (2) is homogeneous of degree one in the quantity of money and the domestic currency price of traded goods. Accordingly, we can write the logarithmic differential of (2) as follows:

$$\hat{P} = \delta(\hat{e} + \hat{P}_T^*) + (1 - \delta)\hat{M}; \quad 0 < \delta < 1 \qquad (3)$$

where government spending is held constant.

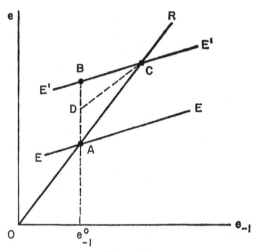

Figure 7

Taking similarly the differential of the asset market equilibrium condition:

$$r(M/P) = r^* + (1 - \pi)(e_{-1}/e - 1) \tag{4}$$

we obtain:

$$\hat{M} - \hat{P} = -\sigma(1 - \pi)(\hat{e}_{-1} - \hat{e}) \tag{5}$$

where the foreign interest rate is held constant. Combining (3) and (5) yields an expression for the change in the spot rate as a function of the disturbances:

$$\hat{e} = \frac{\delta}{\delta + \sigma(1 - \pi)}(\hat{M} - \hat{P}_T^*) + \frac{\sigma(1 - \pi)}{\delta + \sigma(1 - \pi)}\hat{e}_{-1}. \tag{6}$$

In the short run $\hat{e}_{-1} = 0$ and the first term in (6) indicates the impact effect of a monetary or foreign price disturbance. In the long run, $\hat{e} = \hat{e}_{-1}$, and therefore nominal disturbances are reflected in corresponding exchange rate changes.

Consider next the stability question.[1] Substituting the equilibrium price level, $P(\ )$ in (4) yields a final reduced form equation that relates the current spot rate to the past spot rate for given money and foreign prices:

$$r(M/\bar{P}(eP_T^*, M, g)) - (1 - \pi)(e_{-1}/e - 1) = r^*. \tag{7}$$

Eq. (7) is a difference equation in the exchange rate. To determine stability we differentiate (7) and evaluate at equilibrium the derivative to obtain:

$$de/de_{-1} = \frac{\sigma(1 - \pi)}{\delta + \sigma(1 - \pi)} < 1 \tag{8}$$

which ensures stability.

In Fig. 7 we show eq. (7) for an initial nominal quantity of money as the upward

---

[1] There is a growing body of partial equilibrium models exhibiting instability in the foreign exchange market because of a failure to link that sector with the asset markets. See, for example, Allen & Miller (1974) and Britton (1970). Minford (1974) in a very interesting formulation shows that instability can be attributed to a failure to consider the monetary effects of exchange rate changes.

sloping line EE with a slope less than unity. An increase in the nominal quantity of money shifts the schedule upward in the same proportion to $E'E'$. From the initial equilibrium at A, the spot rate immediately jumps to point B and then moves along $E'E'$ until the new equilibrium at point C is reached. We have inserted, too, in Fig. 7 the path of the forward rate ADC. The forward rate by (10) will always lie between the current and past spot rate and therefore consistently underpredicts the actual exchange rate. This departure from rational expectations forms the basis of the transitory real effects of a monetary disturbance.

REFERENCES

ALLEN, W. & MILLER, M.: The stability of the floating exchange rate. Unpublished manuscript, Bank of England, 1974.

ARGY, V. & PORTER, M.: The forward exchange market and the effects of domestic and external disturbances under alternative exchange rate systems. *I.M.F. Staff Papers 19*, No. **3**, 1972.

BLACK, S.: *International Money Markets and Flexible Exchange Rates*. Princeton Studies in International Finance, No. **32**. Princeton University, 1973.

BLACK, S.: Exchange rate policies for less developed countries in a world of floating rates. Unpublished manuscript, Vanderbilt University, 1975.

BRITTON, A. J. C.: The dynamic stability of the foreign exchange market. *Economic Journal 80*, 91–96, 1970.

COLLERY, A.: *International Adjustment, Open Economies and the Quantity Theory of Money*. Princeton Studies in International Finance, No. **28**, Princeton University Press, 1971.

CORDEN, M.: *The Theory of Protection*. Clarendon Press, Oxford, 1971.

DORNBUSCH, R. (1974a): Capital mobility, flexible exchange rates and macroeconomic equilibrium. Forthcoming in *Recent Developments in International Monetary Economics* (ed. E. Claassen and P. Salin), North-Holland, 1976.

DORNBUSCH, R.: Tariffs and nontraded goods. *Journal of International Economics 4*, 177–185, 1974b.

DORNBUSCH, R.: A portfolio balance model of the open economy. *Journal of Monetary Economics 1*, 3–19, 1975.

FLEMING, J. M.: Domestic financial policies under fixed and floating exchange rates. *I.M.F. Staff Papers 9*, 369–379, 1962.

FLEMING, J. M.: *Essays in International Economics*. Allen and Unwin, 1971.

FRENKEL, J. & LEVICH, R.: Transaction costs and interest arbitrage: tranquil versus turbulent periods. *Journal of Political Economy 85*, No. **6**, December, 1977: 1209–1226.

JOHNSON, H. G.: World inflation and the international monetary system. Unpublished manuscript, University of Chicago, 1975.

LAURSEN, S.: The market for foreign exchange. *Economia Internazionale 8*, 762–783, 1955.

MAGEE, S.: U.S. import prices in the currency contract period. *Brookings Papers on Economic Activity 1*, 117–164, 1974.

MINFORD, P.: Structural and monetary theories of the balance of payments. Unpublished manuscript, University of Manchester, 1974.

MUNDELL, R. A.: Exchange rate margins and economic policy. In Murphy, C. (ed.), *Money in the International Order*. Southern Methodist University Press, 1964.

MUNDELL, R. A.: *International Economics*. Macmillan, 1968.

MUSSA, M.: A monetary approach to balance of payments analysis. *Journal of Money, Credit and Banking* (3), 333–351, 1976.

NIEHANS, J.: Some doubts about the efficacy of monetary policy under flexible exchange rates. *Journal of International Economics 5*, 275–281, 1975.

POLAK, J. J.: European exchange depreciation in the early twenties. *Econometrica 12*, 151–162, 1964.

ROBINSON, J.: Banking policy and the exchanges. *Review of Economic Studies 3*, 226–229, 1936.

SWOBODA, A. K.: The dual exchange rate system and monetary independence. In Aliber, R. Z. (ed.), *National Monetary Policies and the International Financial System*. University of Chicago Press, 1974.

SHEEN, J.: Dual exchange rates and the asset markets. Unpublished manuscript, International Monetary Project, London School of Economics, 1974.

WONNACOTT, P.: The floating Canadian dollar. American Enterprise Institute, Foreign Affairs Study 5, 1972.

THE EXCHANGE RATE, THE BALANCE OF PAYMENTS, AND MONETARY AND FISCAL POLICY UNDER A REGIME OF CONTROLLED FLOATING

MICHAEL MUSSA

University of Chicago, Chicago, Illinois, USA

ABSTRACT

This paper considers the extension of the fundamental principles of the monetary approach to balance of payments analysis to a regime of floating exchange rates, with active intervention by the authorities to control rate movements. It makes four main points. First, the exchange rate is the relative price of different national monies, rather than national outputs, and is determined primarily by the demands and supplies of stocks of different national monies. Second, exchange rates are strongly influenced by asset holders' expectations of future exchange rates and these expectations are influenced by beliefs concerning the future course of monetary policy. Third, "real" factors, as well as monetary factors, are important in determining the behavior of exchange rates. Fourth, the problems of policy conflict which exist under a system of fixed rates are reduced, but not eliminated, under a regime of controlled floating. A brief appendix develops some of the implications of "rational expectations" for the theory of exchange rates.

INTRODUCTION

The current system of controlled floating differs significantly from the exchange rate system which existed prior to 1971 and from textbook descriptions of freely flexible rates. Governments no longer seek to maintain fixed parities; neither do they forego direct intervention in the foreign exchange markets. Nevertheless, it is the central contention of this paper that the basic theoretical framework of the monetary approach to the balance of payments, developed for a fixed rate system, remains applicable. This approach emphasizes that both the balance of payments (meaning the official settlements balance) and the exchange rate are essentially monetary phenomena.[1] The proximate determinants of exchange rates and balances of payments are the demands for and the supplies of various national monies. When the demand for

---

Reprinted by permission from *Scandinavian Journal of Economics* 78, No. 2 (May, 1976): 229–248.
[1] A number of recent contributions to the monetary approach to balance of payments analysis are contained in Frenkel & Johnson (1975). See also, Dornbusch (1973), Kemp (1975), and Mussa (1974).

a particular money rises relative to the supply of that money, either the domestic credit component of the money supply must be expanded, or the exchange rate must appreciate, or the official settlements balance must go into surplus, or some combination of the three.

This paper will elaborate on the monetary approach to exchange rate and balance of payments theory and will discuss the applicability of this theory to recent experience. To focus on broader issues, while avoiding excessive concern with formal details, the discussion will proceed at a general level. In addition to summarizing the monetary approach, this paper will make four basic points. First, in accord with the general principles of the monetary approach, exchange rates are best thought of as relative prices of different national monies, rather than as relative prices of different national outputs. Exchange rates are determined primarily by the conditions for equilibrium between the demands for the *stocks* of various national monies and the stocks of these monies available to be held. Second, like all prices determined in asset markets, exchange rates are strongly influenced by asset holders' expectations of the future behavior of asset prices. Since national monetary authorities can exert substantial control over the supplies of national monies, expectations concerning the behavior of these authorities are of critical importance for the behavior of exchange rates. Third, while the exchange rate and the official settlements balance are monetary phenomena, they are not exclusively monetary phenomena. Changes in exchange rates are frequently induced by "real" factors, operating through monetary channels; and, changes in exchange rates usually have real effects which are of legitimate concern to government policy. Fourth, the problems of policy conflict which exist under a system of fixed rates are potentially reduced, but not eliminated, under a regime of controlled floating. The relaxation of the commitment to fixed parities allows greater independence in use of monetary and fiscal policies by introducing an additional policy instrument, the exchange rate, but undesired real effects of exchange rate changes limit the usefulness of this additional instrument.

I. A MONETARY APPROACH TO EXCHANGE RATE THEORY

The monetary approach to balance of payments analysis is built on the assumption that the demand for money is a stable function of a limited number of arguments, at least over periods of a year or two. This money demand function constrains the equilibrium size of the money supply. Under a system of fixed rates, where governments are committed to buy or sell foreign exchange to maintain the par value of their national money, the foreign source component of the money supply is endogenous. If there is a change in one of the arguments of the money demand function which leads to an increase in money demand, and if the domestic source component of the money supply is not increased, the monetary approach predicts that the country will experience a balance payments surplus. Eventually, to prevent the exchange rate from appreciating, the monetary authority will be compelled to purchase foreign exchange and, thereby, to increase the foreign source component of the money supply. On the other hand, if the monetary authority were to increase the domestic source component of the money supply, without any change in the arguments in the money demand function, the result would be an excess of money supply over money demand. Eventually, this would lead to downward pressure on the exchange rate, forcing the monetary authority to contract the foreign source component of the money supply by the amount of the increase in the domestic source component. The process whereby the initial disturbance is transmitted to the balance of payments and the speed with which adjustment occurs will depend on particular circumstances and institutional arrangements. The ultimate result is determined by the condition for equilibrium between money demand and money supply.

This simple theory of the balance of payments under fixed rates is easily converted into a theory of the exchange rate under freely flexible rates. Under freely flexible rates, the foreign source component of the money supply is fixed. Hence, if there is a change in one of the arguments of the money demand function or in the domestic credit component of the money supply, equilibrium cannot be achieved by induced adjustment of the foreign source component of the money supply. Instead, the exchange rate adjusts. These adjustments affect the variables which enter into the money demand function: prices, incomes, expected returns from holding domestic rather than foreign money, etc. Ultimately, the exchange rate must change sufficiently so that money demand is brought into equilibrium with money supply.

The monetary theory of the exchange rate and the balance of payments under a regime of controlled floating is a combination of these two simple theories. Under this regime, monetary authorities actively intervene in the foreign exchange market to control fluctuations in exchange rates, but do not seek to maintain fixed rates. A change in the demand for money relative to the supply available from domestic credit sources puts pressure on the exchange rate. The monetary authorities must decide the extent to which this pressure will be relieved by allowing the exchange rate to change and the extent to which it will be absorbed through variations in foreign exchange reserves. The extent of the initial monetary disequilibrium determines the total adjustment which is required. The authorities must decide on the division of this adjustment between exchange rate changes and foreign exchange reserve changes.

This monetary theory of the exchange rate and the balance of payments is useful in interpreting some of our experience in recent years. First, consider the substantial appreciation of the Swiss franc relative to other European currencies which occurred in 1974. Was this due to an increase in the competitiveness of Swiss industry or to an increase in the demand for Swiss watches and Swiss ski resorts? Clearly not. The explanation is that there was a substantial increase in the demand to hold Swiss money, at the old exchange rates, and that this increase in demand was not met by an increase in the supply of Swiss money, thus requiring an appreciation of the Swiss franc.

Second, consider the relative performance of the German mark and the British pound during 1974. Both countries are large importers of oil, and both suffered from the large increase in the price of oil. Nevertheless, the mark was strong while the pound was weak. The monetary explanation of this result is to be found in the monetary policies of Germany and England. The Bundesbank pursued a very tight policy with respect to domestic credit expansion, while the Bank of England pursued a much easier policy.

Third, consider the balance of payments of Saudi Arabia. The increase in the price of oil has meant a large increase in the real income of Saudi Arabia. This increase in income made possible the large balance of payments surplus of Saudi Arabia. But, the surplus also reflected a choice concerning how to spend the increased income. If the income had all been spent on foreign goods or on shares in foreign companies, Saudi Arabia would not have experienced an official settlements surplus. It is because the Saudis decided to spend a significant portion of their increased income on the accumulation of official foreign exchange assets that they ran a large official settlements surplus.

Finally, consider the appreciation of the U.S. dollar relative to other currencies during the early summer of 1975. The explanation of this event from a monetary perspective, is to be found in the simultaneous tightening of U.S. monetary policy and the loosening of monetary policies in most other countries. In late June and early July, the U.S. Federal Reserve provided convincing evidence of its desire to keep the rate of monetary expansion below $7\frac{1}{2}\%$ per year by clamping down on a previous surge in the money supply and increasing short term interest rates. At virtually the same moment Chancellor Schmidt announced that Germany would pursue a strong reflationary policy, and the governments of France and Japan announced similar policies. The combined effect of these policy changes on asset holders' expectations of future exchange rates was sufficient to induce an approximately 10% appreciation of the dollar.

II. THE EXCHANGE RATE AS THE RELATIVE PRICE OF TWO MONIES

In this brief sketch of the monetary approach, no mention has been made of the traditional elements of exchange rate theory: the demand for foreign exchange and the supply of foreign exchange and the price elasticities of import demands and export supplies. In the traditional theory, the demand for foreign exchange is determined by the amount which domestic residents spend on imports, measured as a *flow* of foreign money, and the supply of foreign exchange is determined by the amount which foreign residents spend on domestic exports, measured as a *flow* of foreign money. Under fixed rates, the excess of the demand for foreign exchange over the supply of foreign exchange is equal to the balance of payments deficit. A devaluation, it is argued, increases the price of imports in terms of domestic money and reduces the price of exports in terms of foreign money. Provided that the Robinson–Metzler–Bickerdike condition on the elasticities of demands for imports and supplies of exports is satisfied, a devaluation improves the balance of payments. Under flexible exchange rates, the balance of payments is zero, and the exchange rate is determined by the condition that the demand for foreign exchange must equal the supply of foreign exchange. The Robinson–Metzler–Bickerdike condition becomes the condition for the stability of the exchange rate.[1]

From the perspective of the monetary approach, however, all of this discussion of elasticities is fundamentally irrelevant since the traditional theory on which it is based contains two serious conceptual errors. First, it views the exchange rate as the relative price of national outputs, rather than as the relative price of national monies. Second, it assumes that the exchange rate is determined by the conditions for equilibrium in the markets for flows of funds, rather than by the conditions for equilibrium in the markets for stocks of assets.

The identification of the exchange rate with the relative price of national outputs is implicit in the assertion that the balance of payments effects of a change in the exchange rate arise because exchange rate changes induce changes in the relative prices of domestic and foreign goods. The fallacy in this view is most easily seen when two countries produce the same goods. Commodity trade still occurs since the pattern of commodity production need not match the pattern of commodity consumption in each country. The law of one price, however, requires that the same good have the same price in both countries, adjusted for the exchange rate, and taking account of transport costs, tariffs, etc. In such a situation, a devaluation by the home country will increase the domestic money price of every good relative to the foreign money price of that good by exactly the amount of the devaluation. But, there is no strong reason to believe that this change in nominal prices should be associated with any particular change in relative commodity prices.

This argument does not deny that there are circumstances in which exchange rate changes do have significant effects on relative commodity prices or that relative price changes affect the balance of payments. But such effects must come through the impact of these relative price changes on the demand for money. Specifically, if a devaluation reduces the relative price of domestic output in terms of foreign output and, thereby, induces an expansion of domestic output and contraction of foreign output, the demand for domestic money should rise and the demand for foreign money should fall. This change in money demands will induce a flow of foreign exchange reserves from the foreign country to the home country. On the other hand, if the demand for money in the home country and the demand for money in the foreign country were unaffected by a devaluation, and if the domestic credit components of the money supplies were held constant, there could be no permanent balance of payments effect from an exchange rate change. A devaluation might lead to a temporary change in relative commodity prices which might induce a temporary flow of foreign exchange. But, this flow would produce an excess of the supply of money over the demand for money in one country and a corresponding deficiency in the other country. Eventually, the restoration of monetary equilibrium would

---

[1]There are a variety of approaches which yield restrictions on price elasticities as the condition for a successful devaluation; see, for instance, Pearce (1970, ch. 4), and Caves & Jones (1973, ch. 4 and 5).

require that any initial foreign exchange flow in one direction be matched by a later foreign exchange flow in the opposite direction.

The second fallacy in the traditional approach is the concentration on the markets for flow of funds and the neglect of the markets for stocks of assets. In the traditional approach, under a system of fixed rates, a "fundamental disequilibrium," created by incorrect relative commodity prices, generates a permanent divergence between the flow demand for and the flow supply of foreign exchange. Since the effects of asset flows on asset stocks are usually not considered in the traditional approach, these deficits and surpluses presumably continue, without repercussions or self-limiting adjustments, until some country exhausts its reserves. In contrast, in the monetary approach, the critical equilibrium condition is the requirement that the demand for the *stock* of each national money must equal the *stock* of that money available to be held. Flows of funds occur in order to correct existing monetary disequilibria or to prevent new disequilibria from emerging. But, the demands and supplies of flows of funds are a reflection of the requirements for asset market equilibrium, rather than the basic determinant of equilibrium.

The distinction between the monetary approach, with its emphasis on stocks, and the traditional approach, with its emphasis on flows comes out most forcefully in analyzing disturbances in the flow markets. Consider an increase in foreign aid payments from one country, the home country, to another, the foreign country. (For simplicity, assume a two country world). The traditional conclusion is that such an increase in foreign aid will create a permanent balance of payments deficit for the home country and a permanent balance of payments surplus for the foreign country. The home country will either have to devalue or pursue policies which improve the competitiveness of its export and import competing industries. The monetary approach takes quite a different view. The increase in the flow of foreign aid will reduce income in the home country and increase income in the foreign country. This will have a once and for all effect on the demand for the stock of money in the two countries which, in the absence of changes in domestic credit, will require a small temporary flow of reserves to restore monetary equilibrium. After this equilibrium is achieved, the official settlements balance of both countries will be zero. The home country will experience a balance of trade surplus and the foreign country will experience a balance of trade deficit. In the balance of payments accounts, the trade surpluses and deficits will be balanced by the payments and receipts of foreign aid.

The traditional approach which emphasizes flows of funds derives much of its appeal from technical details of the operation of foreign exchange rate markets. Traders in foreign exchange markets may take open positions, on a very short-term basis, in order to smooth out very short-run fluctuations in exchange rates. Aside from this very short-run smoothing, however, traders seek to set rates which will balance the inflow and outflow of each national currency. Foreign exchange traders operate in much the same way as specialists on the stock exchange. They make the market. They seek to set a price which will balance purchases and sales.

The perspective of the foreign exchange trader, or the stock market specialist, however, is not the relevant perspective from which to analyze the determination of asset prices. Stock prices can change rapidly, even though the flow through the market is very small. Conversely, the volume of trade can be large and stock prices may remain essentially unchanged. The condition which determines the value of a particular company is that the outstanding shares of that company be willingly held. If sentiment concerning the future profitability of the company changes suddenly, the values of its shares will change suddenly. The volume of trade in the company's shares reflects primarily the divergence of views among asset holders: if sentiment is unanimous, prices will change with little or no trade. If sentiments differ, the volume of trade will be large.

The same principles apply to the foreign exchange markets. If money holders decide that the Deutsche mark is undervalued relative to the U.S. dollar, the mark will appreciate relative to the dollar. The flow through the mark–dollar exchange market may be very small. The circumstances in which the flow through the market becomes large is when opinions regarding the appropriate exchange rate differ. The most spectacular instances occur during exchange crises when official authorities hold one view regarding the appropriate exchange rate and everyone else holds a different view, as, for instance, the day on which the Bundesbank purchased two billion U.S. dollars.

It should be emphasized that the asset market view of the determination of exchange rates does not require that all money holders be prepared to shift their holdings from one money to another on short notice. As in any asset market, all that is required is that there be a sufficient number of active participants to make the market work. As a practical matter, these active participants are most likely to be professional traders, banks and multinational corporations who, in the regular course of business, are used to holding on to a variety of different national monies. These particular money holders are likely to be the most sensitive to exchange rate changes and the most aggressive in shifting their holdings when such changes are anticipated.

III. EXPECTATIONS AND EXCHANGE RATES

The identification of the exchange rate as the relative price of national monies and the emphasis on asset market equilibrium permits the monetary approach to explain one of the major anomalies of the post-1971 period: the large, short-term fluctuations of exchange rates between the currencies of the major developed countries. These movements cannot be explained by changes in the relative prices of different national outputs. However, it has been observed for many years that prices determined in organized asset markets, such as an index of stock prices, can move up and down by significant amounts over short intervals of time. The monetary approach holds that the relative prices of national monies are determined by forces which are similar to those which operate in any asset market and, hence, that substantial short-term fluctuations in exchange rates are to be expected if the forces which lie behind exchange market equilibrium are themselves subject to substantial short-term fluctuations.

The factor which is usually held to be responsible for fluctuations in asset prices is changes in the expectations of asset holders concerning the returns (including capital gains) which are likely to accrue to particular assets. Expectations are also of critical importance in determining exchange rates. If everyone expects a particular currency to appreciate, the increase in the demand to hold that currency will force its appreciation, unless the monetary authorities permit its quantity to expand sufficiently to absorb the increase in demand. The problem is to identify the things which influence expectations concerning the returns to holding particular currencies and to explain why expectations have tended to fluctuate.

If the monetary approach is correct, then *one* of the critical determinants of the equilibrium value of any national money is the supply of that money available to be held. Hence, one of the critical variables influencing asset holders' expectations of future exchange rates is their prediction of the future supplies of various national monies. (This issue is analyzed more thoroughly in the appendix.) Expectations about money demand are also important, as in the case of the Swiss franc. Further, fiscal policy is likely to influence the exchange rate and, hence, expectations about the exchange rate, since budget deficits are frequently financed, at least in part, by the central bank.

The role of expectations in influencing exchange rates during the last four years has a counterpart during the earlier fixed exchange rate period. Normally, during this period, the official commitments to the maintenance of fixed parities led to the expectation that these parities would be maintained. Occasionally, however, people would come to believe that a change in the official parity was imminent, resulting in an exchange rate crisis in which huge flows of reserves would be drained from a country which was expected to devalue or would inundate a country which was expected to revalue. In the traditional approach to balance of payments theory, such "speculative flows of short-term capital" are usually treated as a special phenomenon, outside the scope of the theory. In the monetary approach, the explanation of these flows is an integral part of the theory. If asset holders expect that a currency will be devalued, the demand for that money clearly falls.

IV. REAL CAUSES AND EFFECTS

So far, this paper has emphasized money demand and money supply as the proximate determinants of exchange rates and the balances of payments. "Real" variables are also important. The most important real variable affecting the exchange rate and the balance of payments of developed countries is the level of real income. As pointed out by Mundell, countries which enjoy rapid growth of real income will also experience rapid growth in the demand for money. Unless the domestic credit component of the money supply ·expands more rapidly than the demand for money, high growth countries should experience balance of payments surpluses and/or appreciating exchange rates. Fluctuations of real income around its normal trend also affect the exchange rate and the balance of payments since they affect the demand for money. Further, real disturbances affect the balance of payments and the exchange rate through the induced response of the policy authorities to such disturbances. If output and employment decline, governments are likely to pursue expansionary monetary and fiscal policies. Such policies have monetary consequences in the form of balance of payments deficits and/or depreciating exchange rates.

An important real variable affecting the balance of payments of many developing countries is the price of their primary exports. This has been illustrated dramatically for the oil exporting countries. It is also apparent in the experience of countries where export earnings are heavily dependent on a single commodity. It should be emphasized, however, that while changes in primary export prices are appropriately regarded as real disturbances, such disturbances must operate through monetary channels in order to affect the exchange rate or the official settlements balance. The tendency to run balance of payments surpluses when export prices are high and balance of payments deficits when export prices are low implies that real domestic consumption does not fluctuate by the full amount of fluctuations in export earnings. This dampening effect may not be deliberate. It may simply reflect the extent to which the government calls upon the central bank to finance its own deficit. When government receipts from royalties and taxes on exports are high, the central bank does not have to print much money. When government tax and royalty receipts decline, the central bank must finance the deficit by expanding the domestic credit component of the money supply.

Whatever may be the cause of changes in exchange rates, real or monetary, such changes usually have important real effects. These real effects are apparent in the recent experience of the United States and various Western European countries. The depreciation of the dollar relative to most other currencies has improved the competitive position of U.S. export industries and worsened the competitive position of European export industries. This is apparent in the experience of the steel industry in the United States which has continued to enjoy relative prosperity, despite the current recession. Further, while the auto industry all over the world has been depressed, Volkswagen has been particularly hard hit. One of the reasons appears to be that Volkswagen exports a large fraction of its output to the United States. The large appreciation of the mark relative to the dollar (up to June of 1974) has increased the price of Volkswagens relative to American cars and has reduced the size and profitability of Volkswagen's exports.

The explanation of these real effects of exchange rate changes has to do with the role which money plays in the economy. Domestic money is the unit of account for domestic contracts. For this reason, an important part of an exporter's costs are likely to be fixed, at least in the short run, in terms of domestic money. If the exchange rate of domestic money in terms of foreign money appreciates, the exporter must either increase his prices in terms of foreign money or see his profit margin eroded by a decline in his selling price relative to his production costs. Firms that produce highly standardized goods have little choice but to adjust their prices in terms of foreign money to those that prevail in world markets (unless they have a significant share of the market). Firms which produce more differentiated products have some latitude in increasing their prices in terms of foreign money, at the expense of some decline in sales.[1]

---

[1] Previous discussions of the monetary approach have frequently dealt with the "small country case" in which the prices of traded goods in terms of foreign money are assumed to be given by conditions in world markets. This assumption is primarily a matter of convenience. There is no difficulty in incorporating differentiated national outputs or large countries into the general framework of the monetary approach.

V. POLICY CONFLICT AND POLICY COORDINATION

From the perspective of policy makers, the most important real effects of exchange rate changes are their effects on employment, output and the price level. If prices of domestic outputs and domestic wages tend to be fixed, in the short run, in terms of domestic money, then the expansion of the nominal demand for domestic goods which is induced by a decline in their relative price in world markets expands domestic output and employment. The price level is influenced directly by the impact of exchange rate changes on the prices of standardized internationally traded commodities. Beyond this direct influence, a depreciation contributes to inflation (and an appreciation contributes to deflation) through the gradual adjustment of the prices of non-traded goods and non-standardized traded goods to the new prices of standardized traded goods and through the adjustments of wages to the unexpected changes in real incomes.[1]

The fact that exchange rate changes have real effects makes such changes a concern of government policy. It also implies that governments can use exchange rates as instruments of government policy. This possibility has been recognized for some time. During the thirties, a number of governments devalued in the hope that this would stimulate domestic output and employment. Policy conflicts arose because everyone wanted to devalue relative to everyone else. This problem of policy conflict, however, is not an inevitable consequence of a system of controlled floating. Indeed, a system of controlled floating offers greater possibilities for avoiding policy conflict than a system of fixed rates. Under fixed rates, conflict is likely to arise whenever one government wants to expand and another government wants to contract. These different policies will put a strain on the balance of payments, with the country which is pursuing expansionary monetary and fiscal policies losing reserves to the country pursuing contractionary policies and with these reserve flows interfering with the policies of both countries. Under flexible rates, this source of conflict can be eliminated by permitting the currency of the expansionary country to depreciate relative to the currency of the contractionary country. Policy conflict is likely to arise when two countries want to expand output and employment or reduce inflation simultaneously, and when each wants to use their mutual exchange rate in pursing its objective.

The potential for policy conflict gives rise to the need for policy coordination. What the monetary approach contributes to the discussion of policy coordination is a clear understanding of the policies which must be coordinated. Specifically, to avoid the problem of competitive depreciation which plagued the thirties, it is usually suggested that governments agree not to intervene against their own currencies in the foreign exchange markets. The monetary approach suggests that this rule is fundamentally inadequate. What matters is the supply of money, not whether this money is

---

[1] Recent events in England and Israel indicate that workers have caught on to the fact that a devaluation is likely to reduce the real value of any given nominal wage. Workers appear to be quite prompt in demanding nominal wage increases to compensate for the effects of devaluation.

created by buying domestic or foreign assets. A government can cause its currency to depreciate almost as well by having its central bank buy domestic bonds as by having it buy foreign currency. Thus, policy coordination requires essentially the coordination of monetary policies. Fiscal policies also matter to the extent that such policies are financed by money creation or have an impact on money demand.

Finally, it is worth discussing the insulation from foreign disturbances and independence of domestic monetary policy which a system of flexible rates is supposed to provide. The argument that flexible exchange rates insulate an economy from foreign disturbances is usually presented in a model in which national outputs are distinct and capital is immobile. In such a situation, the only link between the domestic economy and the rest of the world is through the relative price of domestic and foreign goods. Under flexible rates the exchange rate adjusts this relative price so as to keep foreign demand for domestic goods constant, thereby, insulating the domestic economy.

Formally, this argument is correct.[1] As a practical matter, it may be essentially descriptive of the relationships between the United States and China. But, the argument does not apply to relationships between the United States and Canada. If the United States experiences a deep recession, so will Canada, regardless of whether the Canadian dollar floats relative to the U.S. dollar. The reason is that goods markets and capital markets in the United States and Canada are all highly integrated. The automobile industry in the two countries is really a single industry. If the demand for autos falls in the U.S., the output of autos in both countries will fall. The same holds true for many other industries. Further, the integration of the capital markets provides an important channel for the transmission of disturbances. If aggregate demand in the U.S. falls, the U.S. demand for Canadian goods will fall, tending to produce a trade balance deficit for Canada. This deficit, however, need not force a depreciation of the Canadian dollar and a corresponding cheapening of Canadian goods which restores U.S. demand for these goods. Rather, the trade imbalance can be financed by capital inflow into Canada, with the result that part of the reduction in U.S. aggregate demand is transmitted to Canada.

The failure of flexible exchange rates to insulate an economy from foreign disturbances implies that flexible exchange rates do not permit total independence of national stabilization policies. Flexible exchange rates do, however, permit different long-term rates of inflation. The explanation of why flexible rates permit different long-term rates of inflation returns us to the basic theme of this paper: the exchange rate as a monetary phenomenon. It is now a well established principle of monetary analysis that fluctuations in the money supply have real effects on employment and output only if these fluctuations are not anticipated.[2] The same is true for exchange rates. If one country's money depreciates continually relative to another

---

[1] Actually, this argument neglects the Laursen—Metzler effect of a change in the terms of trade on desired saving, and, hence, on aggregate demand.
[2] In connection with this issue, see especially the work of Lucas (1972 and 1973) , Sargent (1973), and Sargent & Wallace (1975).

country's money, these changes in the exchange rate will come to be anticipated. Once they are anticipated, they will cease to have any real effects.

APPENDIX

Rational Expectations, Monetary Policy, and the Exchange Rate

The purpose of this appendix is to develop a simple model which illustrates a number of conclusions concerning the interaction between monetary policy, exchange rates and exchange rate expectations. The model is built on the assumption that the exchange rate is fundamentally an asset price which is proximately determined by the relationship between the willingness to hold domestic money and the stock of domestic money available to be held. Expectations of future exchange rates affect the willingness to hold domestic money. These expectations are assumed to be "rational" in the sense that they reflect asset holders' knowledge of the structure of the economy, in particular, the structure of the stochastic processes generating money demand and money supply.[1]

I. The Model

Suppose that the stock of domestic money which domestic and foreign residents are willing to hold is given by

$$m(t) = \lambda \cdot e(t) - \eta \cdot \pi(t) + \zeta(t), \lambda \text{ and } \eta > 0; \tag{1}$$

where $m(t)$ is the logarithm of the stock of domestic money at time t; $e(t)$ is the logarithm of the exchange rate (defined as the price of a unit of foreign money in terms of domestic money); $\pi(t)$ is the expected rate of change in the exchange rate,

$$\pi(t) \equiv E_t(e(t + 1) - e(t)) \tag{2}$$

where $E_t(\ )$ indicates the expectation at time t, based on the information available to asset holders at that time; and $\zeta(t)$ summarizes all of the influences on the willingness to hold domestic money other than $e(t)$ and $\pi(t)$. The right hand side of (1) should be thought of as the final reduced form of a general equilibrium model with the usual structure of goods and asset market equilibria.[2] The prices, quantities and rates of return on all goods and assets (except m, e and π) have been solved out of the system, and the influence of all of these variables on the willingness to hold domestic money

---

[1] For the application of the concept of "rational" expectations to exchange rate theory, see Black (1972) and (1973). Also see Kouri (1975). For a general survey of the literature on rational expectations in macroeconomic models see Shiller (1975) or Sargent (1973).

[2] The general procedure for deriving such a final reduced form relationship is indicated in Mussa (1975b). A variety of models could be used as the basis for the relationship given in (1), for instance, those of Dornbusch (1976), and Kouri (1975). The simplest model would be one in which there is a single traded good with a domestic price equal to the exchange rate times the foreign price level and where the real demand for money depends on the expected rate of inflation (which is identical to the expected rate of depreciation). This is essentially the model analyzed by Sargent & Wallace (1973) and Mussa (1975a) for the closed economy. The model could be made more realistic by the methods suggested by Dornbusch.

is subsumed in the variable $\zeta(t)$ and in the values of the elasticities, λ and η. In particular $\zeta(t)$ incorporates the effects of disturbances in the foreign money supply, foreign prices, and foreign interest rates on the willingness to hold domestic money.

The assumption that λ and η are positive is plausible for virtually any basic model of exchange rate determination. An increase in the exchange rate increases the domestic price of internationally traded commodities and may also increase domestic output and income, all of which suggests an increase in the desire to hold domestic money. An increase in the exchange rate reduces the ratio of the value of domestic money to foreign money and to all assets denominated in foreign money (or in real terms) and should, from a portfolio balance perspective, increase the nominal demand for domestic money. An increase in the expected rate of depreciation (an increase in π) decreases the attractiveness of domestic money relative to foreign money and relative to assets denominated in foreign money. An increase in π also suggests an increase in the expected rate of inflation which should reduce the demand for money.

Substituting (2) into (1) and solving for $e(t)$ yields

$$e(t) = \left(\frac{1}{\lambda + \eta}\right) \cdot [m(t) - \zeta(t) + \eta \cdot E_t(e(t+1))]. \tag{3}$$

To complete the determination of $e(t)$, it is necessary to know the current expectation of $e(t+1)$. We impose the assumption that expectations are formed "rationally". Specifically, asset holders are assumed to know (or act as if they know) equation (3) and apply it to next period's exchange rate; thus

$$E_t(e(t+1)) = \frac{1}{\lambda + \eta} \cdot E_t[m(t+1) - \zeta(t+1) + \eta \cdot E_{t+1}(e(t+2))]. \tag{4}$$

Using the fact that $E_t(E_{t+1}(e(t+2))) = E_t(e(t+2))$ and applying the same procedure iteratively to $E_t(e(t+2)), E_t(e(t+3))$, etc., it follows that[1]

$$E_t(e(t+1)) = \left(\frac{1}{\lambda + \eta}\right) \cdot \left\{ E_t \left[m(t+j) - \zeta(t+1) + \frac{\eta}{\lambda + \eta}(E_t(m(t+2)) \right. \right.$$

$$\left. \left. - \zeta(t+2) + \dots) \right] \right\}$$

$$= \left(\frac{1}{\lambda + \eta}\right) \sum_{j=1}^{\infty} E_t[m(t+j) - \zeta(t+j)] \cdot \left(\frac{\eta}{\lambda + \eta}\right)^{j-1}. \tag{5}$$

II. Two Examples
It is reasonable to assume that people have relatively little information about events far in the future, except possibly in the form of predictions of long-run average levels or rates of growth. This assumption eliminates all but a finite number of terms from

---

[1]The form of (5) is almost identical to that given by Sargent & Wallace (1973). See, also, Mussa (1975a).

(5). In this section, we consider two examples which focus on short-run deviations of $m(t) - \zeta(t)$ around long-run levels or rates of growth. For simplicity we assume that $\zeta(t) = k$, a constant.

Example 1: A fixed mean with autocorrelated disturbances. Suppose that $m(t)$ is determined by

$$m(t) = \bar{m} + u(t), \quad u(t) = \rho \cdot u(t-1) + \epsilon(t) \tag{6}$$

where $\bar{m}$ is the mean level of the money supply, $u(t)$ is an autocorrelated disturbance with correlation coefficient, ρ, $0 \leqslant \rho \leqslant 1$, and $\epsilon(t)$ is a serially uncorrelated, normally distributed random variable with zero mean and variance σ_ϵ^2. Assuming that asset holders know the properties of the stochastic process generating the money supply, including the mean, $\bar{m}$, and also know $m(t)$ and hence $u(t) = m(t) - \bar{m}$, it follows that

$$E_t(m(t+j)) = \bar{m} + \rho^j \cdot u(t) \tag{7}$$

Substitution of this result into (5) yields

$$E_t(e(t+1)) = \bar{e} + \left(\frac{\rho}{\lambda + \eta(1-\rho)}\right) \cdot u(t), \tag{8}$$

which together with (3) implies

$$e(t) = \bar{e} + \left(\frac{1}{\lambda + \eta(1-\rho)}\right) \cdot u(t) \tag{9}$$

where $\bar{e} \equiv (1/\lambda)(\bar{m} - k)$ is the long-run expected level of e, the value of e which is consistent with $m = \bar{m}$. From (2), (8) and (9), it follows that

$$\pi(t) \equiv E_t(e(t+1)) - e(t) = (1-\rho) \cdot (\bar{e} - e(t)). \tag{10}$$

The intuitive explanation of this result is the following. When ρ is small, money holders expect the exchange rate to converge rapidly to $\bar{e}$. A temporary increase in the money supply will cause $e(t)$ to rise; domestic money depreciates relative to foreign money. However, money holders expect a rapid reappreciation. This expectation induces them to hold larger domestic money balances which, in turn, limits the current depreciation. In contrast, if ρ is large, money holders will not expect a rapid return to $\bar{e}$. The current exchange rate will have to move further in order to equilibrate the current demand and supply of domestic money. In the limit, when $\rho = 1$, any current disturbance to the money supply is expected to persist forever. In fact, m is a random walk, and this makes e a random walk. Any current disturbance to the money supply affects the current and all expected future exchange rates by the same amount. Since money holders do not expect the exchange rate to regress to any normal level, the current exchange rate must absorb the full effect of any change in the current money supply.

Example 2: A random walk on levels and rates of growth. The second example assumes that the rate of growth as well as the level of the money supply is randomly determined. Specifically,

$$m(t) = m(t-1) + \alpha(t) + \epsilon(t) \tag{11}$$

where $\epsilon(t)$ has the same properties as in the first example and $\alpha(t)$ is a random walk,

$$\alpha(t) = \alpha(t-1) + \delta(t) \tag{12}$$

where $\delta(t)$ is a serially uncorrelated, normally distributed random disturbance with zero mean, variance σ_δ^2, and independent of the ϵ's. $\alpha(t)$ should be interpreted as the (expected) long-term rate of growth of the money supply which changes randomly over time. In addition to the randomness in the long-term rate of growth, there are also disturbances to the level of the money supply, the ϵ's.

Assuming that money holders know the properties of the stochastic process generating the money supply, it follows that

$$E_t(m(t+j)) = m(t) + j \cdot \hat{\alpha}(t) \tag{13}$$

where $\hat{\alpha}(t) \equiv E_t(\alpha(t))$ is not necessarily equal to $\alpha(t)$. Whether this equality holds depends on the information available to money holders at time t. Substituting (13) into (5) yields

$$E_t(e(t+j)) = \frac{1}{\lambda} \cdot \left[m(t) - k + \left(\frac{\lambda + \eta}{\lambda} \right) \cdot \hat{\alpha}(t) \right] \tag{14}$$

which together with (3) implies

$$e(t) = \frac{1}{\lambda} \left[m(t) - k + \left(\frac{\eta}{\lambda} \right) \cdot \hat{\alpha}(t) \right]. \tag{15}$$

If money holders always know the current values of α and ϵ as well as the current value of m, it follows that $\hat{\alpha}(t) \equiv E_t(\alpha(t)) = \alpha(t)$ and $\hat{\epsilon}(t) \equiv E_t(\epsilon(t)) = \epsilon(t)$. The effect on the exchange rate of an unexpected increase in the money supply depends on the source of this increase. The expected increase in the money supply from period $t-1$ was $\alpha(t-1) = E_{t-1}(m(t) - m(t-1))$. If m increases by more than this amount because of a positive value of $\epsilon(t)$, money holders will know that is only a disturbance to the level of the money supply. The current value of e will rise by a factor $1/\lambda$ times $\epsilon(t)$. The expected value of $e(t+1)$ will rise by the same amount. However, if the expected increase in $m(t)$ is known to arise from a positive value of $\delta(t)$, money holders know that this portends larger increases in the money supply in every future period. The current value of e will rise by a factor of $(1/\lambda)(1 + (\eta/\lambda))$ times $\delta(t)$. This is a greater increase than for the positive $\epsilon(t)$. Further, the expected value of $e(t+1)$ rises by even more than $e(t)$ because the increase in the expected long-term rate of growth of the money supply leads people to expect more rapid depreciation of domestic money.

On the other hand, suppose that money holders only observe the time path of m and must infer from this information the values of α and ϵ. It can be shown (see, for instance, Mussa, (1975a)) that under rational expectations

$$\hat{\alpha}(t) = \hat{\alpha}(t-1) + a \cdot (m(t) - m(t-1) - \hat{\alpha}(t-1)). \tag{16}$$

The magnitude $m(t) - m(t-1) - \hat{\alpha}(t-1)$ is the difference between the observed change in m, $m(t) - m(t-1)$, and its a priori expected value $\hat{\alpha}(t-1)$. A fraction, a, of this difference is added to last period's $\hat{\alpha}$ in order to obtain the current $\hat{\alpha}$. The fraction, a, is determined by the relative likelihood that a deviation of $m(t) - m(t-1)$ from its a priori expected value is caused by an unexpected change in α rather than by a random disturbance to the level of m; specifically,

$$a = \frac{\theta^2 + \sigma_\delta^2}{\theta^2 + \sigma_\delta^2 + \sigma_\epsilon^2} \tag{17}$$

where

$$\theta^2 = \tfrac{1}{2} \cdot \left[-\sigma_\delta^2 + \sqrt{\sigma_\delta^4 + 4 \cdot \sigma_\delta^2 \cdot \sigma_\epsilon^2} \right].$$

In the present case, an increase in the long-term rate of growth of m (a positive $\delta(t)$) has the same effect as an increase in the level of m (a positive $\epsilon(t)$). The reason is that money holders cannot, at time t, distinguish between a positive $\epsilon(t)$ and a positive $\delta(t)$. The current value of e rises by a factor of $(1/\lambda)[1 + a \cdot (\lambda + \eta/\lambda)]$ times either $\epsilon(t)$ or $\delta(t)$. It should be emphasized, however, that the errors which are made under incomplete information are neither permanent nor irrational. The errors are not permanent because in periods $t+1, t+2$, etc., additional information will be received concerning the true value of α; if there has been a change in α, money holders will ultimately discover it. Further, any errors which are made are not irrational because "rationality" is defined with respect to an information set. People form the best expectations they can, given the limitation on their information.

III. Some Implications
These examples illustrate a number of important conclusions. First, the way in which exchange rate expectations are formed should depend on the underlying economic structure, including the stochastic structure of disturbances to the demand and supply of money. In the first example, if $\rho < 1$, expectations are "regressive" in the sense that a current depreciation of the exchange rate leads to the expectation that the exchange rate will re-appreciate to its average level. On the other hand, if $\rho = 1$, any change in $e(t)$ is believed to be permanent and is reflected in an equal change in $E_t(e(t+1))$. These considerations may have practical relevance. The exchange rate between the Canadian and U.S. dollars has been within 10% of parity for more than 100 years. This may explain the apparent regressivity of exchange rate expectations concerning the Canadian dollar.

Second, since the way in which expectations are formed is likely to depend on the characteristics of monetary and fiscal policy, it is incorrect to assume that the expectations mechanism will long remain unchanged in the face of a significant change in the basic characteristics of policy. This important point has been made in a much broader context by Lucas (1970). In the context of Example 1, exchange rate expectations are highly regressive when ρ is close to zero. However, if policy is changed to make $\rho = 1$, expectations will lose their regressivity as soon as the change in policy is discovered. If policy is changed to that of Example 2, the change in the mechanism of expectation formation will be even more dramatic. At a practical level, if Canada began to pursue a highly inflationary policy, relative to the United States, which drove the exchange rate outside of its usual bounds, it probably would not be very long before the normal regressivity of expectations was eliminated.

Third, the exchange rate which prevails at any instant, and the expectations which are held at that instant concerning future exchange rates, depend on the information available to asset holders at that instant. This principle was illustrated in the second example in the comparison between behaviour with full information and behaviour with limited information. As a practical matter, of course, information is always limited in the sense that we never know the future course of all variables relevant to our current decisions. After the fact, it will appear that errors have been made. However, after the fact is not the appropriate perspective from which to judge the "rationality" of exchange rate expectations or the "efficiency" of the exchange markets. Large up and down movements of exchange rates appear irrational and inefficient, after the fact, but do not provide evidence of a capacity to make better predictions or more profitable transactions, before the fact.

Fourth, the two examples suggest caution in making general assumptions concerning the response of forward rates to variations in spot rates. For simplicity, identify the forward rate with the expected future spot rate. In the first example we have the following results. If $\rho = 0$, the forward rate is constant and changes in the spot rate have no effect on the forward rate. If ρ is between 0 and 1, the forward rate moves in the same direction as the spot rate, but not by as much. If $\rho = 1$, the spot and forward rates move together. In the second example, with full information, the spot and forward rates move together for changes in the level of m, and the forward rate moves more than the spot rate for changes in the rate of growth of m. With incomplete information, the forward rate always responds more strongly than the spot rate to an unexpected change in m.

Fifth, exchange rate fluctuations may be more extensive than fluctuations in the money supply or in money demand. From equation (3) it is apparent that if $\lambda + \eta < 1$, fluctuations in either $m(t)$ or $\zeta(t)$ will have a magnified effect on $e(t)$. Further, if, as in Example 2, disturbances to $m(t)$ lead to the conviction that the rate of growth as well as the level of the money supply have changed, the exchange rate will respond immediately to both the disturbance in $m(t)$ and to the anticipated change in the rate of depreciation.

Sixth, in both examples, the process generating disturbances in the money supply was an arbitrarily prescribed stochastic process, a stochastic black box. In fact, there is likely to be a good deal of economic structure which lies behind the nature of disturbances to the money supply, including the structure of the banking system, the aggressivity of "stabilization" policy, and the extent to which the government resorts to the printing press as a means of financing its deficits. However, so long as the internal workings of the black box continue to generate the same sort of stochastic outcomes, it is not necessary for asset holders to understand these workings in order to form their exchange rate expectations. The internal structure becomes important when something inside the box changes. For instance, in the context of Example 1, suppose that the "structure" is changed by a shift from $\rho = 0$ to $\rho = 1$. If asset holders understand the implications of this change in structure, exchange rate expectations will shift immediately from being regressive to a random walk. If asset holders do not understand the structure, it will probably take some time for them to realize that regressive expectations are no longer appropriate.

Finally, the two examples have strong implications concerning the concept of "stabilizing expectations". Exchange rate expectations are frequently said to be "stabilizing" if they are regressive; that is, if current depreciation (or appreciation) is limited by the expectation that the exchange rate will later re-appreciate (or re-depreciate). In Example 1, with $\rho < 1$, exchange rate expectations are regressive. They are regressive because the underlying behaviour of the money supply makes regressive expectations appropriate. However, in Example 1, with $\rho = 1$, and in Example 2, exchange rate expectations are not regressive. These expectations are, nevertheless, "stabilizing" in the fundamental sense that they are the best possible predictions of future exchange rates, given the nature of monetary policy and the information available to asset holders.

REFERENCES

BLACK, S. The use of rational expectations in models of speculation. *Review of Economics and Statistics*, May 1972.

BLACK, S. *International Money Markets and Flexible Exchange Rates*. Princeton Studies in International Finance, No. 32, 1973.

CAVES, R. E. & R. W. JONES *World Trade and Payments*. Little Brown, Boston, 1973.

DORNBUSCH, R. Money, devaluation, and non-traded goods. *American Economic Review* 63, No. 5, 1973.

DORNBUSCH, R. The theory of flexible exchange rate regimes and macroeconomic policy. *Scandinavian Journal of Economics* 78, No. 2, pp. 255–275, 1976. Reprinted in this volume as Chapter 2.

FRENKEL, J. & H. G. JOHNSON *The Monetary Approach to the Balance of Payments*. George Allen and Unwin, 1975.

KEMP, D. S. A monetary review of the balance of payments. Federal Reserve Bank of St. Louis *Review* 57, No. 4, April 1975.

KOURI, P. Exchange rate expectations, and the short run and long run effects of fiscal and monetary policies under flexible exchange rates. Presented at the Conference on the Monetary Mechanism in Open Economies, Helsinki, August 1975.

LUCAS, R. E. Econometric testing of the natural rate hypothesis. In O. Eckstein (ed.), *The Econometrics of Price Determination*. Board of Governors of the Federal Reserve System, Washington, D.C., 1970.

LUCAS, R. E. Expectations and the neutrality of money. *Journal of Economic Theory* **4**, No. 2, April 1972.

LUCAS, R. E. Some international evidence of output-inflation trade-offs. *American Economic Review* **63**, No. 3, June 1973.

MUNDELL, R. A. *International Economics*. Macmillan, New York, 1968.

MUSSA, M. L. A monetary approach to balance of payments analysis. *Journal of Money Credit and Banking* **6**, No. 3, August 1974.

MUSSA, M. L. Adaptive and regressive expectations in a rational model of the inflationary process. *Journal of Monetary Economics* **1**, No. 4, October 1975*a*.

MUSSA, M. L. Equities, interest, and the stability of the inflationary process. *Journal of Money, Credit and Banking*, November 1975*b*.

PEARCE, I. F. *International Trade*. Norton, New York, 1970.

SARGENT, T. J. Rational expectations, the real rate of interest, and the natural rate of unemployment. *Brookings Papers on Economics Activity*, 1973.

SARGENT, T. J. & N. WALLACE Rational expectations and the dynamics of hyperinflation. *International Economic Review*, June 1973.

SARGENT, T. J. & N. WALLACE Rational expectations, the optimal monetary instrument and the optimal money supply rule. *Journal of Political Economy* **83**, No. 2, April 1975.

SHILLER, R. Rational expectations, and the dynamic structure of macroeconomic models. Paper presented at the Conference on the Monetary Mechanism in Open Economies, Helsinki, August 1975.

CHAPTER 4

CONTRACTING AND SPURIOUS DEVIATIONS FROM PURCHASING-POWER PARITY

STEPHEN P. MAGEE
The University of Texas at Austin

The movement to floating exchange rates has been an important development in our understanding of the interaction between goods markets and securities markets. International trade data permit a comparison of the efficiency of goods markets relative to securities markets which is not possible using domestic data. Each transaction in international trade involves both a real and a financial market.

For example, with perfect efficiency and the absence of transactions costs in both markets, the ratio of the home price to the foreign price (called the "goods price ratio") will equal the units of home currency per foreign currency prevailing on foreign exchange markets. This equality is called "absolute purchasing-power parity (PPP)."[1] Absolute PPP guarantees that changes in the goods price ratio will equal changes in the exchange rate (relative PPP). If changes in the price ratios are serially correlated but changes in the foreign exchange rate are not, then the goods markets can be said to be less efficient than the foreign exchange market. Furthermore, a goods market in which changes in the goods price ratio are highly autocorrelated can be defined as less efficient, in some sense, than a goods market with low autocorrelations.

In this paper we explore the implications of the efficient market hypothesis for our observation of deviations from PPP in international trade data. We show that even when goods markets are just as efficient as foreign exchange markets in eliminating all *ex ante* international profit opportunities, the data can still show spurious inefficiencies because the goods price ratio is frequently set when the goods are contracted (e.g., home currency/unit ÷ foreign currency/unit in January) and this may be very different

The author is indebted to Ken Clements, Frank Vargo, Donald Weinig and seminar participants at the University of Florida, Gainesville, the London School of Economics, and at the University of Texas, Austin, for helpful comments; to Jan Finklea and Karen Mathis for typing various drafts, and to the U.S. Department of Commerce and the National Science Foundation for research support.

[1] For a discussion of the various interpretations of PPP see Frenkel (1976). For a model incorporating the PPP relationship for traded goods see Dornbusch (1976). See also Aliber (1976) for empirical work.

from the exchange rate prevailing when the goods are later delivered and recorded in the international trade statistics (e.g., home currency/foreign currency in April). We simulate explicitly the spurious autocorrelation in the deviations from relative purchasing-power parity as determined by the frequency distribution of order to delivery lags for five products imported into the United States from West Germany.

The results derived here have wide application: the use of actual transactions prices for many markets, domestic as well as international, can cause goods markets to appear spuriously inefficient. Removal of this statistical artifact would help narrow the gap between the research methodologies used in the economics literature for goods markets and in the finance literature for securities markets.

Several terms require clarification. By "efficiency" we mean that current information arrives randomly and is fully incorporated into current price quotations so that successive price changes will follow a random walk.[2] "Transactions (or contract) prices" are the prices paid at the time of delivery for goods negotiated at the time of contract while "spot" prices are quotations currently for goods to be delivered presently or in the future. Examples of contract prices include the well-known "unit values" which appear in international trade data and in the NBER series of prices for goods which are made to order in the study by Stigler and Kindahl (1970). Spot prices include many of the items in the U.S. wholesale price index and many items in the consumer index. The greater the unanticipated change in spot prices over a given period and the longer the lags between orders and delivery of contracted goods, the greater the possible divergence between contract prices and spot prices. Most price indices are some combination of transactions prices and spot prices. Contract prices are important in international trade data because of the pervasive use of unit values (transactions prices) in international empirical studies.[3]

In Section I we examine behavior in the financial market; in Section II we investigate how an efficient goods market would interact with this financial market; in Section III we show how contracting and forecast errors interact to generate spurious empirical inefficiency in transactions data for international goods markets and hence, spurious deviations from purchasing-power parity.

I. THE FINANCIAL MARKET

Assume that spot exchange rates contain all of the information currently available about the currencies in question, that new information affecting the markets arrives randomly, and that as a result, the changes in exchange rates follow a random walk through time. Giddy and Dufey (1975) have shown not only that a random walk describes well the change in exchange rates in the recent floating period but also that it out-performs forward market forecasts.[4] Thus, we assume that the expected exchange rate i periods ahead, $E(e_{t+i})$, is the current rate, e_t:

---

[2] The concept of efficiency is also discussed in the context of foreign exchange markets in Bilson (1978), Frenkel (1976), Levich (1978), and Stockman (1978).

[3] See Kravis and Lipsey (1971).

[4] For further results predicting foreign exchange rates, see Levich (1978).

$$E(e_{t+i}) = e_t \qquad (1)$$

The assumption that new information hits the market randomly permits us to model realized future rates as follows. Let u be a serially independent random variable with mean zero. The sequence of realized exchange rates after time t can be written

$$e_{t+1} = e_t + u_1$$
$$e_{t+2} = e_t + u_1 + u_2 \qquad (2)$$
$$e_{t+i} = e_t + u_1 + u_2 + \ldots + u_i,$$

where u_1 is the forecast error between t and $t + 1$, u_2 is the forecast error between $t + 1$ and $t + 2$, etc. The variance of e_{t+i} can be written as follows:

$$V(e_{t+i}) = V(e_t + u_1 + u_2 + \ldots + u_i)$$
$$= 0 + \sigma_{u_1}^2 + \sigma_{u_2}^2 + \ldots + \sigma_{u_i}^2 \qquad (3)$$
$$= i\sigma_u^2$$

where $\sigma_{u_k}^2$ is the variance of u_k. The second line of (3) assumes independence of the u_i while the third line assumes that the u_k are identically distributed.[5] The independence assumption is particularly important since it means that the covariation between all forecast errors equals zero: i.e.,

$$\text{Cov}\,(u_i, u_j) = 0 \qquad \text{for all } i \neq j \;. \qquad (4)$$

We now examine behavior in goods markets.

II. EFFICIENT GOODS MARKET BEHAVIOR

In order to develop the hypothesis posed at the outset, we make the strongest possible assumptions about the efficiency of goods markets, namely, that each supplier is small and that perfect competition prevails, that there are no costs of changing list prices or quotations for future delivery dates, that there are constant costs (so that prices are independent of quantities sold), that there are no transport costs, and for simplicity, that there are no markups by importers.

Most importantly, we assume complete *ex ante* elimination of geographical deviations from the law of one price, so that in equilibrium, all profit opportunities from international arbitrage are eliminated. This is equivalent to assuming complete *ex ante* purchasing-power parity (PPP) between the home and foreign markets in internationally traded goods contracted at time t and delivered at time $t + i$. Hence, we have

$$P_{t+i} = E(e_{t+i})P_{t+i}^*, \qquad (5)$$

where

$\quad P_{t+i} \quad$ = the home currency price of traded goods contracted at time t for delivery at time $t + i$;

---

[5] For a related characterization of the path of foreign exchange rates, see Stockman (1978).

$E(e_{t+i})$ = the expected exchange rate (home currency per unit of foreign currency) at time $t + i$; and

P^*_{t+i} = the foreign currency price of traded goods contracted at time t for delivery at time $t + i$.

Assume also that both the home and the foreign price are fixed at time t. One of the two prices is always fixed in nominal terms since the contract must be written in either home currency or foreign currency. The assumption implies that the other party always fixes his nominal price at time t by hedging the contract. The random walk assumption made earlier implies no drift in exchange rates (i.e., no international interest rate differentials) so that the forward rates used to hedge contracts equal the current spot rate, e_t.

Let us rewrite Eq. (5) by dividing both sides by P^*_{t+i} and defining d_t to be the normalized deviation from PPP:

$$d_{t+i} \equiv (P_{t+i}/P^*_{t+i}) - E(e_{t+i}). \qquad (6)$$

When financial markets set exchange rates according to (1), we can rewrite (6) as

$$d_{t+i} = (P_{t+i}/P^*_{t+i}) - e_t. \qquad (7)$$

The implication is that traders will adjust their price quotations for all future deliveries until the price ratio equals the current spot exchange rate.

The efficient market assumptions for both the goods and the financial markets assure that prices will adjust until there are no *ex ante* deviations from PPP. That is, the expected deviation, $E(d_{t+i})$, is zero for all contract lengths i. However, the variance of the deviations does depend on the forecast horizon, i. Since (P_{t+i}/P^*_{t+i}) is non-random, only forecast errors in e_{t+i} contribute to the normalized variance in the deviations from PPP, d_{t+i}. Thus, the variance in d_{t+i} equals the variance in e_{t+i} in Eq. (3):

$$V(d_{t+i}) = V(P_{t+i}/P^*_{t+i} - E(e_{t+i}))$$
$$= i\sigma^2_u.$$

We are now equipped to show how perfectly efficient goods markets will appear inefficient in the data.

III. SPURIOUS INEFFICIENCY IN MARKETS FOR INTERNATIONALLY TRADED GOODS

In this section we show explicitly how large and sustained deviations from PPP will be generated if transactions prices are used and multiperiod contracting occurs. Since monthly data are available for the contract length of U.S. imports from Germany in months, let the time subscripts denote months. Assume that we attempted to measure the deviations from PPP using an export price index for German goods exported to the U.S., an import price index for U.S. goods imported from Germany, and the current exchange rate. If the price indexes were spot prices, then from Eq. (7), $d_{t+0} = 0$ and we would observe no deviations from PPP since the ratio of prices in the U.S. (P) to

Table 1
FREQUENCY DISTRIBUTIONS (f_i), AUTOCORRELATIONS (r_k), MEAN CONTRACT LENGTHS AND MULTIPLICATIVE FACTORS, M_{fn}, FOR FIVE MAJOR U.S. IMPORTS FROM WEST GERMANY

	Organic chemicals		Steel plates, sheets		Textile machinery		Cars		Miscellaneous	
Observations (for f)	15		46		16		18		27	
Mean contract length (months)	3.67		4.93		4.03		1.07		4.5	
M_{fn}	2.88		4.17		2.88		1.09		2.44	
Month (i) or Lag (k)	f_i	r_k	f_i	r_k	f_i	r_k	f_i	r_k	f_i	r_k
1	0.07	0.80	0.00	0.86	0.19	0.79	0.69	0.28	0.24	0.76
2	0.20	0.57	0.02	0.69	0.31	0.60	0.31	0.00	0.13	0.59
3	0.27	0.39	0.23	0.51	0.13	0.52	0.00	0.00	0.21	0.43
4	0.13	0.29	0.13	0.36	0.00	0.47	0.00	0.00	0.08	0.34
5	0.07	0.20	0.21	0.23	0.00	0.42	0.00	0.00	0.08	0.26
6	0.07	0.13	0.17	0.15	0.00	0.36	0.00	0.00	0.08	0.19
7	0.13	0.08	0.11	0.11	0.06	0.30	0.00	0.00	0.03	0.16
8	0.00	0.07	0.00	0.09	0.00	0.00	0.00	0.00	0.05	0.12
.9	0.00	0.06	0.04	0.06	0.00	0.21	0.00	0.00	0.00	0.10
10	0.00	0.05	0.00	0.04	0.00	0.00	0.00	0.00	0.00	0.08
11	0.00	0.02	0.00	0.02	0.25	0.25	0.00	0.00	0.00	0.04
12 & over	0.06		0.09		0.06		0.00		0.10	

those in Germany (P^*) of goods quoted this month for current and future delivery would equal this month's exchange rate.

However, if contract prices (the amounts actually received by German exporters and the amounts actually paid by U.S. importers) are used for P and P^*, substantial deviations can be measured. Let f_1 be the proportion of trade arriving in the U.S. this month from Germany which was contracted 1 month ago, f_2 the proportion contracted 2 months ago, etc. The frequencies, f_i, are shown in Table 1 for five categories of U.S. imports from Germany (see Magee, 1974, Tables 1–4 for a more elaborate description of the data in Table 1). Note that the average order to delivery lags range from 1.07 months for autos to 4.93 months for steel plates and sheets.

The ratio of U.S. to German contract prices this month will be an average of past spot price ratios, and the weights will equal the f_i in Table 1. For example, last month's spot price ratio of P_{t-1}/P_{t-1}^* for organic chemicals will have a weight of 0.07, the 2-month-ago price will have $f_2 = 0.20$, etc. Assuming time invariance of the f_i allows us to write the current contract price ratio as

$$\tilde{P}_t/\tilde{P}_t^* = \sum_i f_i(P_{t-i}/P_{t-i}^*) \tag{9}$$

and the *realized* differences of this ratio from the current exchange rate will equal a weighted average of past exchange rate forecast errors:

$$\tilde{d}_t = \tilde{P}_t/\tilde{P}_t^* - e_t$$

$$= \sum_i f_i(P_{t-i}/P_{t-i}^* - e_t) \tag{10}$$

$$= \sum_i f_i(e_{t-i} - e_t) \ .$$

Note that the average realized deviation from PPP still equals zero since $E(e_{t-1}) = E(e_t)$. *However, the variance in $\tilde{d}_t$ will always be greater than or equal to the variance in the monthly exchange rate forecast errors.* This can be seen by rewriting Eq. (10) as

$$\tilde{d}_t = \sum_{i=1}^{n} f_i(e_{t-i} - e_t)$$

$$= \sum_{i=1}^{n} f_i \left(\sum_{j=1}^{i} u_j \right)$$

$$= \sum_{i=1}^{n} u_i \left(\sum_{j=i}^{n} f_j \right) \tag{11}$$

$$= \sum_{i=1}^{n} u_i \phi_i$$

where

$$\phi_i \equiv \sum_{j=i}^{n} f_j \ .$$

The u_i are the realized monthly exchange rate forecast errors, the ϕ_i are the weights, and n is the maximum contract length. The observed variance in $\tilde{d}_t$ is calculated as follows:

$$\text{Var} (\tilde{d}_t) = \sigma_u^2 \left(\sum_{i=1}^{n} \phi_i^2 \right)$$

$$= \sigma_u^2 M_{fn} \tag{12}$$

where

$$M_{fn} \equiv \sum_{i=1}^{n} \phi_i^2 \ .$$

The term M_{fn} is greater than 1 in all cases except when $n = 1$; then it equals 1 (in the latter case, $M_{fn} = 1$ since $\phi_1 = 1$).

Note that we have described the normalized deviations from PPP as a statistical distribution with mean zero and with a variance equal to the product of the monthly variance in the exchange rate (the financial market) and a scalar M_{fn} summarizing the entire frequency distribution, f, of contract lengths whose maximum length is n (the goods market). Since M_{fn} is unit free, the product variances are comparable across products. Note in Table 1 that M_{fn} ranges from 1.09 for autos (69 percent of which are ordered and delivered in one month) to 4.17 for steel (whose mean order-to-delivery lag is 4.93 months). Longer lags are generally associated with larger values of M_{fn}. However, the values of M_{fn} clearly depend upon more than one moment of the distribution f: miscellaneous goods have a longer average lag than textile machinery but a smaller value of M_{fn} (note the difference in their f_i).

We have established that the variance of $\tilde{d}_t$ will generally exceed the variance of u_t. We show next that the measured $\tilde{d}_t$ will be serially correlated, a violation of goods market efficiency. The autocovariation at lag k (i.e., covariation between d_t and d_{t-k}) is calculated as follows:

$$
\begin{aligned}
\mathrm{Cov}\,(\tilde{d}_t, \tilde{d}_{t-k}) &= E[\tilde{d}_t - E(\tilde{d}_t)]\,[\tilde{d}_{t-k} - E(\tilde{d}_{t-k})] \\
&= E[\phi_1 u_{t-1} + \phi_2 u_{t-2} + \ldots + \phi_n u_{t-n}]\,[\phi_1 u_{t-k-1} \\
&\quad + \phi_2 u_{t-k-2} + \ldots + \phi_n u_{t-n}] \\
&= E[\phi_1 \phi_{k+1} u_{t-k-1}^2 + \phi_2 \phi_{k+2} u_{t-k-2}^2 + \ldots + \phi_{n-k}\phi_n u_{t-n}^2] \qquad (13) \\
&\quad + E[0 + 0 \ldots + 0] \\
&= \sigma_u^2 [\phi_1 \phi_{k+1} + \phi_2 \phi_{k+2} + \ldots + \phi_{n-k}\phi_n] \\
&= \sigma_u^2 \sum_{i=1}^{n-k} \phi_i \phi_{i+k}.
\end{aligned}
$$

These autocovariances can be normalized by the variance to yield autocorrelations. The sample autocorrelations of lag k, r_k, are calculated in Eq. (14):

$$
\begin{aligned}
r_k &= \mathrm{Cov}\,(\tilde{d}_t, \tilde{d}_{t-k})/\mathrm{Var}\,(\tilde{d}_t) \\[4pt]
&= \frac{\sigma_u^2 \sum_{i=1}^{n-k} \phi_i \phi_{i+k}}{\sigma_u^2 \sum_{i=1}^{n} \phi_i^2} \qquad (14) \\[4pt]
&= \frac{\sum_{i=1}^{n-k} \phi_i \phi_{i+k}}{\sum_{i=1}^{n} \phi_i^2}.
\end{aligned}
$$

Note that all of the autocorrelations will be positive since all of the ϕ_i weights are non-negative and range from a maximum of 1 to a minimum of zero. In contrast to the variance of $\tilde{d}$, the autocorrelations of the normalized deviations from PPP are completely determined by real factors, namely, the frequency distributions of contract lengths.

The autocorrelations at lag lengths of up to 11 months are shown in Table 1. The short contracts for autos generate only one significant autocorrelation while longer contracts and the outliers for textile machinery (31 percent of trade has contracts of 11 months or longer) generate autocorrelations that are greater than .25 for lags in the deviations from PPP of up to 8 months. The simulations in Table 1 show that the normalized deviations from PPP will be large for products with high M_{fn} and persistent (i.e., long strings of deviations will occur, all of which have the same sign). This contrasts with efficient market behavior, which posits neither the presence of deviations nor their serial correlation. Contract price data coupled with payments lags leads us to observe spuriously the presence of apparently unexploited profit opportunities, even though the pricing mechanism which generated this data was perfectly efficient (and left no such profit opportunity unexploited).

In addition to this analytical point, two implications follow. First, the many *dumping studies* done by the developed country governments *must be done with great care under a floating rate regime* if transactions prices are used. Transactions prices will be lower in one economy than another for prolonged periods, as we have demonstrated, even though no dumping ever occurred *ex ante*. The same caveat holds for studies of international price discrimination. Second, econometric studies which attempt to model "disequilibrium" price situations (using adaptive expectations, etc.) in international markets may be chasing statistical flukes generated by the collectors of international price data.

REFERENCES

ALIBER, ROBERT Z. "The Firm under Pegged and Floating Exchange Rates," *Scandinavian Journal of Economics* 78 (May, 1976): 309–322.

BILSON, JOHN F. O. "Rational Expectations and the Exchange Rate," 1978. Reproduced as Chapter 5 in this volume.

DORNBUSCH, RUDIGER. "The Theory of Flexible Exchange Rate Regimes and Macroeconomic Policy," *Scandinavian Journal of Economics* 78 (May, 1976): 225–275. Reprinted in this volume as Chapter 2.

FRENKEL, JACOB A. "A Monetary Approach to the Exchange Rate: Doctrinal Aspects and Empirical Evidence," *Scandinavian Journal of Economics* 78, No. 2 (May, 1976): 200–224. Reprinted in this volume as Chapter 1.

GIDDY, IAN, and GUNTER DUFEY. "The Random Behavior of the Flexible Exchange Rates: Implications for Forecasting," *Journal of International Business Studies* 6 (Spring, 1975): 1–32.

KRAVIS, IRVING B., and ROBERT E. LIPSEY. *Price Competitiveness in World Trade*. New York: Columbia University Press, 1971.

LEVICH, RICHARD M. "Tests of Forecasting Models and Market Efficiency in the International Money Market," 1978. Reproduced as Chapter 8 in this volume.

MAGEE, STEPHEN P. "U.S. Import Prices in the Currency-Contract Period," *Brookings Papers on Economic Activity* (No. 1, 1974): 117–164.

STIGLER, GEORGE J., and JAMES K. KINDAHL. *The Behavior of Industrial Prices*. New York: National Bureau of Economic Research and Columbia University Press, 1970.

STOCKMAN, ALAN C. "Risk, Information and Forward Exchange Rates," 1978. Reproduced as Chapter 9 in this volume.

CHAPTER 5

RATIONAL EXPECTATIONS AND THE EXCHANGE RATE

JOHN F. O. BILSON

International Monetary Fund

Northwestern University

I. INTRODUCTION

The model of exchange rate determination presented here combines elements of the "efficient market" and "monetary" approaches to asset markets.[1] The monetary aspects of the model arise through the assumption that the exchange rate, as the relative price of two monies, is primarily determined by the relative supplies and demands for these monies, and that the relevant demand and supply functions are stable functions of a small number of variables.[2] An "efficient market" is one in which all opportunities for profit are eliminated, implying, in the absence of transactions costs, that the law of one price will hold and that market price expectations will be unbiased predictors of actual future prices.[3] These principles are embodied in four important arbitrage conditions:

(i) purchasing-power parity: the prices of commodities will always be the same when expressed in a common currency;[4]

This paper is adapted from the second chapter of the author's Ph.D. dissertation at the University of Chicago. The author would like to thank Robert Z. Aliber, Rudiger Dornbusch, Jacob A. Frenkel, Harry G. Johnson, and Stephen P. Magee. The views expressed do not necessarily reflect the views of the International Monetary Fund or Northwestern University.

[1] Mussa (1976) and Barro (1977b) have developed similar models of exchange rate determination under rational expectations. The particular contributions of this paper are the account given of real income variation and the empirical tests of the model. All of these papers follow the seminal work of Sargent and Wallace (1973).

[2] For other papers on the monetary approach to exchange rate determination, see Dornbusch (1976a, 1976b), Frenkel (1976), Hodrick (1978), Mussa (1976). Surveys of this literature have been written by Magee (1976) and Whitman (1975).

[3] For a discussion of the concept of an efficient capital market, see Fama (1976), Chapter 5, and Levich (1978).

[4] The consequences of slow commodity price adjustment are discussed in Dornbusch (1976b), and Bilson (1976), Chapter 3. Frenkel (1976) discusses alternative interpretations of purchasing-power parity and Magee (1978) analyzes deviations from purchasing-power parity due to differences between transactions and contract prices.

(ii) interest-rate parity: the real rate of return on assets will be equal and independent of the currency denomination of the asset;

(iii) the Fisher condition: the nominal rate of interest will be equal to the real rate of interest plus the expected rate of inflation; and

(iv) the rational expectations hypothesis: market price expectations will be equal to the actual predictions of the underlying theoretical model.

These arbitrage conditions are relationships between endogenous variables; the role of the monetary model is to provide a theory of the fundamental determinants of these variables. In the monetary model, the present and expected future values of the money supply and the level of real income determine the present and expected future values of the price level. It is then possible, from the Fisher condition, to find the expected rate of inflation and consequently the term structure of nominal interest rates. Finally, from the interest rate and purchasing-power parity conditions, the values of the spot and forward exchange rates can be derived. The complete model consequently determines all of the present and expected future values of the endogenous variables, given the expected time paths of the money supply and real income.

The relationship between the money supply and the level of real income is established through a simple version of the Lucas-Barro-Sargent and Wallace Phillips Curve model in which deviations of real output growth from trend are related to unanticipated changes in the money supply.[5] This extension of the basic monetary model introduces the possibility that an unanticipated increase in the money supply may appreciate the exchange rate in the short run through the induced movement in real income.

The building blocks of the model are specified in the following eleven equations:

Domestic money demand function: $\quad m^d - p = k + \eta y - \epsilon i \quad$ (1)

Domestic monetary equilibrium: $\quad m^d = m^s = m \quad$ (2)

Foreign money demand function: $\quad m^{*d} - p^* = k^* + y^* - \epsilon i^* \quad$ (3)

Foreign monetary equilibrium: $\quad m^{*d} = m^{*s} = m^* \quad$ (4)

Purchasing-power parity: $\quad p = s + p^* \quad$ (5)

Interest-rate parity: $\quad r = r^* \quad$ (6)

Fisher equations: $\quad i = r + p^e_{t+1} - p \quad$ (7)

$\quad i^* = r^* + p^{*e}_{t+1} - p^* \quad$ (8)

Rational expectations: $\quad p^e_{t+1} = E[p_{t+1}|I(t)] \quad$ (9)

$\quad p^{*e}_{t+1} = E[p^*_{t+1}|I(t)] \quad$ (10)

$\quad f = E[s_{t+1}|I(t)] \quad$ (11)

---

[5] Barro (1976), Lucas (1973), and Sargent and Wallace (1975).

Notation

1. All variables are expressed in logarithms with the exception of the nominal interest rate, i, and the real interest rate, r.
2. An asterisk denotes the foreign country; superscript 'd' demand; superscript 's' supply; superscript 'e' market expectations; and subscript '$t + 1$' indicates the following period. All unsubscripted variables refer to the current period.
3. The interest rate and forward rate are both of one period maturity.

Definitions

m = the stock of nominal money balances
p = the price level
y = the level of real income
i = the nominal rate of interest
η = the income elasticity of the demand for money
ϵi = the interest rate elasticity of the demand for money
s = the spot exchange rate
f = the forward exchange rate
r = the real rate of interest, which is assumed to be exogenous.

Note: for convenience, the parameters η and ϵ are assumed to be the same in both countries.

$E[x|I(t)]$ is the conditional expectation of the variable x, given the information available at time t. All contemporaneous, economy-wide variables are assumed to be observable at time t by asset market participants.

As stated above, this model is a combination of the efficient market and monetary approaches to exchange-rate determination. The monetary nature of the model arises from the first four equations which specify a stable demand for money and instantaneous money-market equilibrium. The efficient market characteristics enter through the last seven equations, since these conditions jointly eliminate any consistent opportunities for profit. For example, purchasing-power parity eliminates opportunities for profit from commodity arbitrage; interest-rate parity from asset arbitrage; the Fisher equation from intertemporal arbitrage in commodities; and the rational expectations assumptions eliminate profit opportunities from exchange speculation and the sale of information.

From the basic equations, the following relationship can be derived:

$$s = \underline{m} - \eta \underline{y} + \epsilon(f - s) \tag{12}$$

where

$$\underline{m} = (m - m^*) - (k - k^*)$$

and

$$\underline{y} = y - y^*.$$

Assuming for the moment that real income is exogenous, Eq. (12) includes two endogenous variables, the spot and forward exchange rates. Both of these variables can adjust in order to clear the foreign exchange market, by which is meant the market for one currency relative to the other. Assuming for simplicity that the foreign country is "large," a depreciation of the exchange rate—an increase in s—will clear the domestic money market by increasing the domestic price level—thus decreasing the real supply of money—and by decreasing the nominal rate of interest—thus increasing the demand for real cash balances. For a given spot rate, an increase in the forward rate will decrease the demand for money by increasing the nominal rate of interest. Potentially, therefore, there exists an infinite number of (s, f) combinations which will maintain money-market equilibrium for given values of $\underline{m}$ and $\underline{y}$. The particular combination which will arise in the market is found by introducing the additional constraint imposed by rational expectations: that the forward rate equal the expected future spot rate.[6] This value of the forward rate may be found by leading Eq. (12) by one period and taking expectations. Generally, the rate expected to prevail in any future period $t + j$ is given by

$$(1 + \epsilon)E[s_{t+j}|I(t)] = E[\underline{m}_{t+j}|I(t)] - \eta E[\underline{y}_{t+j}|I(t)] + f_{t+j}.$$

Repeatedly substituting this result into Eq. (12) yields the following expression relating the current spot exchange rate to the current and expected future values of the money supply and real income:

$$s_t = \frac{1}{1+\epsilon} \sum_{j=0}^{\infty} \gamma^j E[\underline{m}_{t+j}|I(t)] - \frac{\eta}{1+\epsilon} \sum_{j=0}^{\infty} \gamma^j E[\underline{y}_{t+j}|I(t)] \qquad (13)$$

where

$$\gamma = \frac{\epsilon}{1+\epsilon}.$$

This equation establishes that the current spot exchange rate is determined by all of the expected future values of the exogenous variables. The equation stresses that it is necessary to distinguish between anticipated and unanticipated changes in the exogenous variables. If, for example, an increase in the money supply is announced six months prior to the actual increase, then the current spot exchange rate will react immediately. The mechanism by which this reaction occurs is as follows: the announcement will increase the expected future spot rate, and consequently the forward rate. For a given spot rate, this implies that the expected rate of inflation and the nominal interest rate have increased. The consequent decline in the demand for real money balances increases the current price level and the exchange rate. The second implication of this experiment is that the spot exchange rate will not increase proportionately with the money supply at the time at which the policy is implemented, since the necessary depreciation will already have occurred during the time during which the increase was anticipated.

How then are anticipations of future monetary and real income growth formed? This question will occupy the next two sections of the paper.

---

[6] This model assumes that speculators are risk neutral. Stockman (1978) relaxes this assumption.

II. THE MONEY SUPPLY PROCESS

In practice, it is extremely difficult to predict the future path of the money supply. Exchange market participants may look at a wide variety of possible indicators— elections, unemployment and inflation statistics, union wage agreements, past values of exchange rates, and even the announced policy targets of the monetary authority. An examination of these issues is beyond the scope of this paper. Instead, a simple illustrative model of the money supply is constructed which is sufficient to indicate the general conclusions of the rational expectations model. Specifically, the rate of growth of the money supply is assumed to follow a random walk:

$$\Delta \underline{m}_t = \Delta \underline{m}_{t-1} + u_t \tag{14}$$

where u_t is an independently distributed random variable with zero mean, and Δ is the difference operator.[7]

Under these assumptions, the expected future growth rates are simply the growth rate at the time at which the expectation is formed:

$$E[\Delta \underline{m}_{t+j} | I(t)] = \Delta \underline{m}_t \tag{15}$$

and the expected future levels are

$$E[\underline{m}_{t+j} | I(t)] = \underline{m}_t + j\Delta \underline{m}_t. \tag{16}$$

Substituting this expression into the first term on the right-hand side of Eq. (13) yields

$$\frac{1}{1+\epsilon} \sum_{j=0}^{\infty} \gamma^j E[\underline{m}_{t+j} | I(t)] = \underline{m}_t + \epsilon \Delta \underline{m}_t \tag{17}$$

$$= \underline{m}_{t-1} + (1+\epsilon)\Delta \underline{m}_{t-1} + (1+\epsilon)u_t. \tag{18}$$

Equation (17) specifies the relationship between the exchange rate and the level and rate of growth of the money supply. The rate of growth of the money supply is an indicator of the expected rate of inflation in all future periods, and influences the exchange rate through its influence on the term structure of nominal interest rates. In Eq. (18), the monetary variables are divided into the anticipated and unanticipated components. The elasticity relating the innovation—or unanticipated change—exceeds unity, as suggested by the magnification effect.[8] The rationale for the elastic response of the exchange rate is that market participants base their estimates of future monetary growth on the current growth rate. Any unanticipated change in the money supply will consequently influence the forward exchange premium. The increase in interest rates, for example, in response to an increase in the money supply, will require a further increase in the price level, and a depreciation of the exchange rate, in order to maintain money-market equilibrium.

The magnification effect, in this context, is a consequence of the choice of the money-supply process. If, as an alternative, positive money-supply errors tended to be

---

[7] Note that the difference of a variable expressed in logarithms is the rate of growth of that variable.

[8] The term 'magnification effect' in this context was originally coined by Frenkel (1976), in his discussion of the German hyperinflation. The issue is also discussed in Dornbusch (1976a, 1976b).

reversed in future periods, the elasticity relating the exchange rate to the current error would be less than unity. A full knowledge of the relationship therefore requires a detailed knowledge of the money-supply process.

The second feature of Eq. (17) that is worth mentioning is that it describes a distributed lag relationship between the money supply and the exchange rate. The particular contribution of the rational expectations model is the prior specification of the form of the distributed lag relationship based upon the underlying process generating the money supply.

III. THE REAL INCOME PROCESS

In this section, the expected future levels of real income are derived from a simple rational expectations Phillips Curve model in which only the unanticipated changes in the money supply influence unemployment and real income. In developing this theory, it is necessary to assume that the information set possessed by labor-market participants is more limited than the information set of asset-market participants. This segmentation hypothesis appears to be justified by casual observation: speculators in foreign exchange markets profit more from acquiring information rapidly relative to labor suppliers, and have consequently invested a larger quantity of human and non-human capital in information gathering. Operationally, I implement this assumption by assuming that the labor-market information is limited to economy-wide variables in period $t-1$, so that contemporary monetary shocks are unanticipated. With these considerations in mind, real income is assumed to be determined by

$$\underline{y}_{t+j} = \underline{y}^p_{t+j} + \underline{y}^t_{t+j} \tag{19}$$

$$\underline{y}^p_{t+j} = \underline{y}^p_t + \lambda j \tag{20}$$

$$\underline{y}^t_{t+j} = \rho \underline{y}^t_{t+j-1} + z_t \tag{21}$$

$$z_t = \delta u_t + v_t \tag{22}$$

where $\underline{y}^p_{t+j}$ = the log of permanent relative income in period $t+j$,

$\underline{y}^t_{t+j}$ = the log of transitory relative income in period $t+j$,

u_t = the unanticipated growth in the relative money supply, and

v_t = an exogenous shock in relative real income.

In Eq. (22), z_t is a contemporaneous shock which is comprised of an exogenous disturbance, v_t, and the unanticipated growth in the money supply, u_t. The parameter, δ, is the impact elasticity of the variable u_t on real income. The Lucas-Barro theory of the Phillips Curve suggests that the size of this coefficient is determined by the variance of the absolute price level relative to the variance of relative prices. The influence of the money supply on employment arises through the inability of market participants to distinguish between shifts in relative prices and shifts in the price level. Labor-market participants will be more likely to believe that a higher nominal wage is a higher real wage if the price level is stable, so that the response of employment to inflation will be greater. This theory is important for the exchange-market model because the induced movements in real income act as a stabilizing force in the exchange market. A higher level of real income will, in itself, tend to appreciate the exchange rate through the associated increase in the demand for money. This effect will partially offset the excess supply of money due to the unanticipated increase in the money supply. The conclusion to be drawn from this discussion is that a country with a stable monetary policy will tend to have a stable exchange rate in part because of the associated increase in the impact elasticity, δ.[9]

In Eq. (21), transitory income is assumed to follow a first-order autoregressive scheme. This implies that the influence of the disturbance z_t is not only felt in the current period, but will also have an effect on the future values of transitory income. As Barro has argued, the rational-expectations hypothesis does not prohibit this type of adjustment in transitory income. The disturbance may result in changes in the stock of inventories or in the amount of investment undertaken so that the adjustment to the shock is distributed through time.[10] In his empirical investigation, Barro found a significant influence of unanticipated money growth on unemployment with a three-year lag. The strongest impact was found to be felt after a two-year lag.[11]

In Eq. (20) permanent income is assumed to grow at a constant rate, λ.

From these equations, the expected future levels of real income are derived, conditional upon the information available at time t. In calculating these expectations, it is assumed, without loss of generality, that transitory income is zero in period $t-1$. Under this assumption, the expected future levels are

$$E[\underline{y}_{t+j}|I(t)] = y_t^p + \lambda j + \rho^j z_t. \tag{23}$$

Substituting this result into the second term in Eq. (13) yields the reduced-form relationship between the level of real income and the exchange rate:

$$-\frac{\eta}{1+\epsilon}\sum_{j=0}^{\infty}\gamma^j E[\underline{y}_{t+j}|I(t)] = -\eta y_t^p - \epsilon\eta\lambda - \eta\frac{1}{1+\epsilon-\epsilon\rho}z_t. \tag{24}$$

The interpretation of the first two terms on the right-hand side of Eq. (24) is straightforward. The first term represents the demand for money associated with the current level of permanent income while the second term reflects the influence of permanent income growth on the rate of inflation and hence on the demand for money.

The third term captures the effects of transitory income shocks on the exchange rate. These shocks influence both the level and the anticipated growth of real income. A positive shock will increase the level of real income but will decrease the anticipated rate of growth, since transitory income must finally fall back to zero. The total effect will always be to appreciate the exchange rate, although the appreciation will be small if the autoregressive parameter is small.

---

[9] For an extended theoretical and empirical investigation of these issues, see R. J. Barro (1977a).
[10] Ibid. See also R. E. Lucas (1975).
[11] The shape of the distributed lag coefficients in Barro's investigation is triangular, rather than exponentially declining. The assumption of a humped distribution would change some of the conclusions reached in the text, but would add greatly to the complexity of the resulting algebra. The major modifications to the model which occur with a humped distribution will be discussed below.

IV. THE FINAL EXCHANGE RATE EQUATION

The results of the two previous sections will now be combined in order to determine the total influence of the monetary innovations on the exchange rate. The relationship may be found by substituting Eqs. (18) and (24) into Eq. (13) to yield

$$s_t = E[s_t|I(t-1)] + \left[1 + \epsilon - \eta\delta + \frac{\eta\delta\epsilon(1-\rho)}{1+\epsilon(1-\rho)}\right]u_t - \frac{\eta}{1+\epsilon(1-\rho)}v_t, \quad (25)$$

where

$$E[s_t|I(t-1)] = m_{t-1} + \Delta m_{t-1} - \eta y_{t-1}^p + \epsilon(\Delta m_{t-1} - \eta\lambda).$$

The four terms in the coefficient on u_t indicate the four channels through which the unanticipated changes in the money supply influence the exchange rate. They are
(i)   the proportional relationship between the money supply and the exchange rate under strict quantity theory assumptions;
(ii) the influence of the innovation on the anticipated rate of growth of the money supply, hence on the nominal rate of interest, the demand for money, and the exchange rate;
(iii) the direct effect on real income, which increases the demand for money and appreciates the exchange rate; and
(iv) the influence of the increase in transitory income on the anticipated growth of real income, hence on the nominal rate of interest and the exchange rate.

A noticeable feature of the income effects is that they influence the exchange rate in opposite directions. If transitory income is above zero, then this factor will increase the demand for money. However, positive transitory income implies that the anticipated growth of real income is below its long-run level, since transitory income must fall towards its long-run equilibrium level. The negative anticipated rate of growth of transitory income will increase the nominal rate of interest and depreciate the exchange rate.

This conclusion is a consequence of the assumption that transitory income follows a first-order autoregressive process. If Barro's humped adjustment path had been used, it is possible that the anticipated increase in the short-term rate of growth would outweigh the long-term decline so that the two effects would exert an influence in the same direction.

In a similar manner, the elasticity relating the real shock, v_t, to the exchange rate may also be divided into a direct and an indirect influence, the latter arising through the induced movement in the nominal interest rate.

V. THE STABILITY OF THE EXCHANGE RATE

The question of stability will be taken to refer to the size of the elasticities relating the money supply and real-income innovations to the exchange rate. If these elasticities are small, then the exchange rate will be insulated from current disturbances, and the actual rate will not deviate widely from the rate anticipated by the market. The rational expectations model specifies the determinants of these elasticities: higher values of the income elasticity, η, the Phillips Curve impact coefficient, δ, and the auto-regressive parameter, ρ, will reduce the sensitivity of the exchange rate to unanticipated changes in the money supply.

These comments are based upon the structure of the present model. More generally, the point of the analysis is that the elasticities reflect the process which is generating the exogenous variable. If an unanticipated change in the money supply is generally reversed in the near future, then the exchange rate will not be strongly influenced, since nominal interest rates will fall in response to the anticipated future decline in the money supply. On the other hand, if the unanticipated change indicates the beginning of a new period of inflation, the exchange rate will respond elastically. In this sense, exchange rate instability is a consequence of an unstable money supply process, which should be distinguished from an unpredictable money supply. An unstable process implies that a current change leads to future changes in the same direction, thus leading to a large elasticity. On the other hand, an unpredictable money supply simply implies that the variance of the prediction error is large, without carrying any implications for the size of the coefficients.

VI. THE TERM STRUCTURE OF THE FORWARD PREMIUM

In this section, the time path of the forward-exchange premium, and hence of the expected future spot rates, is derived. From Eq. (12), the forward premium is given by

$$f_t - s_t = \frac{1}{\epsilon}[s_t - \underline{m}_t - \eta \underline{y}_t].\tag{26}$$

Substituting the final reduced-form equation for the exchange rate, Eq. (25), into this expression yields the following expression for the forward premium:

$$f_t - s_t = \Delta \underline{m}_t - \eta \lambda + \frac{\eta(1-\rho)}{1 + \epsilon(1-\rho)} z_t.\tag{27}$$

Applying the same method of solution to all the future periods yields the term structure of the forward premium:

$$f_{t+j} - f_{t+j-1} = \Delta \underline{m}_t - \eta \lambda + \frac{\eta \rho^j (1-\rho)}{1 + \epsilon(1-\rho)} z_t.\tag{28}$$

The first two terms in this expression simply reflect the anticipated rate of currency depreciation due to the differential anticipated rate of growth of the money supply and permanent income. The third term reflects both the anticipated change in transitory income and the induced change in the forward premium. After the shock, z_t, the anticipated rate of real transitory income growth is $-\rho^j(1-\rho)z_t$, which is declining with time. Hence the forward premium will initially be above the long-run value given by the first two terms. As time proceeds, the negative rate of growth of transitory income will decline, thus decreasing the forward premium and appreciating the exchange rate.

VII. EXTENSIONS

The present analysis could be continued by deriving the associated values of the nominal interest rates and prices in the two countries. This would require that the innovations discussed in the preceding sections be divided into their domestic and foreign components. It would then be possible to determine the covariance structure of the dependent variables. For example, a domestic money-supply shock will increase the domestic price level and depreciate the exchange rate. It is obvious, therefore, that the covariance between prices and exchange rates will be related to the fraction of the shocks which originates in the domestic economy. The importance for many business decisions of this covariance has been stressed by a number of writers.[12]

It would also be possible to extend the model in order to allow for the possibility that the real rate of interest responds to unanticipated changes in the money supply. The simplest method of doing so would be through an equation similar to that used for real income, in which an unanticipated change in the money supply would decrease the real rate of interest in the short run below that prevailing in the rest of the world. After the change, the rate would move back towards the world real rate at a speed of adjustment determined by an autoregressive parameter. Some tests of this model were carried out using data on the DM/Pound exchange rate. In spite of the evidence from several domestic studies, no significant liquidity effect could be discerned.[13]

The previous section has developed a theoretical model which determines the exchange rate, the price level, interest rates, forward rates, and real income in a two-country model. The analysis provides an explanation of the magnification effect, whereby money supply changes lead to proportionately greater changes in the exchange rate, based upon a theory of rational foreign exchange market speculation. This speculation is destabilizing with respect to the lagged exchange rate, but is stabilizing with respect to the expected equilibrium rate. In fact, the instability is not a consequence of exogenous "bandwagon" speculation, but is a rational anticipation of underlying monetary conditions. From a policy viewpoint, this implies that the cure for exchange market instability should be based upon an attempt to stabilize monetary expansion, rather than an attempt to counter speculative behavior through an active intervention policy.

VIII. EMPIRICAL TESTS OF THE MODEL

In this section, I shall develop and test a number of hypotheses which arise from the monetary approach to the exchange rate. The section will not include tests of the various arbitrage conditions—interest-rate parity, purchasing-power parity, and forecasting efficiency—since these conditions have been examined in a number of excellent

---

[12] For example, P. B. Clark (1973), W. Ethier (1973).

[13] For evidence on the liquidity effect on domestic interest rates, see J. Carr and L. B. Smith (1972).

papers.[14] In the preceding discussion, the market-clearing equation in the foreign exchange market was assumed to be of the following specific form:

$$s = (k - k^*) + (m - m^*) - \eta(y - y^*) + \epsilon(f - s). \tag{29}$$

The object of this section is to test the validity of Eq. (29) as a model of exchange rate determination. In order to describe the tests, the equation is respecified as the following regression relation:

$$s_t = \beta_0 + \beta_1 m + \beta_2 m^* + \beta_3 y + \beta_4 y^* + \beta_5 fp \tag{30}$$

where fp = the forward-exchange premium.

The monetary theory suggests the following priors concerning the coefficients in Eq. (30):

A: $\beta_1 = -\beta_2 = 1$. This hypothesis reflects the presumption that the economic system is homogenous of degree one in money and prices.

B: $-\beta_3 = \beta_4 = \eta$, the income elasticity of the demand for money.

C: $-\beta_5 = \epsilon$, the interest rate coefficient in the demand for money. For the Cagan functional form, the interest elasticity of the demand for money is defined as ϵi, where i is the nominal rate of interest. U.S. studies of the demand for money have found interest rate elasticities of approximately 0.015 if the nominal rate of interest is 10 percent.

D: The equation should predict a large fraction of the variance in the exchange rate, it should have a small standard error relative to alternative models, and it should have serially independent residuals. These characteristics would suggest that the monetary theory has captured the major determinants of exchange rate fluctuations.

These hypotheses fall into two major groups: A, B, and C are statements concerning the values of the regression coefficients, while D is concerned with the ability of the equation to predict the variation in the exchange rate. The hypotheses on the coefficients are complicated by the fact that the exact values of these coefficients are not known, so that a range of values may be considered as consistent with the monetary approach. For this reason, it is proper to formulate the tests by stating the probability limits within which the coefficients are expected to lie. The following statements are assumed to be consistent with the monetary approach to the exchange rate:

A1: The 95 percent confidence limits for the money supply coefficients are 0.9 and 1.1.

B1: The 95 percent confidence limits for the income elasticity of the demand for money are 0.5 and 1.5.

C1: The 95 percent confidence limits for the interest rate coefficient are 0 and

---

[14] The interest arbitrage condition is examined in Aliber (1973), Branson (1969), and Frenkel and Levich (1975, 1977). The efficiency of the forward rate as a forecast of the future spot rate is examined in Levich (1977, 1978), and Bilson and Levich (1977). See Officer (1976) for a review of the literature on purchasing-power parity. In Bilson (1976), the evidence from the DM/Pound experience was found to be consistent with the interest parity and speculative efficiency conditions, but not with the purchasing-power parity condition. The probable consequences of relaxing the purchasing-power parity condition are examined in Bilson (1976), Chapter 3.

-0.03. Using the two sigma rule, these statements imply that the actual coefficients may be described by the following equations:

$$
\begin{array}{ll}
\beta_1 = 1 + v1 & \sigma_{v1} = 0.05 \\
\beta_2 = -1 + v2 & \sigma_{v2} = 0.05 \\
\beta_3 = -1 + v3 & \sigma_{v3} = 0.25 \\
\beta_4 = 1 + v4 & \sigma_{v4} = 0.25 \\
\beta_5 = 0.015 + v5 & \sigma_{v5} = 0.0075
\end{array}
$$

or, more compactly,

$$
R\beta = r + v \tag{31}
$$

where

$$
\beta' = [\beta_0 \quad \beta_1 \quad \beta_2 \quad \beta_3 \quad \beta_4 \quad \beta_5]
$$

$$
r' = [1 \quad -1 \quad -1 \quad 1 \quad 0.015]
$$

$$
R = \begin{bmatrix}
0 & 1 & 0 & 0 & 0 & 0 \\
0 & 0 & 1 & 0 & 0 & 0 \\
0 & 0 & 0 & 1 & 0 & 0 \\
0 & 0 & 0 & 0 & 1 & 0 \\
0 & 0 & 0 & 0 & 0 & 1
\end{bmatrix}.
$$

The covariance matrix of the error vector, v, is simply a diagonal matrix with the variance of the individual equations in Eq. (31) as the diagonal elements:

$$
V_0 = \begin{bmatrix}
0.0025 & & & & \\
& 0.0025 & & & 0 \\
& & 0.0625 & & \\
& 0 & & 0.0625 & \\
& & & & 0.5625\text{E-}04
\end{bmatrix}.
$$

Equation (31) specifies the prior information derived from the monetary approach. The test on the coefficients can now be undertaken by testing whether the prior ideas are contradicted by the information contained in the sample information. The information from the sample is derived from Eq. (30), which is compactly written in Eq. (32):

$$
y = X\beta + u \tag{32}
$$

where

$$
y = s
$$

$$
X = [c \quad m \quad m^* \quad y \quad y^* \quad fp].
$$

Theil proposes the following test of the compatibility of the prior and sample information.[15] If the two information sets are compatible, the following statistic is distributed as $\chi^2(q)$, where q is the number of equations in (31):

$$(r - R\hat{\beta})' [\sigma^2 R(X'X)^{-1} R' + V_0] (r - R\hat{\beta}). \tag{33}$$

To interpret this statistic, recall that r is the "best guess" of the coefficient based upon the prior information, while $R\hat{\beta}$ is the corresponding "best guess" based upon the sample information. The quadratic form $(r - R\hat{\beta})'(r - R\hat{\beta})$ is consequently the sum of the squared differences between the prior and the sample estimates. The covariance matrix of these errors is found by noting that

$$r - R\hat{\beta} = -R(\hat{\beta} - \beta) + v \tag{34}$$

from Eq. (31). Equation (34) indicates the two reasons why r may not equal $R\hat{\beta}$ under the null hypothesis: the error in the sample estimate $\hat{\beta} - \beta$, and the error in the prior estimate, r. The covariance matrix of the difference between the two estimators is given by

$$V(r - R\hat{\beta}) = \sigma^2 R(X'X)^{-1} R + V_0 \tag{35}$$

if the two information sets are independently distributed. The inverse of this matrix is the weighting factor in Eq. (33) which transforms the random errors into standardized normal variates. Thus Eq. (33) is simply the sum of q independent standardized normal variables, and hence is distributed $\chi^2(q)$ under the null hypothesis.

The logic behind Theil's test can now be made clear. Since neither the sample nor the prior information provides complete information about the coefficients, the estimates are expected to differ. The covariance matrix in Eq. (35) indicates the variance in the estimates which would be consistent with the compatibility hypothesis. If the sample and prior information are incompatible, then the sum of standardized squared residuals will exceed the sum suggested by the covariance matrix, since the incompatibility is an additional source of difference between r and $R\hat{\beta}$. If the excess is significant, then the hypothesis that the two information sets are compatible is rejected by the test, so that the sample estimates of the coefficients are significantly different from the values suggested by the monetary approach.

The second set of hypotheses concerns the goodness of fit of the equation. If the monetary model captures the principal determinants of the exchange rate, then the standard error should be small relative to alternative models, and the errors in the equation should be serially uncorrelated. In order to examine these issues, an alternative model of exchange-rate determination is required. In the following, I shall consider two alternative empirical models: the purchasing-power parity model and the random-walk model. In setting up these alternatives, I stress that they are alternatives on empirical, not theoretical, grounds. All of the equations can be derived from a similar theoretical framework. Equation (31), for example, was derived by making use of the theoretical concept of purchasing-power parity. As an empirical question, however, it is an open question whether the purchasing-power parity condition or the reduced form equation from the monetary approach provide the best predictions of the exchange rate. Supporters of the former approach may stress the instability of the

---

[15] Theil (1971), p. 351.

money demand function as a reason for using the price relationship, while supporters of the latter could equally well argue that conventional price indices are inappropriate measures of the true price indices with which the market deflates the nominal quantity of money.

The alternative equations are

$$\text{Purchasing-power parity:} \quad s = \alpha_0 + \alpha_1 p \tag{36}$$

where $p = $ the ratio of the German to the British consumer price index; and

$$\text{Random-walk model:} \quad s = \gamma_0 + \gamma_1 s_{-1} \tag{37}$$

where s_{-1} is the lagged value of the spot exchange rate.

Equations (30), (36), and (37) were estimated by ordinary least squares. The resulting estimates are reported in Table 1.

TABLE 1
ALTERNATIVE EXCHANGE RATE EQUATIONS
GERMANY/U.K.; JANUARY, 1972–APRIL, 1976

The Monetary Approach

$$s = \begin{array}{c} 4.4537 + \\ (4.7878) \end{array} \begin{array}{c} 0.4178m - \\ (0.9414) \\ (1.3120) \end{array} \begin{array}{c} 0.9147m^* - \\ (4.3203) \\ (0.4029) \end{array} \begin{array}{c} 0.2081y - \\ (0.7240) \\ (2.7543) \end{array} \begin{array}{c} 0.1712y^* + \\ (0.5687) \\ (3.8920) \end{array} \begin{array}{c} 0.0015fp + u_1 \\ (0.5965) \\ (5.4990) \end{array} \tag{30}$$

R-squared $= 0.9208$ D.W. $= 0.5088$ N.O.B. $= 52$ S.E. $= 0.047$ F(5, 46) $= 106.89$

Purchasing-Power Parity

$$s = \begin{array}{c} -0.3665 + \\ (-1.818) \end{array} \begin{array}{c} 1.1003p + u_2 \\ (10.9369) \end{array} \tag{36}$$

R-squared $= 0.7052$ D.W. $= 0.1540$ N.O.B. $= 52$ S.E. $= 0.0875$ F(1, 50) $= 119.62$

Random Walk

$$s = \begin{array}{c} 0.0144 + \\ (0.2706) \end{array} \begin{array}{c} 0.9861s_{-1} + u_3 \\ (34.39) \end{array} \tag{37}$$

R-squared $= 0.9594$ D.W. $= 1.8924$ N.O.B. $= 52$ S.E. $= 0.0325$ F(1, 50) $= 1182.83$

Note: The numbers in brackets beneath the coefficients are t-statistics. The second row of t-statistics in the estimates of Eq. (30) tests the hypothesis that the coefficient is equal to the value suggested by the monetary approach.

Sources of Data:

German Money Supply: German Money and Quasi-Money Stock, End of Month, seasonally adjusted, January 1974 revision. Source: Statistical supplement to the *Deutsche Bundesbank Report*.

U.K. Money Supply: U.K. Currency and all U.K. Bank Deposits, Third Wednesday in Month, seasonally adjusted. Source: *Bank of England Quarterly Bulletin*, Table 12.

German Income Series: German Industrial Production Index, all industries. Source: Monthly Report of the Bundesbank, Series 4, seasonally adjusted.

U.K. Income Series: U.K. Industrial Production Index, all industries, seasonally adjusted.

Consider first the test of relative goodness of fit. Although Eq. (30) appears to fit the data more closely than the purchasing-power parity equation, it is noticeably inferior to the random-walk model in terms of R-squared, standard error, and the extent of the autocorrelation of the residuals.[16] Consequently, although the monetary model does explain over 90 percent of the variation in the exchange rate, these results lead to the rejection of the monetary model as a complete description of the determination of the exchange rate.

Consider next the coefficients in the exchange-rate equation. The second row of t-statistics in Eq. (30) tests the hypothesis that the regression coefficients are equal to the values postulated above. Three of the four coefficients are significantly different from the point estimates suggested above and, in addition, only one of the coefficients, that on the British money supply, is significantly different from zero. The insignificance of the coefficients is due, in part, to the strong collinearity among the dependent variables in the equation. The correlation coefficient between the two money supply variables is 0.957; the same statistic for the income variables is 0.719. This strong multicollinearity increases the standard errors of the coefficients so that it is difficult to estimate the true relationship between the variables.

Following the argument above, the correct test of the coefficients is Theil's compatibility test. The expected value of the χ^2 statistic is 5 under the null hypothesis, since, under this hypothesis, the statistic is the sum of squares of five standardized normal variables. The actual value of the statistic is 28.1457. Since $\chi^2(5) = 15.09$ at the 0.01 percent level of significance, the hypothesis that the statistic is drawn from the hypothesized distribution is rejected, thus implying that the sample and prior information are not compatible.

IX. AN ALTERNATIVE FORMULATION

In exploring the reasons for the rejection of the simple monetary model, it is helpful to briefly review attempts to estimate the demand for money using domestic data. The conventional formulation of the demand for money, as suggested by Goldfeld,[17] is one in which actual money holdings adjust slowly to the desired level, and in which the errors in the demand function follow a first-order autoregressive scheme. The conventional equation is of the form:

$$\log\left(\frac{M}{p}\right) = \beta_0 + \beta_1 y + \beta_2 i + \beta_3 \log\left(\frac{M}{p}\right)_{t-1} + \rho u_{t-1} + u. \tag{38}$$

The structure of Eq. (38) differs in three ways from the structure of the simple exchange-rate equation: (i) a lagged dependent variable is included to reflect the partial adjustment of actual money balances to the desired level; (ii) the errors in the equation are assumed to follow a first-order autoregressive scheme; and (iii) the long-run elasticity relating money and prices is assumed to be unity, so that real money balances, rather than prices, are the dependent variable. An additional gain from this procedure

---

[16] The test of the relative autocorrelation is not well defined, since the D.W. statistic is biased in an equation with a lagged dependent variable.

[17] Goldfeld (1973).

is that it reduces the multicollinearity problem that would arise if both the nominal money supply and the lagged price level appeared as dependent variables.

These considerations suggest that the simple monetary model of exchange-rate determination should be extended to allow for a lagged dependent variable and serial dependence in the error structure. The problem of multicollinearity will be handled at a later stage. The exchange rate equation now becomes[18]

$$s = \beta_0 + \beta_1 m + \beta_2 m^* + \beta_3 y + \beta_4 y^* + \beta_5 fp + \beta_6 s_{t-1} + \rho u_{t-1} + u_t. \tag{39}$$

The tests on the coefficients in the extended model now refer to the long-run elasticities relating the exogenous variables to the exchange rate. The hypothesis can be stated as

$$\frac{\beta_j}{1 - \beta_6} = r_j + v_j, \qquad j = 1 \text{ to } 5, \tag{40}$$

where the covariance structure of the errors is the same as that specified in Eq. (31), and r_j are again the "best guesses" of the parameters of the money-demand function. Equation (40) implies the following linear restriction on the coefficients:

$$\beta_j + r_j \beta_6 = r_j + (1 - \beta_6) v_j. \tag{41}$$

The particular feature of Eq. (41) is that the covariance structure of the errors is dependent upon the value of the unknown parameter, β_6. For the moment, this coefficient will be assumed to be known with certainty for the purposes of the covariance matrix. In practice, an estimate from the mixed estimation procedure discussed below is employed.

Equation (39) was estimated using the iterative Cochran-Orcutt procedure.[19] The results from this estimation are reproduced below:

$$s = \begin{array}{cccccc} 3.09746 + & 0.3581m - & 0.5879m^* - & 0.4083y - & 0.0146y^* + & 0.0025fp \\ (2.2131) & (0.9429) & (2.8623) & (1.5895) & (0.0634) & (1.3942) \end{array}$$

$$\begin{array}{c} + \ 0.4235 s_{-1} \\ (2.9527) \end{array}$$

$$u = \begin{array}{c} 0.5475 u_1 + w \\ (4.672) \end{array}$$

R-squared $= 0.9654$ D.W. $= 1.8947$ N.O.B. $= 51$ S.E. $= 0.31$ F(6, 44) $= 204.913$

In terms of the goodness of fit, this equation is superior to the simple model, and the standard error of the regression is less than the standard error of the random-walk model.[20] The equation's residuals are significantly autocorrelated, however, as is evi-

---

[18] Equation (39) is not directly derived from Eq. (38) since the lagged values of the money stocks are excluded. Equation (39) may be considered as a model in which the exchange rate responds to the excess relative supply of money.

[19] To check for any possible bias from this procedure, the Hildreth-Lu scanning technique was also used to estimate the equation. Both procedures gave identical results.

[20] The decrease in the standard error is not due to the fact that this equation includes the random-walk model as a special case, since the statistic is corrected for degrees of freedom.

denced by the significant coefficient on the lagged error. This autocorrelation may sig-
nify the omission from the equation of some significant determinants of the exchange
rate.

The test on the coefficients proceeds as before. There are five restrictions on the
coefficients implied by the long-run elasticities specified in Eq. (40), so that the
expected value of the χ^2 statistic is again five, under the null hypothesis. The actual
value of the statistic is 7.4547, which is less than 15.09, the 0.01 percent confidence
limit of the distribution. The compatibility hypothesis cannot therefore be rejected in
this case.

The extended model passes both of the proposed tests of the monetary approach:
it predicts as well as the simple alternative model and the estimated coefficients are
consistent with prior beliefs based upon the demand for money. In other respects,
however, the estimated equation is still unsatisfactory. Only one of the impact coefficients is significantly different from zero at the 95 percent level of significance, the
long-run elasticity relating the German money supply to the exchange rate is 0.6212,
which is substantially below the expected value of unity, and the long-run income
elasticity for the United Kingdom is of the wrong sign. In part, these problems are a
result of the strong collinearity among the right-hand side variables. Having found that
the prior information and the sample data are compatible, it is now possible to tackle
these problems through the Theil-Goldberger mixed estimation procedure,[21] in which
the two sources of information are combined. The aggregate relationship is written

$$\begin{bmatrix} y \\ r \end{bmatrix} = \begin{bmatrix} X \\ R \end{bmatrix} \beta + \begin{bmatrix} u \\ -(1-\beta_6)v \end{bmatrix} \qquad (42)$$

Two features of the error structure must be taken into account in the estimation of
Eq. (42): the errors from the sample, u, follow a first-order autoregressive scheme, and
the variance of the errors on the prior information depend upon the parameter, β_6.
The variance of the typical restriction is

$$V(-(1-\beta_6)v_j) = V(\beta_6)V(v_j) + (1 - E(\beta_6))^2 V(v_j) + E(v_j)^2 V(\beta_6)$$

if β_6 and v_j are independently distributed.[22] Assuming that the first term is small
enough to be ignored, and recognizing that $E(v_j)$ equals zero, the variance can be
reduced to

$$V(-(1-\beta_6)v_j) \doteq (1 - E(\beta_6))^2 V(v_j). \qquad (43)$$

As it stands, the error vector in Eq. (42) is heteroscedastic. Dividing through the prior
information by

$$k = \frac{(1-\beta_6)\sigma_{vj}}{\sigma_w} \qquad (44)$$

[21] See H. Theil and Goldberger (1961), and the extension in Theil (1963).
[22] For a proof, see Stevens (1971).

where
$$\sigma_{vj} = \text{the standard deviation of } v_j,$$
and
$$\sigma_w = \text{the standard deviation of the white noise residuals, } w,$$

will equalize the variance of the two error vectors so that ordinary least squares estimation is appropriate. In order to carry out this estimation, however, the values of ρ, the first-order autocorrelation coefficient, and β_6 must be known. Since these coefficients are not known, the following iterative procedure is adopted. Using the estimates from Eq. (39) as starting values, the autoregressive and heteroscedastic transformations are carried out, and an initial estimate of the parameter vector β is derived. This estimate is then used to find a new value for ρ and β_6, and the procedure is repeated. The iterations were continued until the change in ρ was less than 0.005 in absolute value. The estimates of the coefficients derived from this procedure are presented below.

	Coefficient	Standard Error	t-statistic
β_0	-0.0018	0.0295	0.0637
β_1	0.1384	0.0670	2.0661
β_2	-0.1393	0.0682	2.0427
β_3	-0.1408	0.0734	1.9181
β_4	0.1381	0.0735	1.8779
β_5	0.0031	0.0015	1.9525
β_6	0.8617	0.0677	12.7292

All of these estimates are consistent with the predictions of the monetary approach as can best be seen by deriving the associated long-run exchange rate equation,[23]

$$s(LR) = -0.0136 + \underset{(14.2656)}{1.0013m} - \underset{(15.4474)}{1.0081m^*} - \underset{(3.6008)}{1.0184y} + \underset{(3.2448)}{0.9990y^*}$$

$$+ \underset{(1.4668)}{0.0228fp} \tag{45}$$

All of the money supply and income elasticities are extremely close to prior expectations. The interest-rate elasticity is a little higher than the prior expectations;

---

[23] To derive the standard errors of the long-run coefficients, the expression is expanded in a Taylor Series around the expected values:

$$\frac{\beta_j}{1-\beta_6} \doteq \frac{\beta_j}{1-\underline{\beta}_6} + \frac{\beta_j}{(1-\underline{\beta}_6)} 2[\beta_6 - \underline{\beta}_6] + \frac{1}{1-\underline{\beta}_6}[\beta_j - \underline{\beta}_j]$$

where $\underline{\beta}_j$ is the point estimate of β_j.
   The variance of this expression is

$$V = \left[\frac{\beta_j}{(1-\underline{\beta}_6)}2\right]^2 V(\beta_6) + \left[\frac{1}{1-\underline{\beta}_6}\right]^2 V(\beta_j) + \frac{2\beta_j}{(1-\underline{\beta}_6)} 3 \operatorname{Cov}(\beta_j, \beta_6)$$

This expression is used to calculate the standard errors of the long-run elasticities in Eq. (45).

at an interest rate of 7 percent, the implied long-run interest elasticity is 0.1596. This elasticity is large, since the M2 definition of the money supply is employed along with the one-month forward premium. Previous studies have only found strong interest-rate elasticities with narrow definitions of money and longer-term interest rates. The strong interest-rate effect found in the international evidence may reflect the phenomenon of currency substitution.[24]

The other interesting characteristic of the mixed estimation is that the results find little evidence of autocorrelation in the residuals. The final estimate of the auto-correlation coefficient yielded the following relation:

$$u = -\ 0.00018 + 0.1454u_{-1} + w$$
$$(0.0431) \quad (1.0356)$$

$$R\text{-squared} = 0.0210 \quad \text{D.W.} = 1.96 \quad \text{S.E.} = 0.0304 \quad F(1, 50) = 1.07$$

The mixed-estimation procedure yields estimates of the coefficients and the auto-correlation coefficient which are consistent with the predictions of the monetary approach. The final question that should be answered is whether it does so at the expense of significantly increasing the standard error of the prediction of the sample data. Since the prior information imposes a restriction on the coefficients, the error from the sample data will always have a large variance when the mixed-estimation technique is used. However, in this particular case, the increase in the standard error is very small: the standard error of the unrestricted equation is 0.031, while the standard error from the mixed-estimation procedure is 0.032. The small increase in the standard error is to be expected, since it has been previously established that the sample and prior information are compatible with each other.

X. CONCLUSION

One of the more perplexing features of the current floating-rate experience has been volatile and erratic movements in the major currencies. Exchange rates, it appears, are behaviorally more akin to stock market prices than to the aggregate commodity indices stressed in traditional versions of the purchasing-power parity theory. With this observation in mind, the theoretical section of this paper attempted to apply the "efficient market" analysis of the financial economists to the recently developed asset approach to the exchange rate. The hybrid model does appear to be helpful in explain-ing the erratic movements in the exchange rate because it emphasizes how current changes in the money supply, or other exogenous variables, influence expectations of future monetary growth and hence the nominal rate of interest. The model also offers a theory of interest-rate differentials and an explanation of the error in the forward rate's prediction of the future spot rate. In this context, exchange-rate uncertainty is seen to be a reflection of the underlying instability in monetary policy, rather than being a consequence of irrational speculative behavior.

---

[24] For example, Calvo and Rodriguez (1977), Girton and Roper (1976).

Technically, the theoretical model combined a number of arbitrage conditions with a relative money demand function. Although the arbitrage conditions have been extensively investigated on an empirical level, there have been few tests of the relative money demand function at this time.[25] The second half of the paper found that the simple instantaneous stock-equilibrium equation was not supported by the evidence from the DM/Pound rate. However, an alternative formulation relating the rate of depreciation to the relative excess supply of money did find strong empirical support. This evidence confirms the conclusions reached in domestic studies that the partial adjustment model is the appropriate model for money-market equations.

REFERENCES

ALIBER, ROBERT Z. "The Interest Rate Parity Theorem: A Reinterpretation." *Journal of Political Economy* **81** (November/December, 1973): 1451–1459.

BARRO, ROBERT J. "Rational Expectations and the Role of Monetary Policy." *Journal of Monetary Economics* **2** (January, 1976): 1–32.

————. "Unanticipated Money Growth and Unemployment in the United States." *American Economic Review* **67** (March, 1977a): 101–115.

————. "A Stochastic Equilibrium Model of an Open Economy Under Flexible Exchange Rates." *Quarterly Journal of Economics* (forthcoming). (1977b).

BILSON, JOHN F. O. *A Monetary Approach to the Exchange Rate.* Unpublished doctoral dissertation, University of Chicago, 1976.

————. "The Monetary Approach to the Exchange Rate–Some Empirical Evidence." Unpublished manuscript, International Monetary Fund, 1977.

BILSON, JOHN F. O., and RICHARD M. LEVICH. "A Test of the Forecasting Efficiency of the Forward Exchange Rate." Unpublished working paper, Northwestern University, 1977.

BLEJER, MARIO I. "Exchange Restrictions and the Monetary Approach to the Exchange Rate." 1978. Reproduced as Chapter 7 in this volume.

BRANSON, W. H. "The Minimum Covered Differential Needed for International Arbitrage Activity." *Journal of Political Economy* **77** (November/December, 1969): 1028–1035.

CALVO, G. A., and C. A. RODRIGUEZ. "A Model of Exchange Rate Determination Under Currency Substitution and Rational Expectations." *Journal of Political Economy* **85**, No. 3 (June, 1977): 617–626.

CARR, J., and L. B. SMITH. "Money Supply, Interest Rates and the Yield Curve." *Journal of Money, Credit and Banking* **4** (August, 1972): 582–593.

CLARK, P. B. "Uncertainty, Exchange Risk, and the Level of International Trade." *Western Economic Journal* **11** (September, 1973): 302–313.

DORNBUSCH, R. "The Theory of Flexible Exchange Rate Regimes and Macroeconomic Policy." *Scandinavian Journal of Economics* **78** (1976a): 255–276, also reprinted in this volume, Chapter 2.

————. "Exchange Rate Dynamics." *Journal of Political Economy* **84** (December, 1976b): 1161–1176.

---

[25] Frenkel (1976), Bilson (1976), and Hodrick (1978) are among the exceptions.

ETHIER, W. E. "International Trade and the Forward Exchange Market." *American Economic Review* **63** (June, 1973): 494–508.

FAMA, EUGENE F. *Foundations of Finance.* New York: Basic Books, 1976.

FRENKEL, J. A. "A Monetary Approach to the Exchange Rate: Doctrinal Aspects and Empirical Evidence." *Scandinavian Journal of Economics* **78** (1976): 200–224; also reprinted in this volume as Chapter 1.

———. "The Forward Exchange Rate, Expectations and the Demand for Money: The German Hyperinflation." *American Economic Review* **67**: 4 (September, 1977): 653–670.

FRENKEL, J. A., and R. M. LEVICH. "Covered Interest Arbitrage: Unexploited Profits?" *Journal of Political Economy* **83** (April, 1975): 325–338.

———. "Transaction Costs and Interest Arbitrage: Tranquil versus Turbulent Periods." *Journal of Political Economy* **85** (December, 1977): 1209–1226.

GIRTON, LANCE, and DON ROPER. "Theory and Implications of Currency Substitution." Federal Reserve Board of Governors, International Finance Discussion Papers, Number 56, August, 1976.

GOLDFELD, S. M. "The Demand for Money Revisited." *Brookings Papers on Economic Activity* **3** (1973): 577–639.

HODGSON, JOHN S., and PATRICIA PHELPS. "The Distributed Impact of Price-Level Variation on Floating Exchange Rates." *Review of Economics and Statistics* **107** (February, 1975): 58–64.

HODRICK, ROBERT J. "An Empirical Analysis of the Monetary Approach to the Exchange Rate." 1978. Reproduced as Chapter 6 in this volume.

LEVICH, R. M. "The International Money Market: Tests of Forecasting Models and Market Efficiency." Unpublished doctoral dissertation, University of Chicago, 1977.

———. "Tests of Forecasting Models and Market Efficiency in the International Money Market." 1978. Reproduced as Chapter 8 in this volume.

LUCAS, R. E. "An Equilibrium Model of the Business Cycle." *Journal of Political Economy* **83** (December, 1975): 1113–1144.

———. "Some International Evidence on Output-Inflation Trade-Offs." *American Economic Review* **63** (June, 1973): 326–334.

MAGEE, STEPHEN P. "The Empirical Evidence on the Monetary Approach to the Balance of Payments and Exchange Rates." *American Economic Review: Papers and Proceedings* **66** (May, 1976): 163–170.

———. "Contracting and Spurious Deviations from Purchasing-Power Parity." 1978. Reproduced as Chapter 4 in this volume.

MUSSA, MICHAEL "The Exchange Rate, the Balance of Payments and Monetary and Fiscal Policy under a Regime of Controlled Floating." *Scandinavian Journal of Economics* **78** (1976): 229–248, reprinted in this volume as Chapter 3.

OFFICER, L. H. "The Purchasing Power Parity Theory of Exchange Rates: A Review Article." *IMF Staff Papers* **23** (March, 1976): 1–61.

SARGENT, T., and N. WALLACE. "Rational Expectations, the Optimal Monetary Instrument, and the Optimal Money Supply Rule." *Journal of Political Economy* **83** (April, 1975): 241–254.

———. "Rational Expectations and the Dynamics of Hyperinflation." *International Economic Review* **14** (June, 1973): 328–350.

STEVENS, GUY. "Two Problems in Portfolio Analysis: Conditional and the Multiplicative Random Variables." *Journal of Financial and Quantitative Analysis* (December, 1971): 1235–1250.

STOCKMAN, ALAN C. "Risk, Information, and Forward Exchange Rates." 1978. Reproduced in this volume as Chapter 9.

THEIL, HENRI. *Principles of Econometrics.* New York: Wiley, 1971.

————. "On the Use of Incomplete Prior Information in Regression Analysis." *Journal of the American Statistical Association* **58** (1963): 401–414.

THEIL, H., and A. S. GOLDBERGER. "On Pure and Mixed Estimation in Economics." *International Economic Review* **2** (March, 1961): 65–78.

WHITMAN, MARINA V. N. "Global Monetarism and the Monetary Approach to the Balance of Payments." *Brookings Papers on Economic Activity* **3** (1975): 491–536.

AN EMPIRICAL ANALYSIS OF THE MONETARY APPROACH TO THE DETERMINATION OF THE EXCHANGE RATE

ROBERT J. HODRICK

*Graduate School of Industrial Administration
and Carnegie-Mellon Institute of Research*

I. INTRODUCTION

This paper develops tests of the monetary approach to the determination of exchange rates using data from the flexible exchange-rate period which followed the collapse of the Bretton Woods fixed-parity system. Two types of time-series models are analysed to test several aspects of the theory.

As usually formulated, the monetary approach stresses that the exchange rate, as the relative price of two monies, is determined by the equilibrium between the demands for and the supplies of the stocks of monies outstanding.[1] This follows since the modern theory of the demand for money is that it is a derived demand for the services that flow from holding a stock of money.

In the second section of this paper the equation that forms the basis of the estimation is discussed and potential problems are reviewed. Section III presents estimates of the coefficients of the stock equilibrium model when the variables are in levels of natural logarithms. This is the traditional linear-regression analysis. Section IV develops estimates of the coefficients when the variables are in rates of growth or first differences of natural logarithms. These equations allow for dynamic models in which the stock equilibrium emerges as a special case. In addition, the exogeneity of the variables can be tested to check the adequacy of the model. Section V presents a summary and conclusions of the tests of the monetary approach to the determination of the exchange rate.

The analysis considers the United States as the home country and examines the determination of the exchange rates for the United Kingdom and Germany. Monthly

---

This paper is adapted from the fourth chapter of the author's Ph.D. dissertation at the University of Chicago. The author would like to thank Jacob Frenkel, Harry G. Johnson, and Arnold Zellner.
[1] The papers by Dornbusch (1976a), Frenkel (1976), and Mussa (1976) reproduced in this volume all consider the stock equilibrium approach. This framework is the dual to the monetary approach to the balance of payments under fixed exchange rates, see e.g., Frenkel and Johnson (1976), Dornbusch (1975), and Frenkel and Rodriguez (1975).

data are used, and the period covers July 1972 to June 1975 for the U.K. and April 1973 to September 1975 for Germany. Exchange rates are in terms of U.S. dollars per unit of foreign currency, and an asterisk will denote the foreign country variables in the equations.

II. EQUILIBRIUM DETERMINATION OF THE EXCHANGE RATE

This section develops the equation that will furnish the tests of the monetary approach to exchange-rate determination. As Frenkel (1976) demonstrates, the purchasing-power parity (PPP) relationship between prices and the exchange rate can be thought of as the ideological antecedent of the current monetary approach. The current approach stresses that equilibrium in the money markets determines the exchange rate. Therefore, one can consider the situation in which the price levels are determined by the money-market equilibrium, the exchange rate being determined simultaneously.[2] The purchasing-power parity equation is set forth in (1) where the natural logarithm of the exchange rate is related to the difference between the natural logarithms of the domestic and foreign price levels.[3]

$$e_t = p_t - p_t^* \qquad (1)$$

The price index which would perform best in estimating PPP would be the one most accurately representing the implicit price index which deflates the nominal money supply in the aggregate demand function for real balances. If the demand for money is dominated by households, one would expect that the consumer price index would be best. There are two reasons why estimates of (1) are not presented here. First, space limitations prevent an examination of PPP, which should be considered as distinct from the monetary approach under consideration, and second, price indexes that are available may not be the true indexes that are used to deflate the aggregate nominal balances of a country to get real balances. Indeed, the price indexes are often made up from list rather than transaction prices, and it is often the case that the prices of all goods composing the index are not samples from one month to the next but are interpolated by the statisticians forming the index. In the case of the U.K. especially, many of the prices entering the index were pegged by the government during a large part of the sample period. These recorded prices cannot measure the true value of money in a country, and consequently their use would lead to poor statistical results. In what follows, the true price index which deflates the nominal magnitudes of a country and satisfies (1) is considered unobservable.[4]

---

[2] See Frenkel (1976), Bilson (1978), Hodrick (1976), and Dornbusch (1976a) for models which rely on the purchasing-power parity formulation in the simultaneous determination of the price level and the exchange rate. For an early monetary analysis see Collery (1971).

[3] Lower-case variables other than interest rates refer to natural logarithms of the variables.

[4] See Hodrick (1976) for an estimate of (1) and other tests of PPP during this period. Magee (1978) examines a model in which PPP holds ex ante (at the time contracts are made), but unanticipated shocks to the exchange rate or one price cause serially correlated deviations from PPP ex post due to the existence of long-term contracts. Isard (1977) demonstrates that at the most disaggregated level of product classification for which price data are available, the tradable goods prices exhibit large and persistent changes in their common-currency prices.

In order to derive the equation to test the monetary approach we write the money-demand function as in Eq. (2).

$$(m_t^d - p_t) = a_0 + a_1 \ln(1 + i_t) + a_2 y_t + u_t \tag{2}$$

This is a standard long-run money-demand function which relates the natural logarithm of per capita real balances demanded $(m_t^d - p_t)$ to the natural logarithm of one plus the interest rate on an alternative asset and to real per capita permanent income y_t. The term u_t is an error term. The particular functional form used for the interest rate is analogous to the semilogarithmic form used by Cagan (1956).[5]

If we assume that the money supply is exogenously determined and money demand equals money supply, we can solve Eq. (2) for the natural logarithm of the price level in each country. If we then substitute into the PPP equation (1), we have an equation which determines the spot exchange rate as in (3) where v_t is the resulting error term.

$$e_t = c_0 + c_1 m_t + c_1^* m_t^* + a_1 \ln(1 + i_t) +$$
$$a_1^* \ln(1 + i_t^*) + a_2 y_t + a_2^* y_t^* + v_t \tag{3}$$

Several problems are presented in estimating (3) with monthly data. Accurate data on the populations of Germany and the United Kingdom are unavailable in monthly data. By not including an estimate of the difference in the populations, we make an error to the extent that the populations of the countries in question grew at different rates. Otherwise, the constant terms will capture the ratio of the populations of the United Kingdom to the United States and Germany to the United States.

The problem of permanent income is potentially more troublesome. Friedman (1957) first postulated that individuals would demand money based on their desired consumption stream, which would be a function of their expected wealth or permanent income. Since permanent income in this sense is truly unobservable, he constructed an exponentially weighted moving-average of past values of current real income which was used as a proxy. An alternative solution would be to construct a model of expected wealth. This could be done by estimating an autoregressive moving-average time-series model of current income, forecasting the expected future values, and discounting them back to the present. The interest rate times expected wealth would then be an alternative proxy for real permanent income.[6] Since both approaches are merely proxies, it is not obvious that the benefits of generating complex measures of

---

[5] The elasticity of real balances with respect to the interest rate for (2) is $a_1 i/(1 + i)$. As the interest rate approaches zero, this quantity approaches zero which a priori rules out a liquidity trap in which the elasticity becomes infinite. Such a situation would be generated by a functional form in (2) of a_1/i_t. This form was tried in the regressions of this section, and the results were so similar to those reported here that the alternative results are not reported. For a discussion of the functional form of the demand for money, see Frenkel (1977).
[6] W. Schwert suggested this time-series approach in a lecture at the Graduate School of Business, University of Chicago. See Box and Jenkins (1970) for the development of the time-series methodology used in this paper and a discussion of the formation of forecasts from estimated autoregressive moving-average models. Bilson and Glassman (1977) use this permanent income approach in estimating a consumption function.

permanent income outweigh the costs. Consequently, in the first part of the study the real-income measure that is used is the seasonally adjusted index of industrial production. The larger the variance of the measurement error of the proxy relative to the variance of true permanent income, the more biased will the estimates of the coefficients be from the true coefficients. In the second part of the study a time-series one-step-ahead forecast of the index of industrial production is also used to test an alternative proxy for permanent income.

The other variables in the study are the interest rates on three-month Treasury bills from the U.S. and the U.K., and the three-month money-market interest rate for Germany. The exchange rates and U.S. and U.K. interest rates are all taken from the *Harris Bank Weekly Review*. They are spot observations on a given day, usually the Friday closest to the end of the month. The German interest rate is an average of money-market rates in Frankfurt. As such, it too will be subject to measurement error. The money supplies are seasonally unadjusted M_2 for the U.S. and Germany, and M_3 for the U.K. These, too, are end-of-month observations which do not correspond to the quantity of money on a given day, but are averages over a week of daily data.

Since the model uses monthly data, the issue of seasonality must be addressed.[7] The basic issue one must confront is how does seasonality enter the model. A priori, it is clear that true permanent income is not seasonal. Hence, the choice of some form of seasonal adjustment of real income is necessary. On the other hand, it seems somewhat clear that the demand for consumption and consequently the demand for money throughout the year is seasonal, peaking during the December shopping spree. If the central banks did nothing to counteract this change in the functional form of the demand for money, interest rates and exchange rates would have a seasonal component, i.e., there would be significant autocorrelations in the series at the twelve-month lag. On the other hand, to the extent that high-powered money is changed in excess of the desired increase or decrease in the demand for money, when the money-market equilibrium was established the market forces on the interest rate and exchange rates would be in the opposite direction than if the central bankers under-shot or did nothing about the change. Since there was no seasonality found in the autocorrelations of any of the interest-rate or exchange-rate series used in this study, it seemed reasonable to conclude that the central bankers were perhaps on target. In this case the use of seasonally unadjusted money stocks would more closely approximate the true functional form of the demand for money.

In Eq. (3) the coefficients of the natural logarithms of the money supplies, c_1 and c_1^*, are expected to be plus and minus unity. This reflects the fact that the model is an equilibrium model, and it incorporates the standard homogeneity postulate which requires that economic actors formulate their demands for and supplies of goods, assets, and labor in real terms. To the extent that results from money-demand studies based on a longer time interval can be expected to apply to this

---

[7] See Plosser (1976) for a discussion of one possible way of dealing with seasonality in a macro-economic monetary model.

analysis, the coefficients of the interest rates, a_1 and a_1^*, are expected to be around 1.5 and -1.5. At a level of the interest rate of 10 percent this implies an elasticity of real balances with respect to the interest rate of $-.13$.[8] The elasticity of real balances with respect to real permanent income is usually estimated to be slightly less than unity, implying estimated parameter values for a_2 and a_2^* of $-.8$ and $.8$, respectively. The next section presents estimates of equations derived from (3) for the U.K. and Germany.

III. TESTS WITH VARIABLES IN THE LEVELS OF NATURAL LOGARITHMS

Results for the United Kingdom

The basic equation (3) developed in the last section is not estimated for the United Kingdom for two reasons. The first is that multicollinearity is a problem in this case, and the second is a general problem of the monetary approach to the determination of the exchange rate. In the last section Eq. (3) was developed in a very simplistic manner. In his "Quantity Theory of Money – A Restatement" Friedman (1956) states that the demand for money will depend on many more variables than the two mentioned in Section II. In particular, if assets are not perfect substitutes, more than one of the interest rates on alternative assets will enter the demand for money. In the case of the U.K. it is desirable to include a variable which reflects the difference between domestic interest rates and Eurocurrency interest rates, that is, interest rates on assets denominated in the currency of one country but issued in a second country. The notation for the Eurodollar interest rate will be j, and j^* will represent the Europound or Eurodeutschemark interest rate. In Eq. (4) the money supplies and incomes are constrained to have the same coefficient and the differential between the Europound interest rate and the U.K. Treasury bill interest rate is included as an additional explanatory variable.[9]

$$\hat{e}_t \;=\; 1.74 + .27\,(m_t - m_t^*) + 1.93\,\ln\,(1 + i_t) - .83\,\ln\,(1 + i_t^*) \qquad (4)$$
$$\phantom{\hat{e}_t \;=\;} (.35)\ (.10) \qquad\qquad (.40) \qquad\qquad (.48)$$

$$\phantom{\hat{e}_t \;=\;} -.66\,(y_t - y_t^*) + 1.00\,(\ln\,(1 + j_t^*) - \ln\,(1 + i_t^*))$$
$$\phantom{\hat{e}_t \;=\;} (.15) \qquad\qquad (.34)$$

$$R^2 \;=\; .73 \quad F(5,30) = 15.77 \quad \text{D.W.} = 1.81 \quad \text{S.E.R.} = .018$$

---

[8] For demand for money studies which generate elasticity estimates whose magnitudes are analogous to those suggested here see Goldfeld (1973), Chow (1966), and Cagan and Schwartz (1975) for the U.S.; and Laidler (1969) and Haache (1974) for the U.K.

[9] R^2 is the coefficient of determination corrected for degrees of freedom; D.W. is the Durbin–Watson statistic; and S.E.R. is the standard error of the regression. The term $\hat{e}_t$ signifies the explained part of the endogenous variable e_t.

						Lag							
1	2	3	4	5	6	7	8	9	10	11	12	Estimated $\hat{\sigma}$ for row
A .03	−.05	−.01	.17	−.07	−.12	−.14	.04	−.17	.08	−.11	.00	.17
P .03	−.05	−.00	.17	−.09	−.10	−.14	.01	−.17	.13	−.12	−.01	.17

A = Autocorrelation   P = Partial Autocorrelation

The autocorrelations and partial autocorrelations of the residuals of Eq. (4) are presented above. None of the autocorrelations are statistically different from zero at the 5 percent level of significance.

The explanatory power of Eq. (4) is quite good, and all of the estimated coefficients have the anticipated sign and are statistically different from zero at the 5 percent level of significance except the U.K. interest rate coefficient which is significantly different from zero at the 10 percent level. The data in this case do not support the hypothesis that the coefficient of the difference in the money supplies is unity. A 95 percent confidence interval for the coefficient of the money-supply differential is .07 to .47. The coefficient of the income differential has a 95 percent confidence interval that is given by − .36 to − .96. This is consistent with the hypothesis that an increase in income in the domestic (foreign) country will increase the demand for money, causing the exchange rate to fall (rise) since the exchange rate is in terms of domestic currency per unit of foreign currency. The coefficients of the interest rates on domestic and foreign Treasury bills also have the expected signs, although the magnitude of the coefficient of the U.K. interest rate is somewhat low. The 95 percent confidence intervals for these coefficients are 1.13 to 2.73 for the U.S. and +.13 to −1.79 for the U.K. An increase in expected inflation in the U.S. that caused the interest rate to rise from 10 percent to 11 percent *ceteris paribus* would depreciate the exchange rate of the U.K. pound in terms of the U.S. dollar by 1.7 percent based on the point estimate in Eq. (4).

The last term in Eq. (4), the differential between the three-month Europound interest rate and the three-month U.K. Treasury bill interest rate, has a coefficient whose 95 percent confidence interval is .32 to 1.68. This strong positive influence can be explained by reference to the interest parity theorem and the institutional structure of the period.

The interest-rate parity theorem states that the interest differential between assets which are equivalent except for the currency of denomination is equal to the forward premium as in Eq. (5).

$$\ln (1 + i_t) - \ln (1 + i_t^*) = f_t - e_t \qquad (5)$$

Aliber (1973) and Stoll (1966) have stressed that the equality will not hold if the assets are issued in different countries and there is an expectation of the imposition of exchange controls. It was for that reason that Frenkel and Levich (1975, 1977) chose a neutral center where the expectation of the imposition of controls is the same for both currencies. Frenkel and Levich demonstrate that $\ln (1 + j) - \ln (1 + j^*) = f_t - e_t$ within the neutral bounds of transactions costs. With these considerations in mind we can determine the expected influence of the last term in Eq. (4).

The positive coefficient can be explained by adding and subtracting $\ln (1 + i_t)$ to the interest differential as in Eq. (6).

$$
\begin{aligned}
\ln (1 + j_t^*) - \ln (1 + i_t^*) &= [\ln (1 + j_t) - (f_t - e_t)] + [\ln (1 + i_t) - \ln (1 + i_t)] \\
&\quad - \ln (1 + i_t^*) \\
&= [\ln (1 + j_t) - \ln (1 + i_t)] \\
&\quad + [\ln (1 + i_t) - \ln (1 + i_t^*) + f_t - e_t]
\end{aligned}
\tag{6}
$$

The first term on the right-hand side of Eq. (6) is the differential between the three-month Eurodollar interest rate and the three-month U.S. Treasury bill interest rate. This differential can be expected to widen with portfolio shifts out of dollar-denominated assets if Eurodollars become more risky than Treasury bills. In addition, as the expected rate of inflation rises in the U.S., a certain amount of disinter-mediation takes place because of Regulation Q. This too would contribute to an increased differential as the dollar depreciates, contributing to the positive relation-ships found in Eq. (4). The second term on the right-hand side of Eq. (6) is the interest-parity relationship between U.S. and U.K. Treasury bills. In periods when there are no expectations of capital controls or possible default by either government, this relation-ship holds fairly well. However, a large differential in favour of the U.S., that is, $\ln (1 + i_t) < \ln (1 + i_t^*) + f_t - e_t$, can develop as a risk premium necessary to com-pensate for the risk of capital controls or possible default by the British government. Such an effect would be most likely when the pound was depreciating; that is, when e_t is falling. Therefore, both terms in Eq. (6) contribute to the significant positive coefficient found in Eq. (4).

In the next part of this section the basic equation (3) is estimated for the case of the United States and Germany.

Results for Germany

The basic stock or long-run money-demand formulation of Eq. (3) for the U.S. dollar-German deutschemark spot exchange rate is presented in Eq. (7).

$$
\begin{aligned}
\hat{e}_t = {} & 7.85 + 1.52m_t - 1.39m_t^* + 2.53 \ln (1 + i_t) + \\
& (3.03) \quad (.512) \quad (.563) \quad (1.17) \\
& 1.93 \ln (1 + i_t^*) - 2.23y_t + .073y_t^* \\
& (.669) \qquad\qquad (.456) \quad (.384)
\end{aligned}
\tag{7}
$$

$$
R^2 = .662 \quad F(6,23) = 7.50 \quad \text{D.W.} = 1.61 \quad \text{S.E.R.} = 0.37
$$

Lag												
1	2	3	4	5	6	7	8	9	10	11	12	Estimated $\hat{\sigma}$ for row
A .16	−.10	−.32	−.27	−.32	−.22	.29	.29	.23	.09	−.02	−.05	.18
P .16	−.13	−.29	−.22	−.39	−.48	−.05	−.23	−.24	−.14	.01	−.92	.18

A = Autocorrelation   P = Partial Autocorrelation

The estimated autocorrelations and partial autocorrelations of the residuals of Eq. (7) are presented above. The assumptions about the residuals of the model are that they are independently and identically distributed. This implies that the estimated auto-correlations and partial autocorrelations of the residuals must be zero. The partial autocorrelations of the residuals of Eq. (7) at lag 5 and lag 6 are significantly different from zero at the 5-percent level of significance. However, none of the estimated autocorrelations are significantly different from zero at this standard level of significance. Consequently, it is ambiguous whether or not standard inferences based on the standard errors of the coefficients of Eq. (7) are valid. Proceeding under the hypothesis that the residuals satisfy the assumptions stated above, we find that we cannot reject at the 5-percent level of significance the hypothesis that the coefficients of the money supplies are equal to plus and minus unity. A 95-percent confidence interval for the U.S. money supply coefficient is given by .46 to 2.62 while a 95-percent confidence interval for the coefficient of the German money supply is given by −.23 to −2.55.

The coefficients of the income terms indicate a much stronger influence of the U.S. income than expected and a much weaker influence of the German income. The 95-percent confidence interval for the U.S. income coefficient is −1.74 to −3.36 while the 95-percent confidence interval for the German income coefficient is −.721 to +.816. The imprecision of these estimates and the fact that all of the explanatory power of the two income terms is given to one coefficient may indicate that the income terms should be entered in ratio form to avoid possible problems with multi-collinearity.[10] Later equations in Section IV use this approach.

The coefficients of the interest rate terms are contained in the following 95-percent confidence intervals: .11 to 4.95 for the U.S. and .55 to 3.31 for Germany. The U.S. coefficient is consistent with the hypothesis of a positive influence for the U.S. interest rate as expected; however, the positive influence of the German interest rate is contrary to the expected negative influence. The problem of the German

---

[10]When the income terms in Eq. (7) were entered in ratio form the residuals of the model were autocorrelated. The estimates in Section 4 allow for deviations from the traditional assumptions of the stochastic structure of the residuals.

interest rate may be attributable to the strong capital controls which Germany employed throughout much of the sample period.

In the beginning of the period the capital controls which Germany used were quite extensive. These controls, adopted in February 1973 as a consequence of the massive capital inflows into Germany at the end of the Bretton Woods fixed-parity system, required authorization by the Deutsche Bundesbank for the acquisition of domestic securities by nonresidents. The effect of these controls was to drive a wedge between the real interest rate in Germany and the real interest rate in the U.S. and the rest of the world. Additionally, these controls prevented the deutschemark from appreciating relative to the dollar to the full extent that it would have.[11]

This concludes the analysis using variables in the levels of the natural logarithms of the basic equation (3) of the monetary approach to the determination of the exchange rate. Section IV represents equations which are estimated with variables in the first difference of the natural logarithms or rate-of-change formation.

IV. TESTS USING RATES OF CHANGE OF VARIABLES

In this section tests of the monetary approach to the determination of the exchange rate will be presented when the variables of the equation are in rate-of-change form. This allows a relaxation of the hypothesis of stock equilibrium allowing a dynamic response of the exchange rate to changes in the exogenous variables. The results were derived by testing the general transfer-function model given in Eq. (8) where D is the difference operator, $Dx_t = x_t - x_{t-1}$, and L is the lag operator, $L^i x_t = x_{t-i}$.[12]

$$De_t = c_1 + c_2(L)[D(m_t - m_t^*)] + c_3(L)[D(y_t - y_t^*)] \\ + c_4(L)[D(i_t - i_t^*)] + c_5(L)a_t \tag{8}$$

The coefficients $c_i(L)$ were allowed to be both numerator and denominator polynomials such as Eq. (9).

$$c_i(L) = \frac{w_0 - w_1 L - w_2 L^2}{1 - \delta_1 L - \delta_2 L^2} \tag{9}$$

The use of $c_i(L)$ polynomials such as Eq. (9) allows a wide variety of distributed lag effects of the input variables on the endogenous variable.

Three diagnostic checks were performed to determine the adequacy of the transfer-function models. First, the residuals of the model $\hat{a}_1 \ldots \hat{a}_T$, were checked for autocorrelation where the estimated autocorrelation at lag k is given by Eq. (10).

---

[11] See Hodrick (1976) for an analysis in which a proxy for the real interest rate differential between the U.S. and Germany is constructed and used in an equation like (7). For a theoretical model which generates real interest rate differentials without capital controls see Dornbusch (1976b).

[12] See Box and Jenkins (1970) for a discussion of identification and estimation of transfer-function models of the type used here.

$$r_{\hat{a}\hat{a}}(k) = \frac{\sum\limits_{t=1}^{T-k} \hat{a}_t \hat{a}_{t+k}}{\sum\limits_{t=1}^{T} \hat{a}_t^2} \tag{10}$$

These sample autocorrelations may be checked individually against their large sample standard error, $1/\sqrt{T}$, where T is the number of observations, to test the hypothesis that a given autocorrelation is zero. Also, the Q statistic in Eq. (11) can be used to test the hypothesis that a set of k autocorrelations is zero.[13]

$$Q(k) = \frac{N(N+2)}{N-\frac{h}{2}} \sum\limits_{t=1}^{k} r_{\hat{a}\hat{a}}(i) \tag{11}$$

Under the null hypothesis of no autocorrelation, $Q(k)$ is asymptotically distributed as a $\chi^2(k-l)$ where $N = T - h$, and h is the number of parameters estimated in the transfer-function model. The value of l is set equal to the number of parameters estimated in the autoregressive moving average (ARMA) noise model, the $c_5(L)$ term in Eq. (8). The term preceding the summation in Eq. (11) is a degrees-of-freedom correction which increases the value of $Q(k)$ in small samples. A value of $Q(k)$ greater than the value of the $\chi^2(k-l)$ chosen for the appropriate level of significance allows the rejection of the hypothesis of no autocorrelation in the first k lags.

The other two diagnostic checks rely on the cross correlation of the residuals of the model with the residuals of the input variables, $\hat{u}_{x_t}$, found by estimating a univariate time-series model for those variables. "Prewhitening" the exogenous variables in this way is done to eliminate autocorrelation of the input series which would contaminate the cross correlations of the input series with the residuals of the model. The cross correlation at lag k of the prewhitened input variable, x_t, with the residuals of the model is given by Eq. (12).

$$r_{\hat{u}_x\hat{a}}(k) = \frac{\sum\limits_{t=1}^{T-k} \hat{u}_{x_t} \hat{a}_{t+k}}{\left[\sum\limits_{t=1}^{T} \hat{u}_{x_t}^2 \sum\limits_{t=1}^{T} \hat{a}_t^2 \right]^{1/2}} \qquad \text{for } k > 0 \tag{12}$$

$$\frac{\sum\limits_{t=1}^{T-k} \hat{u}_{x_{t+k}} \hat{a}_t}{\left[\sum\limits_{t=1}^{T} \hat{u}_{x_t}^2 \sum\limits_{t=1}^{T} \hat{a}_t^2 \right]^{1/2}} \qquad \text{for } k < 0$$

---

[13] See Box and Pierce (1970) for the development of the Q statistic. The degrees of freedom correction was suggested by Haugh (1972).

These sample cross correlations can be used to form the Q statistic as in Eq. (11) which is distributed as $\chi^2(k - (h - l))$ when k is positive and $\chi^2(|k|)$ when k is negative. If the Q statistic calculated for positive k is greater than the value from the χ^2 distribution for the chosen level of significance, the hypothesis that the cross correlation between the input and the future residuals of the model is zero can be rejected. This would indicate that the $c_i(L)$ polynomial was improperly specified since there was more information available from the movement of the input variable that can be used to determine the movement of the endogenous variable.

When Eq. (12) is calculated for negative k, the resulting Q statistic tests for the presence of feedback from the endogenous variable to the input variable. A value of the Q statistic greater than the value from the χ^2 distribution for the chosen level of significance would indicate rejection of the hypothesis that the cross correlation of the input with past residuals of the model was zero. This result indicates that the input variable cannot be considered exogenous because it is being simultaneously determined with the endogenous variable of the model. With these tests in mind, the next part of this section examines the transfer functions for the United Kingdom.

Results for the United Kingdom

The results of estimating Eq. (8) with the U.K. as the foreign country are presented in Table 1. Table 2 presents the diagnostic tests which check the adequacy of the models in Table 1 regarding the functional form of the polynomials and the exogeneity of the inputs. In all cases the superior models were those in which the $c_i(L)$ polynomials were constrained to be of degree zero, i.e., constants. This finding supports the hypothesis that money markets and other asset markets are in stock equilibrium. A distributed-lag effect of the rates of change of money supplies, incomes, or interest rates on the rate of change of the exchange rate would be evidence of significant costs of adjustment which prevent equilibrium from obtaining. However, we cannot conclude that the data fully support the hypothesis of stock equilibrium since the Q statistics of the cross correlation between the change in the interest-rate differential and the past residuals of models M1 and M2 indicate that we can reject the hypothesis of exogeneity of the interest-rate differential. Since past values of the exchange rate are significant in explaining contemporaneous values of the interest-rate differential, a change in the exchange rate will imply a change in the interest differential in future months. A risk-neutral investor could profit from this knowledge by appropriately altering his portfolio. If international asset markets are efficient, such profit opportunities would be arbitraged away. Consequently, the existence of feedback implies either that markets are inefficient, investors are not risk neutral, or transaction costs in changing a portfolio are significant.[14]

Since M3 is nested in the models M1 and M2 we can test the hypothesis that the coefficients of the variables excluded from M3 are zero. In no case can we reject the

---

[14] For an analysis of the efficiency of the foreign exchange market see Levich (1978); for the implications of risk see Stockman (1978); for an analysis of slow adjustment of asset markets see Bilson (1978) and Ujiie (1978).

Table 1

ESTIMATED TRANSFER FUNCTIONS FOR THE UNITED KINGDOM SPOT EXCHANGE RATE: DEPENDENT VARIABLE: De_t; INDEPENDENT VARIABLES: $D(m_t - m_t^*)$, $D(y_t - y_t^*)$, $D(i_t - i_t^*)$, $D(i_t^* - i_t^*)$

Model	RSS	DF	$\dfrac{RSS}{DF}$	EIRF for $D(m_t - m_t^*)$	EIRF for $D(y_t - y_t^*)$	EIRF for $D(i_t - i_t^*)$	EIRF for $D(i_t^* - i_t^*)$	Estimated ARMA noise model	Constant
M1	.000347	30	.1157 $\times 10^{-4}$	.167 (.203)	−.454 (.169)	.550 (.356)	.267 (.290)	NE	−.00147 (.0033)
M2	.000345	31	.1112 $\times 10^{-4}$	.159 (.202)	−.395 (.156)	.620 (.367)		NE	−.00169 (.0033)
M3	.000369	32	.1153 $\times 10^{-4}$	.281 (.196)	−.415 (.161)			NE	−.00134 (.0034)

Note: In this table and succeeding tables where the following abbreviations appear:

RSS　　=　　Residual Sum of Squares
DF　　=　　Degrees of Freedom
EIRF　　=　　Estimated Impulse Response Function
ARMA　　=　　Autoregressive Moving Average
NE　　=　　Not Estimated in this model

Standard errors are in parentheses below the coefficients.

Table 2

BOX-PIERCE TEST STATISTICS FOR AUTOCORRELATION OF RESIDUALS AND CROSS CORRELATION BETWEEN RESIDUALS AND PREWHITENED INPUTS FOR MODELS M1–M3 OF TABLE 1.

Model	$r_{\hat{a}\hat{a}}$	$r_{\hat{u}_m\hat{a}}$		$r_{\hat{u}_y\hat{a}}$		$r_{\hat{u}_i\hat{a}}$		$r_{\hat{u}_j*\hat{a}}$	
	k $Q(12)/(P)$	k $Q(12)/(P)$	$-k$ $Q(12)/(P)$	k $Q(12)/(P)$	$-k$ $Q(12)/(P)$	k $Q(12)/(P)$	$-k$ $Q(12)/(P)$	k $Q(12)/(P)$	$-k$ $Q(12)/(P)$
M1	8.23 (.767)	6.79 (.237)	11.6 (.316)	10.9 (.053)	12.4 (.257)	7.94 (.160)	19.7 (.032)	8.11 (.151)	9.06 (.527)
M2	11.1 (.520)	6.02 (.421)	11.0 (.354)	10.4 (.109)	13.4 (.201)	6.37 (.383)	19.5 (.034)		
M3	7.97 (.787)	5.73 (.572)	13.0 (.226)	8.06 (.327)	14.7 (.145)				

Note: In this table and succeeding tables the following notation is employed:
$Q(k)$ is the χ^2 test of the significance of the first k correlations; the number in parentheses is the P-value of the χ^2 test showing the remaining probability in the right tail of the χ^2 above the Q statistic.

$r_{\hat{a}\hat{a}}(k)$ is the cross correlation of the residuals of the model.

$r_{\hat{u}_x\hat{a}}$ is the cross correlation of the innovation in input x_t with future residuals $\hat{a}_{t+k}$ of the model.

$r_{\hat{u}_x\hat{a}}(-k)$ is the cross correlation of the innovation in input x_t with past residuals $\hat{a}_{t-k}$ of the model.

hypothesis since the F statistics are approximately zero in both cases;[15] hence M3 is the superior model. The positive effect of the difference in the rates of growth of the money supplies in the U.S. and the U.K. is estimated to be less than unity, a 95-percent confidence interval being $-.119$ to $.681$. Similarly, the influence of the difference in the rates of growth of real income is negative as expected, and a 95-percent confidence interval for this coefficient is $-.087$ to $-.743$. This concludes the analysis of the U.K., and the next part of this section considers Germany as the foreign country.

Results for Germany
The estimates of Eq. (8) for the rate of change of the German spot exchange rate are presented in Table 3, and Table 4 gives the diagnostic statistics which check the adequacy of the models. Since M1 is nested in M2, the F statistic which tests the validity of the constraint can be found, and its value is 0.2. Consequently, we cannot reject the hypothesis that the simple model is correct.

In this case the point estimate of the coefficient of the differential rate of change of the money supplies between the U.S. and Germany is 1.09, very close to the expected value of unity. The standard error of the estimate is large, implying a 95-percent confidence interval of $-.40$ to 2.58. The coefficient of the difference in the rates of growth of income again has a negative coefficient as anticipated. Since the estimated coefficient of the income terms was low, a different proxy for the permanent income term was constructed. This variable was the one-step-ahead forecast of the difference in the rates of growth of real incomes in the two countries formed from the univariate time-series model of $D(y_t - y_t^*)$.[16] The coefficient of this variable in M3 is much closer to its anticipated value, and a 95-percent confidence interval for it is given by $-.650$ to 2.334. Although these estimates are not very precise, the data do seem to lend support to the theory.

As a final test of the adequacy of the models relating the rate of change of the exchange rate to the differential in the rates of change of money supplies and incomes in the two countries involved, we examine the univariate time-series properties of the

---

[15] The F-statistic is formed in the following way as in Theil (1971).

$$F(c, n-k) = \frac{(RSS_{con} - RSS)/c}{RSS}$$

where
c	=	the number of constraints
$n-k$	=	the number of degrees of freedom in the unconstrained case
RSS	=	the unconstrained residual sum of squares
RSS_{con}	=	the constrained residual sum of squares.

[16] The one-step-ahead forecast of x_t at time $t-1$ is the mathematical expectation $E_{t-1}(x_t)$ using the time-series model that has been estimated. For example, if $(1-\phi L)x_t = (1-\theta L)a_t$ is the ARMA process of x_t, the one-step-ahead forecast of x_t is $E_{t-1}(x_t) = \phi x_{t-1} - \theta a_{t-1}$.

Table 3

ESTIMATED TRANSFER FUNCTION FOR THE GERMAN SPOT EXCHANGE RATE: DEPENDENT VARIABLE: De_t; INDEPENDENT VARIABLES: $D(m_t - m_t^*)$, $D(y_t - y_t^*)$, $D(i_t - i_t^*)$, $E_{t-1}D(y_t - y_t^*)$

Model	RSS	DF	$\dfrac{\text{RSS}}{\text{DF}}$	EIRF for $D(m_t - m_t^*)$	EIRF for $D(y_t - y_t^*)$	EIRF for $D(i_t - i_t^*)$	EIRF for $E_{t-1}D(y_t - y_t^*)$	Estimated ARMA noise model	Constant
M1	.000904	22	.411 $\times 10^{-4}$	1.09 (.747)	-.373 (.403)			$1 - .799L^2 - .774L^3 - .780L^5$ (.222) (.268) (.186)	.0165 (.004)
M2	.000726	21	.346 $\times 10^{-4}$	.386 (.690)	-.722 (.349)	-1.76 (.701)		$1 - .527L^2 - 1.02L^3 - .900L^5$ (.294) (.304) (.239)	.0157 (.005)
M3	.00149	25	.596 $\times 10^{-4}$	.751 (.613)			-.842 (.746)	NE	

Note: See Table 1 note for definitions of abbreviations.

Table 4

BOX-PIERCE TEST STATISTICS FOR AUTOCORRELATION OF RESIDUALS AND CROSS CORRELATION BETWEEN RESIDUALS AND PREWHITENED INPUTS FOR MODELS M1–M3 OF TABLE 3

Model	$r_{\hat{a}\hat{a}}$	$r_{i_m \hat{a}}$		$r_{i_y \hat{a}}$		$r_{i_i \hat{a}}$		$r_{u_E y}\hat{a}$	
	k Q(12)/(P)	k Q(12)/(P)	-k Q(12)/(P)	k Q(12)/(P)	-k Q(12)/(P)	k Q(12)/(P)	-k Q(12)/(P)	k Q(12)/(P)	-k Q(12)/(P)
M1	7.09 (.628)	11.6 (.114)	14.4 (.155)	3.02 (.883)	3.45 (.969)				
M2	7.36 (.600)	10.1 (.119)	7.95 (.633)	1.30 (.972)	3.63 (.963)	6.14 (.408)	11.0 (.354)		
M3	17.8 (.122)	14.9 (.195)	11.1 (.517)					13.2 (.152)	7.58 (.817)

Note: See note of Table 2 for definitions of the terms.

Table 5

UNITED STATES AND UNITED KINGDOM UNIVARIATE TIME-SERIES MODELS OF De_t, $D(m_t - m_t^*)$, and $D(y_t - y_t^*)$

	RSS	DF	$\dfrac{\text{RSS}}{\text{DF}}$	$Q(12)$ (P)
(a) $De_t = -.0018 + (1 - .013L - .236L^2$ $\quad$ (.0004) $\quad$ (.216) (.217) $-.074L^3 -.297L^4 -1.38L^5 -.251L^6)a_t$ (.215) $\quad$ (.216) $\quad$ (.281) $\quad$ (.195)	.000415	29	$.143 \times 10^{-4}$	12.1 (.376)
(b) $D(m_t - m_t^*) = -.005 + [1 - .09L + .24L^2$ $\quad$ (.16) (.14) $-.13L^3 + .10L^4 -.43L^5 + .60L^6]a_t$ (.15) $\quad$ (.15) $\quad$ (.13) $\quad$ (.14)	.000169	34	$.497 \times 10^{-5}$	14.0 (.001)
(c) $D(y_t - y_t^*) = .0004 + (1 + .318L)a_t$ $\quad$ (.004) $\quad$ (.162)	.000396	33	$.120 \times 10^{-5}$	9.4 (.397)

Table 6

UNITED STATES AND GERMAN UNIVARIATE TIME-SERIES MODELS OF De_t, $D(m_t - m_t^*)$, and $D(y_t - y_t^*)$

	RSS	DF	$\dfrac{\text{RSS}}{\text{DF}}$	$Q(12)$ (P)
(a) $De_t = (1 + .4895L - .506L^5)a_t$ $\quad$ (.1317) (.121)	.001143	30	$.38 \times 10^{-4}$	10.8 (.371)
(b) $D(m_t - m_t^*) = -.0013 + [1 - .094L + .069L^2$ $\quad$ (.0009) $\quad$ (.118) $\quad$ (.096) $-.196L^3 + .289L^4 -.994L^5]a_t$ (.092) $\quad$ (.119) $\quad$ (.080) $(1 - .967L)$	.000106	23	$.461 \times 10^{-5}$	12.0 (.035)
(c) $D(y_t - y_t^*) = .00003 + \dfrac{(.048)}{1 - .536L} a_t$ $\quad$ (.0008) (.178)	.000438	26	$.168 \times 10^{-4}$	11.5 (.176)

exogenous and endogenous variables. Zellner and Palm (1974) demonstrated that one can derive implications about the time-series properties of the univariate model of the endogenous variable from the estimated transfer function and the univariate time-series models of the exogenous variables.

Specifically, our estimates of the transfer function relating the rate of change of the exchange rate to the differential rates of change of money supplies and incomes was given by Eq. (8) where c_2 and c_3 were estimated to be constants. Table 5 presents estimates of the univariate time-series processes for the United Kingdom and the United States; and Table 6 presents estimates of the univariate time-series processes for Germany and the United States.

From Table 5 we see that substitution of the univariate processes of $D(m_t - m_t^*)$ and $D(y_t - y_t^*)$ into Eq. (8) implies that the rate of change of the exchange rate should follow a univariate process which is at least a sixth-order moving average. In (a) of Table 5 a sixth-order moving average process is estimated for the rate of change of the exchange rate. Unfortunately, none of the coefficient estimates are statistically different from zero at the standard levels of significance. However, this may not be evidence that the model is incorrect since the changes in the money supplies which caused the sixth-order moving average may have been in response to perceived changes in money demand. Consequently, the effect on the exchange rate is dampened. In the extreme, it might be possible for the money-demand function to be stochastic and the money-supply process to perfectly offset it, causing no stochastic structure in the exchange rate.

From Table 6 we see that substitution of the univariate time series processes for $D(m_t - m_t^*)$ and $D(y_t - y_t^*)$ in the German case indicates that the univariate time-series process for the rate of change of the dollar-deutschemark exchange rate should be a first-order autoregressive and fifth-order moving average process. The process that was identified and estimated for the variable De_t was a fifth-order moving average. This is an indication of model inadequacy since the autoregressive process of the differential in the rates of growth of the two incomes fails to appear in the rate of change of the exchange rate.

One possible solution to this dilemma is to recall that the real-income variable which is being used in this study is a proxy for the concept of permanent income, which it was argued earlier will follow a random walk. Consequently, if we view the term $D(y_t - y_t^*)$ in Eq. (8) as the differential in the rates of growth of permanent income in the two countries, substitution of its stochastic process will contribute only a white noise term, a_t, to the stochastic structure of De_t. Under this consideration the fifth-order moving average which was identified and estimated for De_t is the correct structure.

This completes the estimates of the rate of change of the exchange rate for the German and U.K. case. Section V presents the conclusions of the analysis.

V. CONCLUSIONS

The two preceding sections have empirically examined the monetary approach to the determination of the exchange rate in two different forms. The results of the analysis when the variables were in the levels of the natural logarithms and when the variables were in rate of change form were broadly consistent with the predictions of the theory.

The first prediction of the theory is that in the long run the rate of change of the exchange rate will be the rate of growth of per capita nominal money balances in the domestic country minus the rate of growth of per capita money balances in the foreign country. The data offered mixed support for this proposition. In the case of the United Kingdom we can reject the hypothesis at standard statistical levels. The influence of the differential rate of growth of the money supplies was positive, but it was significantly different from unity. For Germany the data clearly support the hypothesis, but the confidence that we can have in these estimates is not strong given the large confidence intervals of the coefficients. It seems reasonable to conclude that based on the limited data that we examined one would not want to reject the hypothesis that the exchange rate will move at the difference between the rates of growth of nominal money supplies, *ceteris paribus*. However, the data also do not allow us to distinguish whether or not the rate of change of the exchange rate will overshoot or undershoot the difference in the rates of growth of the money supplies.

The second proposition of the theory was that a decline in real permanent income per capita in a country would lead to a decline in the demand for domestic money and a depreciation of the exchange rate. Strong evidence of this effect was found in both kinds of tests and for both the dollar-pound and dollar-deutschemark exchange rates.

The third proposition was that an increase in anticipated inflation that caused an increase in the nominal interest rate would lead to a depreciation of the currency. Investigation of this hypothesis is hampered by possible simultaneous equation bias, but the results of the tests indicate that this proposition can also be accepted.

REFERENCES

ALIBER, ROBERT Z. "The Interest Rate Parity Theorem: A Reinterpretation." *Journal of Political Economy* **81** (November/December, 1973): 1451–9.

BILSON, JOHN F. O. "Rational Expectations and the Exchange Rate." 1978. Reproduced in this volume as Chapter 5.

BILSON, JOHN F. O., AND JAMES E. GLASSMAN. "A Consumption Function with Rational Forecasts of Permanent Income." Northwestern University discussion paper, 1977.

BOX, G. E. P., AND G. M. JENKINS. *Time Series Analysis*. San Francisco: Holden-Day, 1970.

BOX, G. E. P., AND DAVID PIERCE. "Distribution of Residual Auto-correlations in Auto-regressive-Integrated-Moving Average Time Series Models." *Journal of the American Statistical Association* **65** (December, 1970): 1509–26.

CAGAN, PHILLIP. "The Monetary Dynamics of Hyperinflation." In Milton Friedman (ed.), *Studies in the Quantity Theory of Money*. Chicago: University of Chicago Press, 1956, pp. 25–120.

CAGAN, PHILLIP, AND ANNA SCHWARTZ. "Has the Growth of Money Substitutes Hindered Monetary Policy?" *Journal of Money, Credit, and Banking* **7** (May, 1975): 137–59.

CASSEL, GUSTAV. "The Present Situation of the Foreign Exchange." *Economic Journal* 26 (March, 1916): 62–5.

CHOW, GREGORY C. "On the Long-Run and Short-Run Demand for Money." *Journal of Political Economy* 74 (April, 1966): 111–31.

COLLERY, ARNOLD. *International Adjustment, Open Economies, and the Quantity Theory of Money.* Princeton Studies in International Finance, No. 28. Princeton, N.J.: Princeton University Press, 1971.

DORNBUSCH, RUDIGER. "A Portfolio Balance Model of an Open Economy." *Journal of Monetary Economics* 1 (January, 1975): 1–20.

———. "The Theory of Flexible Exchange Rate Regimes and Macroeconomic Policy." *Scandinavian Journal of Economics* 78, No. 2 (1976a): 255–75. Reproduced in this volume as Chapter 2.

———. "Exchange Rate Dynamics." *Journal of Political Economy* 84 (December, 1976b): 1161–76.

FRENKEL, JACOB A. "A Monetary Approach to the Exchange Rate: Doctrinal Aspects and Empirical Evidence." *Scandinavian Journal of Economics* 78, No. 2 (1976): 200–24. Reproduced in this volume as Chapter 1.

———. "The Forward Exchange Rate, Expectations, and the Demand for Money: The German Hyperinflation." *American Economic Review* 67 (September, 1977): 653–670.

FRENKEL, JACOB A., AND HARRY G. JOHNSON (eds.). *The Monetary Approach to the Balance of Payments.* London: Allen and Unwin, and Toronto: University of Toronto Press, 1976.

FRENKEL, JACOB A., AND RICHARD M. LEVICH. "Covered Interest Arbitrage: Unexploited Profits?" *Journal of Political Economy* 83 (April, 1975): 325–38.

———. "Transaction Costs and Interest Arbitrage: Tranquil vs. Turbulent Periods." *Journal of Political Economy* 86 (December, 1977): 1209–1226.

FRENKEL, JACOB A., AND CARLOS A. RODRIGUEZ. "Portfolio Equilibrium and the Balance of Payments: A Monetary Approach." *American Economic Review* 65 (September, 1975): 674–89.

FRIEDMAN, MILTON. "The Quantity Theory of Money – A Restatement." In Milton Friedman (ed.). *Studies in the Quantity Theory of Money.* Chicago: University of Chicago Press, 1956, pp. 1–21.

———. *A Theory of the Consumption Function.* National Bureau of Economic Research, No. 63 General Series. Princeton, N.J.: Princeton University Press, 1957.

GOLDFELD, STEPHEN. "The Demand for Money Revisited." *Brookings Papers on Economic Activity* 3 (1973): 577–638.

HAACHE, G. "The Demand for Money in the UK: Experience Since 1971." *Bank of England Quarterly Bulletin* 14 (September, 1974): 284–97.

HAUGH, LARRY D. "The Identification of Time Series Interrelationships with Special Reference to Dynamic Regression Models." Ph.D. Dissertation, University of Wisconsin, Madison, 1972.

HODRICK, ROBERT J. "The Monetary Approach to the Determination of Exchange Rates: Theory and Empirical Evidence." Ph.D. dissertation, University of Chicago, 1976.

ISARD, PETER. "How Far Can We Push the 'Law of One Price'?" *American Economic Review* 67 (December, 1977): 942–948.

LAIDLER, DAVID. *The Demand for Money: Theories and Evidence*. Scranton, Pa.: International Textbook Co., 1969.

LEVICH, RICHARD M. "Tests of Forecasting Models and Market Efficiency in the International Money Market." 1978. Reproduced in this volume as Chapter 8.

MAGEE, STEPHEN P. "Contracting and Spurious Deviations from Purchasing-Power Parity." 1978. Reproduced in this volume as Chapter 4.

MUSSA, MICHAEL. "The Exchange Rate, The Balance of Payments and Monetary and Fiscal Policy under a Regime of Controlled Floating." *Scandinavian Journal of Economics* 78, No. 2 (1976): 229–248. Reproduced in this volume as Chapter 3.

PLOSSER, CHARLES. "Time Series Analysis and Seasonality in Econometric Models with an Application to a Monetary Model." Ph.D. dissertation, University of Chicago, 1976.

STOCKMAN, ALAN C. "Risk, Information, and Forward Exchange Rates." 1978. Reproduced in this volume as Chapter 9.

STOLL, HANS. "The Determinants of Forward Exchange Rates." Ph.D. dissertation, University of Chicago, 1966.

THEIL, HENRI. *Principles of Econometrics*. New York, John Wiley and Sons, 1971.

UJIIE, JUNICHI. "A Stock Adjustment Approach to Monetary Policy and the Balance of Payments." 1978. Reproduced in this volume as Chapter 10.

ZELLNER, ARNOLD, AND FRANZ PALM. "Time Series Analysis and Simultaneous Equation Models." *Journal of Econometrics* 2 (April, 1974): 17–54.

CHAPTER 7

EXCHANGE RESTRICTIONS AND THE MONETARY APPROACH TO THE EXCHANGE RATE

MARIO I. BLEJER
Hebrew University of Jerusalem and Boston University

I. INTRODUCTION

The importance of monetary variables in the determination of the exchange rate in a regime of floating rates has recently been the object of careful theoretical and empirical studies, some of which are collected in this volume.[1] Many of these studies, however, have been carried out under the stated or the implicit assumption that restrictions to the international movement of capital are not present and, therefore, that market forces are the overwhelming determinants of the exchange rate. This paper presents an extension to the monetary approach to the exchange rate that analyzes the experience of countries where the presence of exchange restrictions leads to the development of a black market for foreign money. We postulate that in those cases the exchange rate in the black market is freely determined by market forces and responds to disequilibria in the domestic money market while the official exchange rate is administratively determined by the government responding to a reaction function that may be derived from a condition of utility maximization.

Black-market behavior and equilibrium determination with price controls have been analyzed, among others, by Boulding (1937), Bronfenbrenner (1947), and Michaely (1954). The specific behavior of the black market for foreign exchange was considered by Einzig (1937), and more recently by Sheikh (1976) and Culbertson (1975), who also presents an empirical test of his model. Those models, however, do not consider the importance of monetary factors in the determination of the

---

Part of this paper is based on work done by the author at the Center for Latin American Monetary Studies in Mexico City. The author is thankful to the Center for its assistance and support.

[1] See especially Frenkel (1976), Dornbusch (1976), and Mussa (1976) which are reprinted in this volume as Chapters 1, 2, and 3, respectively, and the papers by Hodrick (Chapter 6) and Bilson (Chapter 5). See also Kouri (1976).

equilibrium exchange rate in the black market (and of its rate of depreciation).[2] In this paper, we present a model in which the behavior of monetary variables is the main factor underlying the behavior of the black market exchange rate.

After presenting the formal model in Part II, the results of an empirical analysis of the experience of several Latin American countries are reported in Part III. In that section, the behavior of the black market exchange rate is explained on the basis of the theoretical considerations of Part II. Part IV consists of a brief summary.

II. THE MODEL

Several assumptions are used throughout the paper, particularly regarding the institutional framework and the functioning of the black market. We consider the black market as an outlet for capital transactions that are barred from the official market. In other words, foreign exchange is bought and sold in the black market because the public desires to alter the composition of its portfolio of financial assets and not for the purpose of carrying out international sales and purchases of commodities.[3] That is so because most of the current-account operations are really channeled through the official market. We also assume in this context that there are no tight controls on the foreign-trade sector (tariffs or quotas), so we do not have to consider the effects of smuggling.[4]

We assume a small country (in the sense that the international price of its traded goods is exogenously determined) and allow for the existence of nontraded goods (defined as those whose price responds, at least in the short run, to domestic monetary disequilibria). We also assume full employment and that monetary disequilibrium does not affect the rate of growth of real income.

A. The Money Market and the Excess Supply of Money in an Open Economy
The basic relationships of the monetary sector are the following:

$$M_s = a(R + D) \tag{1}$$

$$M_d = P \cdot m_d \tag{2}$$

$$m_d = f(y, \Pi^e) \tag{3}$$

where M_s is the nominal supply of money, a is the money multiplier, R the foreign-exchange reserves of the Central Bank, D the domestic-credit component of the

---

[2] A test of the monetary hypothesis, using black-market data for Israel, is presented by Fishelson (1976).

[3] That assumption implies that the expected rate of depreciation should influence the demand for domestic money and for other financial assets. This aspect, which is not pursued here, is empirically investigated by the author elsewhere (See Blejer (1978)).

[4] Alternatively, it is possible to assume that the penalties and/or the probability of being caught are high enough to discourage illegal trade activities. This assumption is needed because in the presence of smuggling, foreign exchange will be demanded in the black market not only for financial transactions but also in order to pay for goods and services that are imported without declaring them to the authorities.

monetary base; M_d is the demand for nominal cash balances, P stands for a price index that includes traded and nontraded goods, and m_d is the real demand for money, which is a function of real permanent income (y) and of the expected rate of domestic inflation (Π^e).[5]

The condition for stock equilibrium in the money market is that the nominal quantity of money equals, *ex post*, the demand for nominal cash balances. That condition will be maintained if the market clears in each period, which requires the following flow equilibrium:

$$M_s^* = M_d^*, \tag{4}$$

where the symbol (*) indicates the percentage rate of change of the variable. Differentiating logarithmically Eqs. (1) and (2) and substituting into Eq. (4) we obtain

$$a^* + (1 - \gamma)R^* + \gamma D^* = \Pi + m_d^*, \tag{5}$$

where γ is a factor of proportionality equal to $D/(D + R)$ and Π is the domestic rate of inflation.

As is being increasingly recognized,[6] in a small open economy under fixed exchange rates the nominal money supply is, in fact, an endogenous variable beyond the control of the monetary authority. The Central Bank can only determine the *ex ante* quantity of money by changing the domestic-credit component of the base or manipulating variables under its control to affect the money multiplier. These actions, in conjunction with the flow demand for real balances (generated by adjustments in the desired stock), create an *ex ante* excess flow supply of money. It is to that *ex ante* disequilibrium that the public reacts and, in order to restore monetary balance, changes the level of the reserves component of the base through the balance of payments and, in the short run, the rate of domestic inflation. It is the public, therefore, that determines the *ex post* nominal quantity of money in an open economy.

From the above discussion, it appears that the operative measure of money-market disequilibrium should be an *ex ante* measure which excludes the endogenous reaction of the foreign component of the monetary base. Therefore, in what follows, we measure flow monetary disequilibrium as the difference between the expansion of the domestic-credit component of the base (and variations in the money multiplier) and the changes in the demand for real cash balances.

B. The Domestic Rate of Inflation

The rate of domestic inflation is here measured as a weighted average of the rate of change of the prices of traded and nontraded goods:

$$\Pi = \beta P_T^* + (1 - \beta)P_{NT}^*, \tag{6}$$

---

[5] For simplicity we implicitly assume here that the margin of choice is between money and goods. In the presence of a capital market, however, a second margin, i.e., the margin between money and bonds, should also appear in the formulation of the money demand. We emphasize here the first margin of choice because given the magnitude of the inflationary process in the countries to which the model is applied in the empirical section, it appears to be the more relevant.

[6] See, for example, Johnson (1972) and Mundell (1971).

where P_T is the price of traded goods and P_{NT} the price of nontraded goods. The term β stands for the share of traded goods in total expenditure. Since we assume that this is a small economy, the price of traded goods is exogenously given and its rate of change (in domestic currency) is determined by the world rate of inflation (Π_w) and by variations in the official exchange rate (ρ_0^*):

$$P_T^* = \Pi_w + \rho_0^*. \tag{7}$$

On the other hand, and since an excess supply of money implies an excess demand for goods (both traded and nontraded goods), by assuming that the excess demand for nontraded goods varies monotonically with excess demand throughout the economy, we can postulate the following equation for the rate of change of the prices of nontraded goods:

$$P_{NT}^* = P_T^* + \lambda(\gamma D^* + a^* - M_d^*), \tag{8}$$

where λ is the elasticity of the relative prices to monetary imbalance.[7]

Substituting Eq. (7) into (8) and then Eq. (8) into (6) we obtain after some manipulations an expression for the rate of domestic inflation as a function of world inflation, of changes in the official exchange rate, and of the rate of *ex ante* disequilibrium in the money market:

$$\Pi = \theta(\Pi_w + \rho_0^*) + (1 - \theta)[\gamma D^* + a^* - m_d^*], \tag{9}$$

where $\theta = \dfrac{1}{1 + \lambda(1 - \beta)}$.[8]

C. The Black-Market Exchange Rate

The black-market exchange rate is determined by the interaction between the supply of and the demand for foreign money in that market. The main sources of foreign-exchange supply to the black market are receipts from the over-invoicing of imports and under-invoicing of exports as well as receipts from tourism. The main incentive for engaging in over- and under-invoicing is provided by the differential between the official and the black-market rates. The greater the differential, the larger the profit possibilities, and the higher the incentive for defeating the system. This leads to a diversion of transactions from one market to the other which even a comprehensive control network may not be able to stop. Discrepancies between the official and the black-market rates also increase the supply of foreign exchange to the black-market by tourists since this differential tends to spur the flow of visitors to the country.

Therefore, we can postulate the following supply function of foreign exchange to the black-market:

---

[7] Changes in the domestic price of traded goods affect the price of nontraded goods through substitutions in production and consumption. For a complete model of domestic-price determination with traded and nontraded goods, see Blejer (1977).

[8] Note that if all goods are traded ($\beta = 1$), θ equals unity and the domestic rate of inflation in a fixed-exchange-rate country is pegged to the world rate.

$$\log S_B^{fe} = c_1 + a \log \left(\frac{\rho_B}{\rho_0}\right), \tag{10}$$

where S_B^{fe} is the supply of foreign exchange to the black market and ρ_B is the black-market exchange rate.

On the other hand, as is the case for the demand for domestic currency, the demand for foreign currency at a given level of income is positively related to the return derived from holding this asset and negatively related to the return derived from holding alternative assets.

The return from holding foreign currency as an asset is a function of the expected rate of depreciation in the black market. Indeed, when at any particular moment of time people compare the past behavior of the exchange rate with the behavior of the ratio between the domestic and foreign level of prices and conclude that domestic prices have been rising faster than foreign prices and that this has not led to a corresponding increase in the black-market exchange rate, they will expect as large a depreciation of the black-market rate as is the observed inflation rate differential.[9] In addition, since expectations are formed for the future, people are likely to anticipate that any expected excess of domestic over foreign inflation will also be transmitted to the exchange rate.

From these considerations we can postulate the following expression for the expected depreciation of the black-market exchange rate:[10]

$$(\overset{*}{\rho}_B) = (\log P - \log P_w - \log \rho_B) + (\Pi^e - \Pi_w^e), \tag{11}$$

where P and P_w are, respectively, the domestic and the world price level and Π and Π_w^e are their expected rate of change.

Given that foreign exchange which is acquired through the black market may be used to buy foreign assets, the nominal holding return of those assets, namely the foreign nominal interest rate, also has to be considered as part of the return from the purchase of foreign exchange. On the other hand, since the alternative to holding foreign assets is to hold domestic ones, the opportunity cost of buying foreign exchange will be given by the nominal return of domestic assets, i.e., the domestic nominal interest rate. Assuming that variations in domestic and foreign nominal

---

[9] If the black-market exchange rate is freely determined by market forces, it may be expected that the rate of depreciation will follow closely the trend of the differential between domestic and foreign inflation rates. It is possible, however, to observe short- and medium-run discrepancies between actual black-market depreciations and inflation differentials. Such discrepancies may result from a variety of reasons, mainly imperfect information, government interventions, and seasonality.

[10] In countries with functioning forward exchange markets the expected rate of depreciation could be proxied by the observed forward premium. Although some forward operations are carried out in the black market, no data are available for empirical estimation. For the incorporation of data from the forward foreign-exchange market in empirical analysis, see the studies by Bilson and Dornbusch in this volume (Chapters 5 and 2, respectively) and Frenkel (1977). For the relationship between the forward exchange rate and the expected future exchange rate, see Stockman's study, Chapter 9 of this book.

interest rates are dominated by variations in the expected rate of inflation, the demand function for foreign exchange in the black market will be specified as follows:[11]

$$\log D_B^{fe} = c_2 + b[(\rho_B^*)^e + \Pi_w^e] - d\Pi^e \tag{12}$$

and using Eq. (11), that is equal to

$$\log D_B^{fe} = c_2 + b[(\log P - \log P_w - \log \rho_B) + (\Pi^e - \Pi_w^e) + \Pi_w^e] - d\Pi^e. \tag{12'}$$

If we assume that the own-return elasticity (b) is equal to the alternative-cost elasticity (d), we can rewrite $(12')$ as

$$\log D_B^{fe} = c + b(\log P - \log P_w - \log \rho_B). \tag{13}$$

Differentiating Eqs. (10) and (13) we obtain:

$$(S_B^{fe})^* = a(\rho_B^* - \rho_0^*) \tag{14}$$

and

$$(D_B^{fe})^* = b(\Pi - \Pi_w - \rho_B^*). \tag{15}$$

The flow-equilibrium condition on the foreign-exchange black market requires that

$$(S_B^{fe})^* = (D_B^{fe})^* \tag{16}$$

which, using (14) and (15), can be solved for the rate of black-market exchange-rate depreciation:

$$\rho_B^* = \frac{1}{a+b} [a\rho_0^* + b(\Pi - \Pi_w)] \tag{17}$$

and replacing Π by its value in Eq. (9) we finally obtain

$$\rho_B^* = \left(\frac{a+b\theta}{a+b}\right)\rho_0^* + \frac{b(1-\theta)}{a+b}(\gamma D^* + a^* - \Pi_w - m_d^*), \tag{18}$$

which formulates the rate of depreciation of the black-market exchange rate as a weighted average of the rate of devaluation of the official exchange rate and of flow-monetary disequilibrium.[12]

D. The Official Exchange Rate
Except in the presence of free floating, the official exchange rate is regarded by governments as a policy instrument and its fluctuations generally follow policy decisions. That seems to be particularly true in those cases in which the interaction of market

---

[11] This specification assumes no exchange-rate changes abroad. Although black-market activities are in general illegal, not all governments enforce the prohibition. If black-market transactions are effectively penalized, a risk coefficient should be included. However, we will assume that no legal risk is involved in dealing in the unofficial market since the operation of this market is tolerated by the government (the same result obtained if we assume that the probability of being caught is negligible). That assumption appears to be realistic in the empirical context to which the model is applied.

[12] The coefficient of the official exchange rate variable will be higher, and the coefficient of the excess supply of money will be lower, the higher the elasticity of supply of foreign exchange in the black market and the lower the price elasticity of the demand for foreign exchange in that market.

forces in the official market is restricted by exchange controls. It is likely, therefore, that policy decisions regarding the exchange rate are taken following some sort of reaction function that is aimed at maximizing a government utility function.[13] A plausible simple specification for such a reaction function, which will relate the official exchange rate to deviations from relative purchasing-power parity, can take the following form:[14]

$$\rho_0^* = \alpha(\Pi - \Pi_w). \tag{19}$$

The parameter α takes values ranging from zero to unity. When $\alpha = 1$, there will be a free-floating exchange rate and the model approaches the one presented by Frenkel (in Chapter 1 of this volume) since the rate of devaluation will be fully determined by the differential between domestic and foreign inflation rates. The other extreme case ($\alpha = 0$) implies a fixed-exchange-rate system where monetary disequilibria and domestic inflation are not transmitted to the official exchange rate.

E. Summary of the Model and Equilibrium Conditions

If the official exchange rate is endogenously determined by the reaction function defined by Eq. (19) we can rewrite Eq. (18) as follows (using (9)):[15]

$$\rho_B^* = \frac{(\alpha a + b)(1 - \theta)}{(a + b)(1 - \theta\alpha)} (\gamma D^* + a^* - m_d^* - \Pi_w). \tag{20}$$

In that form, the rate of depreciation of the black-market exchange rate may be expressed as a function of the relationship between domestic monetary disequilibrium and the world rate of inflation. The black-market exchange rate will depreciate faster the higher the rate of domestic credit expansion relative to the increases in the demand for domestic real cash balances and it will depreciate more slowly the higher is the world rate of inflation.

---

[13] For an elaborated analysis and different forms of reaction functions of the monetary authority, see Ujiie's study, Chapter 10 of this volume.

[14] A more general form for the reaction function is the following:

$$(\rho_0^*)_t = \alpha_j(\Pi - \Pi_w)_t + \sum_{i=1}^{n} \alpha_{j+i}(\Pi - \Pi_w)_{t-i} \tag{10'}$$

where, in order to maintain relative purchasing-power parity, it is required that

$$\left(\alpha_j + \sum_{i=1}^{n} \alpha_{j+i}\right) = 1.$$

[15] Replacing ρ_0^* by its value in Eq. (19), the domestic rate of inflation can be rewritten as

$$\frac{\theta(1 - \alpha)}{1 - \theta\alpha} \Pi_w + \frac{1 - \theta}{1 - \theta\alpha} (\gamma D^* + a^* - m_d^*). \tag{9'}$$

Note that the higher the value of α, the higher the weight of the *ex ante* excess supply of money relative to the weight of world inflation. With a free-floating exchange rate ($\alpha = 1$) the domestic rate of inflation is isolated from the world rate and solely determined by domestic monetary disequilibrium.

Equilibrium will be maintained in this system when the monetary authority expands the money supply at the rate necessary to satisfy the growth of the real demand and to replace the depreciated value of the nominal stock. That is achieved when the *ex ante* excess flow supply of money is equal to the world rate of inflation, i.e., when the exogenous components of the supply of money (domestic credit and the money multiplier) are expanded at a rate that exceeds the growth in the demand for real balances by the world rate of inflation. In that case the domestic rate of inflation will not depart from the world rate, the balance of payments will be in equilibrium, and the official as well as the black-market exchange rates will be constant.

III. EMPIRICAL RESULTS

A test of the model presented in Part II was conducted using annual data for Brazil (1952–1973), Chile (1955–1970), and Colombia (1953–1973). The behavior of the black-market exchange rate is analyzed by estimating an equation similar to Eq. (20). However, in order to account for the lagged effects of monetary disequilibria on the dependent variable, the following specification was used:

$$\rho_B^* = \sum_{i=0}^{n} h_i (\gamma D^* + a^* - m_d^* - \Pi_w)_{t-i}. \tag{21}$$

Changes in the U.S. wholesale price index were used as a proxy for the world rate of inflation and the domestic credit component of the monetary base was defined as the claims of the Central Bank on the government, on the publicly-owned financial institutions, and on the private banking system. To obtain m_d^*, a money-demand function of the following form was estimated:

$$\log (M_i/P) = n_0 + n_1 \log y^P + n_2 \Pi^e, \qquad i = 1, 2, \tag{22}$$

where y^P is real permanent income (a proxy for wealth)[16] and Π^e is the proxy used for the opportunity cost of holding money.[17] The term M_1 is defined as currency plus

---

[16] Permanent income is defined as follows:

$$y_t^P = \phi y_t + (1 - \phi) y_{t-1}^P$$

where y_t is current income at constant prices and y_t^P permanent income at constant prices. Several values of ϕ were tried and m^* was calculated on the basis of the values of ϕ that maximized R^2 ($\phi = 0.35$ for Chile; $\phi = 0.4$ for Brazil and Colombia). To calculate the initial value, a GNP-at-constant-prices series for the period 1945–1970 was used. The initial value was obtained by regressing the log of real GNP on a trend and using the fitted values.

[17] To estimate the expected rate of inflation, a traditional adaptive expectations hypothesis is used as follows:

$$\pi_t^e = \delta \pi_t + (1 - \delta) \pi_{t-1}^e,$$

where the rate of inflation is measured by the percentage change in the consumer price index (a yearly average of quarterly percentage changes), and δ is a given constant. To obtain the best fit several values of δ were tried. The results used in the subsequent regressions correspond to $\delta = 0.3$ for Chile and Colombia, and $\delta = 0.4$ for Brazil.

demand deposits and M_2 as M_1 plus time and savings deposits. For each of these definitions m_d^* is calculated by taking first differences of the estimated values from Eq. (22).[18,19]

The data sources were the I.M.F.'s *International Financial Statistics* and the relevant Central Bank bulletins of the various countries. Data on black-market exchange rates were obtained from *Pick's Currency Yearbook*.

The results of the estimations of Eq. (21) are presented in Tables 1, 2, and 3. They indicate that in the three countries studied, monetary disequilibria have a significant effect on the rate of depreciation of the black-market exchange rate. In Chile and Brazil the adjustment of the black-market rate to monetary imbalance appears to take longer than one period since both the current and the one-period lagged coefficients of the excess-flow supply of money are significant at the 0.05 level.[20] When additional lags of the independent variable were included in the estimation, their coefficients, in all cases, were not significantly different from zero and their introduction did not contribute to the explanatory power of the equations. According to the obtained values of the F statistic, the equations are statistically significant at the 0.05 level and

Table 1

BLACK-MARKET EXCHANGE RATE EQUATIONS–BRAZIL (1952–1973)

$$\rho_B^* = c + h_1(\gamma D^* + a^* - m_d^* - \Pi_w)_t + h_2(\gamma D^* + a^* - m_d^* - \Pi_w)_{t-1} + \mu \quad (21)$$

Money definition used	Constant	h_1	h_2	R^2	F	D.W.
M_1	8.015 (1.25)	0.846# (4.25)		0.475	18.12	1.65
M_2	8.824 (1.35)	0.822# (4.05)		0.451	16.44	1.58
M_1	4.500 (0.60)	0.655# (2.25)	0.301# (1.58)	0.496	9.37	1.63
M_2	5.199 (0.69)	0.616# (2.08)	0.326# (1.39)	0.476	8.64	1.56

Notes: # Significant at the 0.05 level.

t-values are in parentheses below the coefficients.

[18] Both the consumer price index and the wholesale price index were used as deflators. However, the values of m_d^* employed to calculate flow disequilibria in the money market correspond to the estimations that used the consumer price index, which gave, in general, better results.

[19] All the variables are calulated as first differences of natural logs. Therefore, γD^*, a^* and Π_w are compatible expressions which can be used together with the estimated m_d^* to calculate the rate of *ex ante*, excess flow supply of money that is used as the independent variable.

[20] In no case is multicollinearity in the independent variable detected when both the current and the lagged values of monetary disequilibrium are included. In these estimations, n of Eq. (21) was set equal to 1.

Table 2

BLACK-MARKET EXCHANGE RATE EQUATIONS–CHILE (1955–1970)

$$\rho_B^* = c + h_1(\gamma D^* + a^* - m_d^* - \Pi_w)_t + h_2(\gamma D^* + a^* - m_d^* - \Pi_w)_{t-1} + \mu \quad (21)$$

Money definition used	Constant	h_1	h_2	R^2	F	D.W.
M_1	10.358 (0.99)	0.923[#] (2.76)		0.545	7.63	1.56
M_2	11.906 (1.08)	0.885[#] (2.43)		0.498	5.94	1.47
M_1	23.901[#] (2.16)	0.721[#] (3.37)	0.173[#] (2.13)	0.653	5.97	1.78
M_2	27.60[#] (2.34)	0.826[#] (3.05)	0.137[#] (2.31)	0.634	5.39	1.65

Notes: See Table 1.

Table 3

BLACK-MARKET EXCHANGE RATE EQUATIONS–COLOMBIA (1953–1973)

$$\rho_B^* = c + h_1(\gamma D^* + a^* - m_d^* - \Pi_w)_t + h_2(\gamma D^* + a^* - m_d^* - \Pi_w)_{t-1} + \mu \quad (21)$$

Money definition used	Constant	h_1	h_2	R^2	F	D.W.
M_1	9.598[#] (1.91)	0.327 (1.31)		0.132	0.61	2.20
M_2	9.085[#] (1.79)	0.374 (1.31)		0.143	0.81	2.24
M_1	4.086 (0.75)	0.233 (0.92)	0.770[#] (1.96)	0.412	2.29	1.97
M_2	2.817 (0.51)	0.308 (1.04)	0.813[#] (2.15)	0.448	2.81	2.06

Notes: See Table 1.

they explain about one-half—and in the case of Chile, two-thirds—of the variations of the black-market rate. In the case of Colombia, the current rate of money-market flow disequilibrium does not yield a significant coefficient and it appears that all the explained variation is accounted for by the one-year lag. With the exception of Colombia, the results indicate that a better fit is obtained when M_1 rather than M_2 is used as the definition of money. The Durbin-Watson statistics indicate, in the majority of the cases, the absence of first-order serial correlation.

It is important to notice that the sum of the estimated coefficients of the current and lagged independent monetary variables is very similar in the three countries studied and in all cases is remarkably close to unity—which seems to indicate that almost all flow disequilibria created in the money market are transmitted to the black-market exchange rate after a period of two years has elapsed.

IV. SUMMARY

The central aim of this study is to develop a testable model in order to analyze the behavior of the exchange rate in an economy where exchange-controls are present and lead to the development of a black market for foreign exchange. The black market rate is taken to be freely determined by market forces and to respond, as do the rate of domestic inflation and the money account of the balance of payments, to monetary disequilibria. On the other hand, the official exchange rate is considered to be a policy instrument that varies according to a reaction function on the part of the authorities.

The empirical results are presented in Part III, and deal with the cases of Brazil, Chile, and Colombia. They lend support to the hypotheses derived from the theoretical model. In particular, the black-market exchange rate appears to be significantly affected by current and one-year-lagged excess supply of money. From the values of the estimated coefficients we can conclude that almost all *ex ante*, money-market flow disequilibria are transmitted to the black-market rate within a two-year period.

REFERENCES

BILSON, JOHN F. O. "Rational Expectations and the Exchange Rate," 1978. Reproduced in this volume as Chapter 5.

BLEJER, MARIO I. "Short-Run Dynamics of Prices and the Balance of Payments," *American Economic Review* 67, No. 3 (June, 1977): 419–28.

BLEJER, MARIO I. "Black-Market Exchange-Rate Expectations and the Domestic Demand for Money: Some Empirical Results," *Journal of Monetary Economics*, forthcoming (1978).

BOULDING, KENNETH E. "A Note on the Theory of the Black Market," *Canadian Journal of Economics and Political Science* (March, 1937): 153–155.

BRONFENBRENNER, MARTIN. "Price Control under Imperfect Competition," *American Economic Review* 37, No. 1 (March, 1947): 107–120.

CULBERTSON, WILLIAM P., JR. "Purchasing Power Parity and Black-Market Exchange Rates," *Economic Inquiry* 13, No. 2 (May, 1975): 287–296.

DORNBUSCH, RUDIGER, "The Theory of Flexible Exchange Rate Regimes and Macro-economic Policy," *Scandinavian Journal of Economics* **78**, No. 2 (May, 1976): 255–275. Reprinted as Chapter 2 of this volume.

EINZIG, PAUL. *The Theory of Forward Exchange*, London: Macmillan, 1937.

FISHELSON, GIDEON. "The Exchange Rate in a Controlled Foreign Exchange Market (Israel)." The Foerder Institute for Economic Research, Tel Aviv University. Working Paper No. 32–76, 1976.

FRENKEL, JACOB A. "A Monetary Approach to the Exchange Rate: Doctrinal Aspects and Empirical Evidence," *Scandinavian Journal of Economics* **78**, No. 2 (May, 1976): 200–224. Reprinted as Chapter 1 of this volume.

FRENKEL, JACOB A. "The Forward Exchange Rate, Expectations and the Demand for Money: The German Hyperinflation," *American Economic Review* **67**, No. 4 (September, 1977): 653–670.

HODRICK, ROBERT J. "An Empirical Analysis of the Monetary Approach to the Determination of the Exchange Rate," 1978. Reproduced as Chapter 6 of this volume.

International Monetary Fund, *International Financial Statistics*, Washington D.C. Various Issues.

JOHNSON, HARRY G. "The Monetary Approach to the Balance of Payments," in his *Further Essays in Monetary Theory*, London: Allen and Unwin, 1972.

KOURI, PENTTI J. K. "The Exchange Rate and the Balance of Payments in the Short Run and in the Long Run: A Monetary Approach," *Scandinavian Journal of Economics* **78**, No. 2 (1976): 280–304.

MICHAELY, MICHAEL. "A Geometrical Analysis of Black-Market Behavior," *American Economic Review* **44** (September, 1954): 627–637.

MUNDELL, ROBERT A. *Monetary Theory*, Pacific Palisades, Calif.: Goodyear, 1971.

MUSSA, MICHAEL. "The Exchange Rate, the Balance of Payments and Monetary and Fiscal Policy under a Regime of Controlled Floating," *Scandinavian Journal of Economics* **78**, No. 2 (1976): 229–248. Reprinted as Chapter 3 in this volume.

PICK, FRANZ. *Pick's Currency Yearbook*, New York: Various Issues.

SHEIKH, M. A. "Black-Market for Foreign Exchange, Capital Flows and Smuggling," *Journal of Development Economics* **3**, No. 1 (March, 1976): 9–26.

STOCKMAN, ALAN C. "Risk, Information, and Forward Exchange Rates," 1978. Reproduced as Chapter 9 of this volume.

TESTS OF FORECASTING MODELS AND MARKET EFFICIENCY IN THE INTERNATIONAL MONEY MARKET

RICHARD M. LEVICH
New York University

I. INTRODUCTION

Over the last twenty years, a substantial research effort has been directed toward developing and testing the efficient-market hypothesis. Stated simply, an efficient market is one "in which prices always 'fully reflect' available information" (Fama, 1970). Investors collect and process information in order to assess the value of an asset. Trading occurs so that market prices continuously reflect the information set; as a consequence, unusual profit opportunities are quickly eliminated.

The main laboratory for testing the efficient-market hypothesis has been the market for financial claims (primarily equities) in the United States.[1] The motivation for the research presented in this paper is to test the efficient-market hypothesis on a uniform set of data from the international money market. Stated in this manner, the hypothesis is too general for empirical testing. Therefore, two more specific hypotheses are formulated:[2]

1. Prices of particular financial claims imply accurate and consistent forecasts of future spot exchange rates.

This paper relies heavily on Chapter seven of the author's doctoral dissertation. The author has benefited through discussions with Robert Z. Aliber, Jacob Frenkel, Charles Nelson, Rudiger Dornbusch, Arthur Laffer, and Myron Scholes. Other participants in the International Business and International Trade Workshops at the University of Chicago made many helpful suggestions. Financial assistance from the Oscar Meyer Foundation and the Chicago Mercantile Exchange is gratefully acknowledged. New York University provided additional research support. The graphs were completed while the author was a Visiting Scholar at the Federal Reserve System. The views expressed here are his own and do not reflect the opinions of any of the sponsoring institutions.

[1] For a survey of the efficient markets literature see Fama (1970, 1976). Surveys with special reference to international financial markets are in Kohlhagen (1976) and Levich (1978).

2. Unusual speculative profits should not be earned by investors who use exchange-rate forecasts based on publicly available information.

The first hypothesis draws on the assumption that prices reflect information. Since investors' expectations of the future spot exchange rate are part of the information set, observed prices of spot rates, forward rates, and interest rates, for example, should reflect the market's consensus estimate of the future spot rate. A test of this hypothesis can be based on the statistical properties of exchange-rate forecasts implied by market prices. Under the null hypothesis that the international money market is efficient, these statistical properties should agree with our theoretical expectations.

The second hypothesis considers the usefulness of exchange-rate forecasts based on publicly available information. One risky investment opportunity is speculation in forward contracts. Market efficiency suggests that publicly available forecasts of the future spot rate should not lead to unusual profits in forward speculation.

These ideas are definitely not new. Statements describing the speed of foreign-exchange traders and the efficiency of foreign-exchange markets can be found in Ricardo (1811), Goschen (1862), and Walras (1874). This paper makes its contribution by applying a thorough statistical analysis on a large, uniform data base covering nine major industrial countries in the sample period 1967–1975.

Overall this research suggests that we cannot reject either hypothesis. First, although exchange-rate forecasts based on market prices are not perfect, they do display many statistical properties consistent with efficient use of available information. Second, publicly available forecasts do not lead to unusual profits in forward speculation. This research, therefore, cannot reject the hypothesis that the international money market is efficient.

II. STATISTICAL METHODS AND EXCHANGE-RATE FORECASTING

One approach to the exchange-rate forecasting problem is to specify a structural model of the economy.[3] If the spot rate can be expressed as a function of lagged endogenous variables and exogenous variables, and if forecasts of the future values of the exogenous variables are available, then a conditional forecast of the future spot rate can be generated. This is not the approach adopted here.

---

[2] A more fundamental hypothesis is that unusual profit opportunities in covered interest arbitrage are quickly eliminated. This hypothesis is more fundamental in the sense that efficiency here rests on the relatively simple process of policing a boundary condition; all inputs for this single period model are known with certainty. Earlier research reported by Frenkel and Levich (1975, 1977) indicates that when transaction costs are included and the financial assets are comparable in terms of risk, unusual arbitrage profits are quickly eliminated. It is therefore appropriate to test hypotheses which consider uncertainty.

[3] Alternative models of exchange-rate determination are described in Bilson (1978), Dornbusch (1976), Frenkel (1976) and Hodrick (1978).

Alternatively, forecasting can rely on principles associated with spot and forward currency speculation. An early statement that the interest-rate differential between assets denominated in two currencies should reflect anticipated exchange-rate changes is associated with Irving Fisher (1896).[4] The basic thrust of Fisher's analysis is that for the asset market to clear, investors demand a higher nominal return on assets denominated in a (relatively) depreciating unit of account; investors accept a lower nominal return on assets denominated in a (relatively) appreciating unit of account. In a world of certainty, the market's implied one-period ahead forecast of the spot rate is given by:

$$\hat{S}_{t+1} = S_t \frac{1 + r_d}{1 + r_f} \tag{1}$$

where

S_t = Spot exchange rate (in domestic currency per unit foreign currency) at time t,

r_d = One-period interest rate on domestic currency asset, and

r_f = One-period interest rate on foreign currency asset.

Equation (1) represents a great simplification; to forecast the future spot rate we need only two inputs—the interest rates. The cost is that we no longer see how underlying economic variables effect the exchange rate. Implicitly, we are acting as though Eq. (1) is the reduced form equation for the spot rate in a correctly specified structural model. In effect, we are relying on asset markets to be efficient processors of information on exchange-rate expectations.[5]

In the case where interest rate parity holds, spot speculation and forward speculation are equivalent investments.[6] Equation (1) can then be re-written as

$$\hat{S}_{t+1} = F_t \tag{2}$$

---

[4] Fisher presents data for the period 1865–1895 on Indian debt, partly denominated in silver and partly denominated in gold. Interest on the silver bonds is paid by draft on India (in rupees) and interest on the gold bonds is paid in gold. Both securities are traded in London. Fisher also presents a matching time series on rupee exchange rates. He concludes:

> From 1884 exchange fell much more rapidly than before, and the difference in the two rates of interest rose accordingly, amounting in one year to 1.1%. Since the two bonds were issued by the same government, possess the same degree of security, are quoted side by side in the same market and are in fact similar in all important respects *except in the standard in which they are expressed,* the results afford substantial proof that the fall of exchange (after it once began) was discounted in advance. Of course investors did not form perfectly definite estimates of the future fall, but the fear of a fall predominated in varying degrees over the hope of a rise. (p. 390, emphasis added.)

[5] For a further elaboration of the role of expectations, see Bilson (1978), Mussa (1976), and Stockman (1978).

[6] A proof of the statement assuming uncertainty is in Tsiang (1959), pp. 86–92.

where F = one-period forward rate at time t. The formulation assumes that the forward market efficiently reflects information on exchange-rate expectations.[7]

Both Eqs. (1) and (2) assume a world of certainty and no transaction costs. When transaction costs exist it is easily shown that the forecast point estimate becomes a neutral band with upper bound (U) and lower bound (L) given by

$$U = \hat{S}_{t+1}/\Omega$$
$$L = \Omega\hat{S}_{t+1}$$

where

$$\Omega = \prod_{i=1}^{n} (1 - t_i),$$

$$t_i = \text{cost of transaction } i,$$

and n is the number of transactions required to take the speculative position. The presence of transaction costs may therefore lead to forecast errors even under perfect foresight and rational behavior.

If market forces are efficient in assessing information about the future spot exchange rate, then a large fraction of sample observations should be bounded by the neutral band. In this case, we will not reject hypothesis one. However, if the fraction of observations bounded is low, there are two alternative conclusions. First, it may be that market participants are inefficient in processing exchange rate expectations. Second, it may be that Eqs. (1) and (2) are not the correct reduced-form models of exchange rates which market participants use to set prices. This conundrum is common to any data which reject market efficiency and empirically, there is no technique for distinguishing the correct conclusion.

When uncertainty exists, forecast errors may arise because unanticipated events occur after the forecast is formulated. In this case, Eqs. (1) and (2) should be modified to include an error term, u_{t+1}. If the mean of the error term is zero, the forecast is unbiased. Furthermore, if the market is efficient, the error terms will be serially uncorrelated.

It is, however, possible for the forecasts to be biased with a nonzero mean error term.[8] It should be underscored that the existence of bias does not necessarily imply market inefficiency. It is conceivable that equilibrium expected returns are set so that the compensation for bearing exchange risk is nonzero.

Another explanation for bias is currency preference (Aliber, 1973). The currency preference argument is that there may be a convenience or other nonpecuniary yield associated with a currency. For example, a London importer (who is risk averse) may hold dollar balances to lessen exposure to exchange risk and to reduce transaction

---

[7] There is substantial literature to support this assumption. For example, Working (1961) argues that "Futures prices tend to be highly reliable estimates of what should be expected on the basis of contemporarily available information . . . ."

[8] For a theoretical description of the sources of bias, see Stockman (1978). An alternative explanation based on international portfolio theory is in Solnik (1973).

costs from trading in and out of sterling. A U.S. investor may hold Swiss franc assets to benefit from anonymity in the Swiss banking system. In both examples, the nominal interest rate does not adequately measure the desirability of these assets for investors.

The empirical evidence on forecasting bias in Eqs. (1) and (2) is mixed.[9] The issue will be examined again in this paper.

Another approach to forecasting which uses market data is based on time-series analysis.[10] In an efficient market, the price of spot exchange itself will reflect the information set. If the underlying factors determining exchange rates are generated by a stationary process, the time-series description of the spot rate may be useful for forecasting. One possible description of the spot series is a random-walk model with zero drift which leads to the forecast

$$\hat{S}_{t+1} = S_t. \tag{3}$$

It should be emphasized that the random-walk description of the exchange rate is not the only model consistent with market efficiency. Equation (3) was selected because it is a naïve model that may have been postulated by market participants during this period.[11]

The Data Base

The data for this paper are taken exclusively from the Harris Bank *Weekly Review*. Data for nine countries (Canada, United Kingdom, Belgium, France, Germany, Italy, Netherlands, Switzerland, and Japan) and the United States are reported. End-of-week bid quotations from the interbank market are reported for the spot rate, the forward premium, the domestic treasury bill rate and the external or Eurocurrency deposit rate. All quotations reported as a percent per annum are converted to their per period equivalents.[12]

Forecasts of the future spot exchange rate, $S(i, j, k, l)$, in U.S. dollars per foreign unit are generated for $i = 1, \ldots 9$ countries, $j = 1, \ldots 4$ forecasting models, $k = 1, \ldots 3$ forecasting horizons, and $l = 1, \ldots 430$ weekly observations. The four forecasting models are: model (1a) using treasury bill rates (Fisher domestic), model (1b) using Eurocurrency deposit rates (Fisher external) and models (2) and (3).

The 430 weeks cover the period January 3, 1967 through May 9, 1975. The

---

[9] Fisher (1896) observed that a 0.2 to 0.3 percent interest rate differential between gold and silver assets existed, even when the exchange rate was unchanged. A reexamination of this data (Levich, 1977) indicates that, under the 25-year sample period, the null hypothesis that the error terms have mean zero and are serially uncorrelated cannot be rejected. For evidence on other periods see Kohlhagen (1975), Bilson (1976) and Frenkel (1977).

[10] For an explanation of time-series estimation methods, see Box and Jenkins (1970) and Nelson (1973). For a comprehensive analysis of the determination of exchange rates implementing a time-series analysis approach, see Hodrick (1978).

[11] A time-series analysis of weekly spot exchange rates over the period 1973–1975 indicates that the strict random-walk model is valid only for the Italian lira and the Swiss franc. However, the precise time-series specification could only be learned using in-sample observations. See Levich (1977).

[12] For a discussion of the problems introduced by using annualized data in models of a shorter horizon, see Frenkel and Levich (1975, 1977).

forecasting horizons analyzed are one, three, and six months. These horizons are consistent with the maturity of interest rates and forward contracts in the data base. However, since the *Weekly Review* is published weekly, it is necessary to translate the forecasting horizons to 4, 13, and 26 weeks. For example, today's one-month forward rate is compared to the spot rate 4 weeks from today. The three- and six-month forward rates are compared to spot rates 13 and 26 weeks in the future. This compromise may increase the magnitude of forecast errors at the one-month horizon. For the three- and six-month horizon, the effect should be small.

Percentage forecast errors, e_t, are calculated using

$$e_t = (S_{t+n} - \hat{S}_{t+n})/S_{t+n}.$$

Therefore, positive (negative) forecast errors indicate underestimation (overestimation). Note also that the forecast errors are subscripted for time t—the time when the forecast was made. Therefore, when forecasts are aggregated over some time period, say 1974, the summary statistics describe errors of forecasts which were formulated in 1974.

In the case of missing observations, the forecast is omitted. Data points are not interpolated or estimated using other sources. Missing observations sometimes resulted because an exchange "crisis" forced official markets to close. At other times, the Harris Bank observed that no single number could adequately represent the hectic trading observed during the day.[13] Omitting observations of this type does not bias the results in any apparent way.

For all countries, methods, and horizons for which data is available, a forecast and percentage forecast error is calculated. If all the data for all 430 weeks were available, we could construct 426 four-week ahead forecasts, 417 thirteen-week ahead forecasts and 404 twenty-six-week ahead forecasts for each of the nine countries and four forecasting methods, for a total of 44,892 forecasts. Because of missing observations (mainly one- and six-month domestic interest rates), the number of forecasts actually constructed is 37,393.

III. STATISTICAL PROPERTIES OF FORECAST ERRORS

A. Forecasting Performance and Forecasting Model

The forecasts that were generated can be analyzed across the four alternative models. Table 1 displays the mean squared error (MSE) statistic for each model. From Table 1 it appears that, given the currency, time period, and horizon, the MSE is similar across

---

[13] For example, in the week ending 11/21/67 a number of forward quotations were omitted. The *Weekly Review* commented, "The foreign exchange markets this week were steadier and more real than they have been since the devaluation of the Pound Sterling on November 18. The forwards, however, were still quoted rather than traded." On 3/1/68 most forward quotations were omitted with the warning "the Forward Market was too erratic for a meaningful quotation." A number of quotations were omitted for the week of 3/18/68 when the two-tier gold system was introduced. Finally, during the week ending 11/22/68 the *Weekly Review* reported that most forward prices were "By Negotiation." They commented "The markets were nervous as the week opened and became chaotic by Tuesday . . . . By Wednesday the major European foreign exchange markets were closed and remained closed for the week."

Table 1

MSE ACROSS FORECASTING HORIZONS: 1967–1975

Country	Horizon (months)	Fisher domestic	Fisher external	Forward	Lag spot
Canada	1	0.374	0.380	0.385	0.365*
	3	1.491	1.486	1.517	1.463*
	6	3.501	3.179*	3.291	3.243
United Kingdom	1	3.968*	4.144	4.052	3.982
	3	15.520	15.924	15.983	15.065*
	6	33.180	29.779*	33.783	32.039
Belgium	1	–	4.406	4.434	4.110*
	3	17.247	18.064	17.935	16.714*
	6	–	36.087	38.525	34.093*
France	1	–	6.277	5.881	5.460*
	3	32.053	22.803	22.280	21.493*
	6	–	53.252	54.189	50.555*
Germany	1	–	5.590*	5.636	5.687
	3	24.112	23.550*	23.737	24.501
	6	–	45.158*	45.415	49.972
Italy	1	–	2.094	2.241	2.067*
	3	13.421	8.557	8.395	7.408*
	6	–	12.909	13.907	12.110*
Netherlands	1	–	4.481*	4.554	4.545
	3	16.681	15.282*	15.385	16.135
	6	–	28.728*	32.717	31.768
Switzerland	1	–	5.448*	5.469	5.458
	3	1.255[a]	20.864*	21.057	20.952
	6	–	45.881*	46.347	47.819
Japan	1	–	5.623*	5.671	5.704
	3	24.248	23.605*	23.788	24.500
	6	–	46.687	45.892*	49.947
Column total of*		1	13	1	12

Notes: * – Entries marked (*) are lowest MSE given country and horizon.

a – Based on only 34 observations.

MSE is in units of percent squared.

Table 2

MSE BY YEAR AND HORIZON, GERMANY

Period	Model	1–month	Horizon 3–month	6–month
1967	(1a)	–	0.455	–
	(1b)	0.096	0.291	0.451
	(2)	0.089	0.297	0.431
	(3)	0.076*	0.181*	0.198*
1968	(1a)	–	1.222	–
	(1b)	0.300	1.250	2.506
	(2)	0.265	1.161	2.457
	(3)	0.192*	0.526*	0.282*
1969	(1a)	–	10.842	–
	(1b)	2.695*	9.641*	14.662
	(2)	2.798	9.799	14.364*
	(3)	3.057	13.224	29.667
1970	(1a)	–	0.228*	–
	(1b)	0.098*	0.447	2.170*
	(2)	0.105	0.470	2.258
	(3)	0.098	0.462	2.380
1971	(1a)	–	12.066	–
	(1b)	1.614*	10.363*	33.110*
	(2)	1.637	10.605	33.680
	(3)	1.860	11.710	37.144
1972	(1a)	–	17.360*	–
	(1b)	0.424	17.724	70.886
	(2)	0.430	17.512	69.823*
	(3)	0.312*	17.900	78.154
1973	(1a)	–	100.050*	–
	(1b)	30.121	100.691	186.070
	(2)	30.059*	100.691	185.989*
	(3)	31.255	105.544	193.670
1974	(1a)	–	46.822*	–
	(1b)	9.272	48.219	47.366*
	(2)	9.447	48.552	47.424
	(3)	8.844*	47.448	55.220
1975	(1a)	–	3.070*	–
	(1b)	3.842	3.188	–
	(2)	3.837	3.148	–
	(3)	3.072*	3.488	–

Note: * – Lowest MSE given year and horizon.

models. Considering the entire sample period, Table 1 indicates that there is little difference among the models. For all 27 country-horizon episodes, the average ratio of the highest MSE to the lowest MSE is 1.05. Therefore, in their overall performance, the models are very similar.

Nevertheless, for most countries, the model which produces the lowest MSE at one horizon also produces the lowest MSE at other horizons. For example, the Fisher external model leads to the lowest MSE forecast for Germany, Netherlands, and Switzerland. For Belgium, France, and Italy, the lagged-spot forecast leads to the lowest MSE at all horizons. One interpretation of this result is that markets are integrated across maturities. For example, investors in external security markets collect information about exchange-rate changes. They set prices so that the term structure of relative interest rates reflects their term structure of exchange-rate expectations. If their expectations about one horizon are correct, internal consistency of prices suggests they may be correct about other horizons as well. In this sense, many models may be "horizon blind"—they work well regardless of forecast horizon.

It does not follow that a model is "time blind." The model which produces the lowest MSE in the overall sample does not necessarily produce the lowest MSE in every subperiod. For example, in forecasting the German mark the Fisher external forecast (1b) produces the lowest MSE in the overall, 1967–1975 sample period. However, in several yearly subperiods, Table 2 indicates that there is often a model with a lower MSE.

The data in Table 1 can be collapsed further. The lowest MSE model in each of the 27 country-horizon episodes is marked with an asterisk. The totals indicate that on 13 episodes, the Fisher external model has the lowest MSE, 12 for the lagged-spot model and one each for the remaining two models.

This is a surprising result given the empirical evidence on interest parity. If interest parity holds exactly, then the Fisher external and forward rate forecasts are identical. Therefore, it was anticipated that the two models would be very similar. While the Fisher external regularly outperforms the forward rate, the difference is generally small enough to be explained by transaction costs or sampling errors. Still, the data suggest that if forecasting must rely on a single model, then either the Fisher external or lagged-spot model should be selected. Across all countries, horizons, and time periods, these two models tend to produce the lowest MSE forecast.

B. Forecasting Performance and Currency
In this section, forecast errors are analyzed in the currency dimension. This classification raises the intuitive question, "Which currency is 'easiest' to forecast?" A more careful analysis suggests that an unambiguous standard for comparison is lacking, and therefore the question cannot be answered.

In part, forecast errors are a function of transaction costs and risk premia. If these factors differ across currencies, then the conclusion that a currency is difficult to forecast is not necessarily justified. Investors may have formed accurate expectations; but they have decided that it is not profitable to act on these expectations. Therefore, prices remain unchanged and (apparent) forecast errors result.

Table 3

LOWEST MSE AND RANKING FOR COUNTRY AND HORIZON

Country	Horizon 1–month	3–month	6–month
Canada	0.365 (1)	1.463 (1)	3.179 (1)
United Kingdom	3.968 (3)	15.065 (3)	29.779 (4)
Belgium	4.110 (4)	16.714 (5)	34.093 (5)
France	5.460 (7)	21.493 (7)	50.555 (9)
Germany	5.590 (8)	23.550 (8)	45.158 (6)
Italy	2.067 (2)	7.408 (2)	12.110 (2)
Netherlands	4.481 (5)	15.282 (4)	28.728 (3)
Switzerland	5.448 (6)	20.864 (6)	45.889 (7)
Japan	5.623 (9)	23.605 (9)	45.892 (8)

Note: Rank in parentheses.

To argue the same point in another way, it is observed that some exchange-rate series are (statistically) more volatile than others. In part, this is because changes in exchange rates reflect underlying variables including changes in monetary policy. Monetary policies differ widely across countries and over time. As a purely theoretical matter, the increased variability in underlying (monetary) factors will not (necessarily) lead to a decrease in forecasting precision. The reason is that some of this variability will be anticipated and therefore reflected by forecasters. It is therefore possible for a series to become more volatile (statistically) and yet the forecast errors for that series may decline. For these reasons, intercountry comparisons must be viewed with caution.

Table 3 presents data on the lowest MSE forecast for each country and horizon. Canada has the lowest MSE of all countries at each horizon. The MSE for the one-month horizon is 0.365% which implies an average forecast error (or root mean squared error) of 0.6%. At the six-month horizon the MSE increases to 3.179% and the average error increases to 1.78%. Four countries (France, Germany, Switzerland, and Japan) have MSEs greater than 5.0% at the one-month horizon and 45.0% at the six-month horizon, or approximately 15 times as great as for Canada. It follows that the average forecast error is three to four times as great for these countries as for Canada.

An alternative measure of forecasting performance is to record the percentage of forecast errors bounded within a neutral band.[14] This technique is especially appropriate for models (1) and (2) where forecast errors are directly associated with transaction costs so that

$$L \leq \hat{S}_{t+n} \leq U. \qquad (4)$$

To illustrate that the mean forecast error may give misleading results, assume that transaction costs are 1.0%. Then, persistent 0.5% forecast errors would not be disturbing in the sense that they represent a market inefficiency. Knowledge of these serially

[14] This technique was used to analyze deviations from interest parity in Frenkel and Levich (1975).

Table 4

PERCENTAGE OF 3-MONTH FORWARD RATE FORECASTS WITHIN 0.5%, 1.0%, AND 2.0% OF FUTURE SPOT RATE

Country	1967			1971			1972			1973			1974			1975			1967–1975		
	0.5	1.0	2.0	0.5	1.0	2.0	0.5	1.0	2.0	0.5	1.0	2.0	0.5	1.0	2.0	0.5	1.0	2.0	0.5	1.0	2.0
Canada	57	83	100	45	61	100	31	43	92	33	60	87	16	36	92	0	17	83	44	66	90
United Kingdom	66	68	70	4	37	50	12	24	34	2	6	14	6	14	38	17	34	67	25	44	61
Belgium	91	100	100	34	38	42	47	68	86	6	14	20	4	8	16	17	34	83	48	60	69
France	57	100	100	53	61	71	22	47	75	4	10	16	2	4	26	0	0	0	28	48	63
Germany	54	98	100	8	12	24	29	56	72	6	8	12	4	10	16	17	50	67	28	45	60
Italy	98	100	100	36	42	74	59	69	85	10	20	34	8	18	40	0	0	0	48	62	75
Netherlands	94	100	100	14	28	42	22	42	77	6	10	20	6	10	20	17	34	100	36	56	70
Switzerland	64	94	100	25	29	56	12	30	72	4	8	16	4	8	14	17	50	67	38	58	70
Japan	–	–	–	47	57	57	15	28	43	10	14	31	10	18	30	17	17	34	29	36	46
Average	73	93	96	30	41	57	28	45	71	9	17	28	7	14	32	11	26	56	36	53	67

correlated, nonzero errors cannot lead to a profit opportunity through spot or forward speculation.[15] Alternatively, forecast errors may be $+ 2.0\%$ and $- 2.0\%$ in equal proportion. The market appears inefficient since equation (4) never holds; still, the mean forecast error is zero. Similarly, the MSE may appear greater than what is necessary for profitable speculation. This overall result could be caused by the domination of a few large outliers in the sample. This might be the case since exchange-rate changes and forecast errors are nonnormal.[16] For these reasons we consider a neutral band analysis. A summary of forecast errors bounded by neutral bands of width 0.5%, 1.0%, and 2.0% is presented in Table 4.

In Table 4, the data for the 1967–1975 period indicate that the forecast errors for Canada and Italy fall within narrower bounds than for the United Kingdom, France, Germany, or Japan. The methods therefore differ in their rankings of Switzerland and the United Kingdom. Table 4 indicates that nearly twice as many forecasts fall within the 1% or 2% bounds for Canada as for Japan. This is an alternative measure of the relative difficulty in forecasting currencies.

C. Forecasts and Currency Preference

In Section II, it was demonstrated that if investors prefer to hold assets denominated in a particular currency, then exchange-rate forecasts based on interest rates may result in forecast errors that are systematically positive or negative. In this section, the mean forecast errors are analyzed. When the mean error is significantly different from zero, forecast bias exists. According to the Fisherian theory, if the forecast exchange-rate change is greater than the actual exchange-rate change, then the foreign currency is preferred. If the forecast exchange-rate change is less than the actual exchange-rate change, then the domestic currency (U.S. dollar) is preferred. In this study, *negative* forecast errors correspond to a preference for the *foreign* currency; significant positive forecast errors correspond to a preference for the *domestic* currency.

Information on the *t*-statistic of the mean forecast error is summarized in Table 5.[17] Entries marked with an asterisk are *not significantly different from zero* at the 5% level. Therefore, it appears that in most cases, the forecasts display a positive bias,

---

[15] This knowledge may be important when a point estimate of the expected future spot rate is used as an input for a balance-of-payments model or corporate-cash-management model.

[16] The distribution of exchange-rate changes is discussed in Westerfield (1975).

[17] Higher moments of the distribution of forecast errors were also estimated. In most cases the skewness statistic is small (near zero), indicating a symmetric distribution of forecast errors. The kurtosis statistic is large, indicating a peaked distribution with fat tails. A Kalmogorov–Smirnov test confirms that for most currencies the distribution is nonnormal. The economic significance of this result is that exchange-risk management models that rely on a normal distribution of speculative returns or forecast errors will not be appropriate.

It is important to note that the standard errors were calculated using a dependent sample of, at most, 426 observations for the one-month forecast, 417 observations for the three-month forecast, and 404 observations for the six-month forecast. Using an independent, nonoverlapping sample, the sample sizes, at most, would be 105, 32, and 15, respectively. Consequently, using an independent sample, the sample *t*-statistics would fall by at least one-half. In this case, bias is significant for only six cases in Table 5.

Table 5

MEAN FORECASTING ERROR ACROSS FORECASTING HORIZON: 1967–1975

Country	Horizon (month)	Fisher domestic	Fisher external	Forward	Lag spot
Canada	1	0.062	0.004[*]	0.043	0.050[*]
	3	0.309	0.107[a]	0.178	0.212
	6	0.640	0.345[a]	0.458	0.487
United Kingdom	1	0.017[*]	0.005[*]	0.054[*]	− 0.184
	3	0.073[*]	− 0.001[*]	0.078[*]	− 0.567
	6	0.088[*]	0.166[*]	− 0.021[*]	− 1.229
Belgium	1	−	0.262[a]	0.340	0.309
	3	1.027	0.941[a]	1.040	1.029
	6	−	1.784[a]	2.145	1.976
France	1	−	0.194[*]	0.339	0.137[*]
	3	1.027	0.862	0.937	0.402[*]
	6	−	1.313	1.644	0.568[*]
Germany	1	−	0.269[*]	0.292	0.453
	3	1.167	1.031[a]	1.060	1.520
	6	−	2.130[a]	2.156	3.036
Italy	1	−	0.118	0.238	− 0.021[*]
	3	0.070	0.283	0.527	− 0.075[*]
	6	−	0.359	0.802	− 0.245[*]
Netherlands	1	−	0.212[a]	0.247	0.352
	3	0.695[a]	0.844	0.899	1.195
	6	−	1.691[a]	2.026	2.314
Switzerland	1	−	0.263[a]	0.291	0.468
	3	− 1.017[a]	1.075	1.096	1.587
	6	−	2.219[a]	2.251	3.136
Japan	1	−	0.233[a]	0.254	0.444
	3	1.082	0.984[a]	1.015	1.510
	6	−	2.317	2.294[a]	3.060
Column total of ([*] and a)		5	19	4	7

Note: [*] – Entries marked ([*]) are *not* significantly different from zero at 5% level.

   a – Model with lowest absolute mean bias.

indicating that the U.S. dollar was the preferred currency during this period.[18] The most prominent clustering of unbiased forecasts is in the United Kingdom. Both Fisher forecasts and the forward rates appear to be unbiased forecasters in the United Kingdom. The lagged-spot forecast also appears to be unbiased in France and Italy.

Estimates of transaction costs in the spot and 90-day foreign exchange market range between approximately 0.05% in the 1962–1967 period to about 0.5% in the 1973–1975 period.[19] Transaction costs in Eurocurrency deposits are smaller, between 0.03% and 0.1%. During the sample period 1967–1975, it seems likely that a bias of 0.5% or 1.0% could be consistent with transaction costs. Most mean forecast errors at the three-month horizon fall within this range. It is therefore possible to conclude that while the bias may be statistically significant, it is not economically significant.

Note also that there is a general tendency for bias to increase, approximately, in proportion to horizon. This agrees with the result in Moses (1969) that currency preferences may be expressed as a constant rate per unit time.

In Table 5 the country-horizon episodes which did not contain an unbiased fore-casting model were considered separately. In this group (of 16) the model with the smallest bias (in absolute value) is marked by the letter "a." In 13 of these 16 cases the Fisher external model produces the smallest bias. This result could be expected since the Fisher external models tended to have low MSE and bias is one of the two components in MSE.

The data in Table 5 can be collapsed further by adding the number of entries that are marked (* or a) in each column. There are 19 entries marked for the Fisher external model; the next highest is the lag spot model with seven. This result indicates that overall, the Fisher external model leads to a greater number of unbiased or smallest bias forecasts among the models that are tested. In this overall sense, the Fisher external model appears to be best.

From a purely forecasting viewpoint, bias is important as a correction factor for the naïve model. For example, a watch which is consistently five minutes fast is a very good forecaster of the correct time. If Fisher external consistently overestimates the future spot rate by 1%, it will be a very helpful forecasting model. In both of these examples the important factor is the consistency or stationarity of the forecast errors over time.

This issue is analyzed using two approaches. First, weekly Fisher external fore-casts for the three-month horizon were aggregated by calendar year. Significant positive mean forecast errors are recorded as (+); significant negative mean forecast errors are recorded as (−). When the mean forecast error is not significantly different from zero, a (0) is entered. Table 6 summarizes these results.

Table 6 indicates that the sign of forecast errors changes over time. Significant positive and negative errors exist for each country during some time period. The bias does not appear to follow any clear time pattern. A formal runs analysis of the series

---

[18] The one exception is Swiss Treasury bills. Holders of these securities yielded about 1% less per three-month period than if they had held U.S. Treasury bills.

[19] See Frenkel and Levich (1977).

Table 6

TIME PATTERN OF FORECASTING BIAS WITH THE FISHER EXTERNAL MODEL, THREE-MONTH HORIZON

Country	1967	1968	1969	1970	1971	1972	1973	1974	1975	1967–1975
Canada	0	+	−	+	0	0	0	−	−	0
United Kingdom	−	+	+	+	+	−	0	+	0	0
Belgium	+	−	+	−	+	+	0	+	+	+
France	0	0	−	+	+	+	0	+	+	+
Germany	−	−	+	+	+	0	0	+	0	+
Italy	−	−	−	+	+	+	−	+	+	+
Netherlands	0	−	−	0	+	0	0	+	+	+
Switzerland	−	−	−	−	+	+	0	+	−	+
Japan	NA	NA	NA	+	+	0	0	−	0	+

Note: + = Significant (at 5% level) positive forecast bias.
  − = Significant (at 5% level) negative forecast bias.
  0 = Forecast bias not significantly different from 0.
  NA = Not available.

Table 7

Q-STATISTIC TO TEST SERIAL
CORRELATION OF FORECAST ERRORS

Country	1–month	Horizon 3–month	6–month
Canada	47.4	17.4	7.5
United Kingdom	–	20.4	11.5
Belgium	–	18.1	12.2
France	49.9	11.3	8.6
Germany	47.4	11.3	8.6
Italy	–	14.8	15.6
Netherlands	25.5	12.9	9.5
Switzerland	48.1	19.5	9.4
Japan	–	–	–
	$N = 105$	$N = 32$	$N = 15$

Note: Entry in table is

$$Q = N \sum_{i=1}^{k} \hat{r}_i \text{ where } k = 24$$

for 1-month and 3-month forecast and $k = 12$ for 6-month forecast. Entry is for method (2), and forward rate. Results for other methods were very similar.
Sample points from the chi-square distribution are:

	d.f. 23	10
Significance 10%	32.0	17.3
Level 5%	35.2	19.7

in Table 6 was not performed, however, since a dependent sample of weekly forecasts was aggregated to calculate yearly bias.

Instead, the second approach calculates the serial correlation of forecast errors in an independent sample. For example, at the one-month horizon, the sample consists of every fourth forecast error; at the three-month horizon, the sample consists of every thirteenth forecast error, etc. Table 7 summarizes these results.

At the three-month and six-month horizons, serial correlation of forecast errors is not significant. At the one-month horizon, serial correlation is significant. However, it seems likely that this correlation is the result of using one-month interest rates to forecast spot exchange rates four weeks in the future. If forecast errors are serially

Table 8

RATIO OF MSE FOR PAIRS OF FORECAST HORIZONS

Country	Ratio[a]	Fisher domestic	Fisher external	Forward	Lag spot
Canada	3/1	3.99	3.91	3.94	4.01
	6/3	2.35	2.14	2.17	2.22
United Kingdom	3/1	3.91	3.84	3.94	3.78
	6/3	2.14	1.87	2.11	2.13
Belgium	3/1	–	4.10	4.04	4.07
	6/3	–	2.00	2.15	2.04
France	3/1	–	3.63	3.79	3.94
	6/3	–	2.34	2.43	2.35
Germany	3/1	–	4.21	4.21	4.31
	6/3	–	1.92	1.91	2.04
Italy	3/1	–	4.09	3.75	3.58
	6/3	–	1.51	1.66	1.63
Netherlands	3/1	–	3.41	3.38	3.55
	6/3	–	1.88	2.13	1.97
Switzerland	3/1	–	3.83	3.85	3.84
	6/3	–	2.20	2.20	2.28
Japan	3/1	–	4.20	4.19	4.30
	6/3	–	1.98	1.93	2.04

[a]3/1 = Ratio of 3-month to 1-month MSE.
 6/3 = Ratio of 6-month to 3-month MSE.

uncorrelated, as the data suggest, the implication is that bias (i.e., significant forecast errors) cannot be predicted; currency preferences are likely to be random. In this case, the standard approach of correcting the naïve forecasting model for bias will not necessarily improve forecasting performance because the bias is not stationary.

D. Forecasting Performance and Horizon

The relationship between forecasting accuracy and forecast horizon is easily developed using time-series methods. A standard result is that the variance of the forecast error is proportional to the forecast horizon. It follows that the MSE is also proportional to forecast horizon.

The data in Table 1 are used to test the theoretical relationship between MSE and horizon. First, the ratio of three-month MSE to one-month MSE is calculated; the theoretical value of this ratio is 3.0. Second, the ratio is calculated for six-month and three-month forecasts; the theoretical value of this ratio is 2.0. Table 8 summarizes the results.

Table 9

PERCENTAGE OF FORWARD RATE FORECAST ERRORS
WITHIN NEUTRAL BANDS[a]

Width of neutral band	Horizon		
	1–month	3–month	6–month
0.5%	47	28	13
1.0%	68	45	26
2.0%	80	60	47
3.0%	87	66	55
4.0%	92	72	59
5.0%	94	77	66

[a]Germany only, 1967–1975.

The three-month to one-month ratio is consistently greater than 3.0. In part, this may be because we are comparing 13-week and 4-week forecasts, and so, the theoretical value of the ratio may be 3.25. However, the sample ratios are even greater than this number.

The results of the six-month and three-month comparison are more consistent with theory. The sample values are generally near two. At these maturities, the data support the hypothesis that MSE rises in proportion to forecast horizon. The economic significance of this result is that the market-based forecasts display a property of a time-series forecast which is a minimum MSE forecast. This is another piece of evidence to support the view that market prices efficiently forecast the future spot rate.

An alternative technique for measuring the horizon effect is illustrated in Table 9, which reports the percentage of forward-rate forecast errors inside a given neutral band. As the forecast horizon lengthens, this percentage decreases. For example, the percentage of forecast errors within a 0.5% band drops from 47% to 13% as the forecast horizon increases from one to six months. For a 2.0% band, the decrease is not as sharp—from 80% to 47%.

E. Forecasting Performance and Time
In this section, forecast errors are analyzed in the time dimension. Graph 1 presents a time-series plot of the weekly forecast errors using the three-month forward rate for Germany. This graph is representative of the forecast errors using other forecasting models on other currencies and horizons.

The graph suggests several qualitative observations. First, for each country large forecast errors are associated with discrete changes in exchange rates or exchange rate systems (e.g., Germany, 1969). Second, forecast errors tend to be smaller during pegged rate periods—except when there is a discrete change in the rate. In the managed float period, forecast errors have become larger and more volatile. The graphs for Belgium, France, Germany, Italy, and Netherlands show the large forecast errors associated with the oil crisis of 1973–1974. However, both positive and negative errors are observed; the errors tend to fluctuate about some value near zero. The graphs for

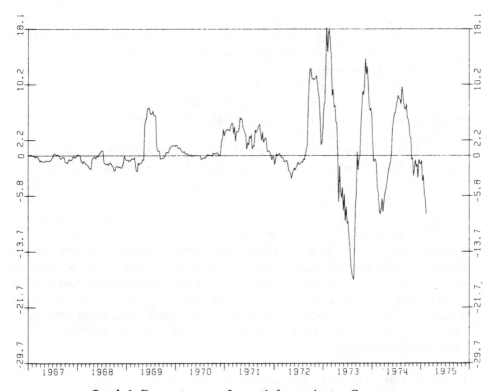

Graph 1. Forecast errors, 3-month forward rate—Germany.

the United Kingdom, Germany, Netherlands, and Japan seem to indicate that forecast errors have decreased during the managed float period.

A quantitative examination of the time dimension begins with Table 4, which reports the fraction of forecast errors within a neutral band. The estimates of transaction costs in Levich (1977) suggest a neutral band of no more than 0.5% during the quiet period. With transaction costs increasing during speculative periods and during the managed float, a 2.0% neutral band is a reasonable estimate.

Table 4 indicates that in 1967, the three-month forward rate was within 0.5% of the future spot rate on 73% of the sample weeks. As the width of the band increases to 1% and 2%, the number of forecasts meeting this tolerance rises to more than 90%.

In later periods, 1971 and 1973, the spot exchange rate is more volatile. Concurrently, the forward rate becomes a less precise forecast of the future spot rate. In 1973, the first year of managed floating, the number of forecast errors within the 2% band is 34% compared with 72% in the previous year. In 1974, forecasting performance is unchanged and in 1975, accuracy improves so that 50% of the weekly forecasts fall within a 2% band. Statistically, therefore, there is some evidence that forecast errors are becoming smaller as the managed float continues.

Since the percentage of forecast errors inside a 0.5% neutral band has decreased over the sample period, we could conclude that the predictive power of the forward rate has declined. However, transaction costs have increased over the period. The data suggest that transaction costs account for a similar, large percentage of forecast errors in most yearly subperiods. In many cases, therefore, the forward rate will be an accurate forecast of the future spot rate.

Table 2 conveys a similar picture. The MSE statistic is smallest during pegged-rate periods except in years when the exchange rate changes. MSE tends to increase with the introduction of floating rates. However, MSE tends to decline in 1974 and 1975 from the levels reached during 1973.

Graph 1 indicates positive serial correlation in the weekly series of three-month (13 week) forecast errors. This is expected since the observations are a dependent series.[20] Therefore, an independent sample of forecast errors was selected to check for serial correlation. The calculation for the Box-Pierce Q-statistic appears in Table 7. At the three-month and six-month horizon, serial correlation appears insignificant. Significant autocorrelation is present in the one-month forecasts. Earlier it was suggested that this may be because the forward-rate and interest-rate maturities are one-month while the differencing interval for spot rates is four weeks. It should be reiterated that serial correlation of forecast errors is not a sufficient condition to reject market efficiency. Serial correlation of unprofitable investment opportunities is consistent with market efficiency. Since the mean forecast error at the one-month horizon is very small (see Table 5), it is possible that this serial correlation is not economically significant.

F. Forward-Rate Forecasts—an Alternative Test for Bias

In Levich (1977), a theory of the time pattern of forecast errors is developed. The theory predicts that positive forecast errors (underestimates) will be most common when the spot rate is rising and negative forecast errors (overestimates) will be most common when the spot rate is falling.

Graph 2 plots the spot exchange rate and the lagged forward rate at the three-month maturity. The data are for Germany and are representative of the experience of other countries and horizons. The graph supports the theory. It is especially clear in the managed floating period that the forward rate is commonly an underestimate (overestimate) of the future spot rate when the spot rate is rising (falling).

One way to test the theory statistically is to classify each time period along two dimensions: (1) the forecast error, positive or negative, and (2) the change in the spot rate, positive or negative. Accordingly, a 2 x 2 contingency table can be constructed for each country-horizon episode. A sample table for the German one-month episode appears in Table 10. The null hypothesis is that the sign of the forecast error is independent of the sign of the rate of change in the spot rate. The test statistic

---

[20] Using time-series methods, it is easily shown that the weekly (dependent) series of k-week ahead forecasts follows a moving average process of order k-1. Using a dependent sample, Bilson and Levich (1977) demonstrate that the forward rate efficiently reflects the time dependence in the spot exchange rate.

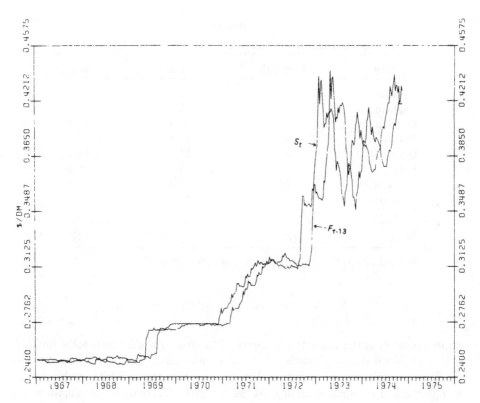

Graph 2. Germany, spot rate and forward-rate forecast, 3-month horizon.

Table 10

FORWARD RATE BIAS IN GERMANY: ONE-MONTH HORIZON

	$S_{t+1} > S_t$	$S_{t+1} \leqslant S_t$	Row total
$S_{t+1} > F_t$	$A_{11} = 60$	$A_{12} = 6$	
	$E_{11} = 40$	$E_{12} = 26$	66
$S_{t+1} \leqslant F_t$	$A_{21} = 4$	$A_{22} = 35$	
	$E_{21} = 24$	$E_{22} = 15$	39
Column total	64	41	105

A_{ij} = Actual number of observations in cell (i, j).
E_{ij} = Expected number of observations in cell (i, j).

Table 11
SUMMARY OF X^2 TESTS FOR FORWARD BIAS[a]

Country	1–month	3–month	6–month
Canada	71.2	20.7	10.9
England	–	15.2	8.0
Belgium	–	6.4	11.4
France	37.3	14.8	3.2
Germany	67.0	21.1	11.2
Italy	–	9.7	6.6
Netherlands	44.7	12.6	5.6
Switzerland	63.2	14.5	15.0
Japan	–	–	–
Nobs	105	32	15

[a]Critical values of $\chi^2(1) = 3.84$ at 5%, and 6.63 at 1% level.

$$\sum_{I=1}^{2} \sum_{J=1}^{2} (A(I,J) - E(I,J))^2 / E(I,J)$$

is approximately chi-square with one degree of freedom. The chi-square value for Table 10 is 67.0, which is highly significant. Table 11 summarizes these chi-square statistics for all nine sample countries. Independent samples were selected for each horizon so the observations are nonoverlapping. At the 5% level, all country-horizon episodes are consistent with the forward rate bias described by our theory. The results are particularly significant for the one-month maturity.[21]

Although the data support our theory, this pattern does not imply profit opportunities since the forecast errors are a function of transaction costs. The theory will be useful for currencies following a trend rate of growth. In these cases, the forecast can be improved by adjusting the forward rate for transaction costs.

G. Composite Models
The theory of composite forecasting is to combine several alternative forecasts of the future spot rate. Even if the overall results are similar across models, the composite forecast can increase accuracy if the correlation of error terms across models is less than one.[22]

---

[21] The blanks in Table 11 indicate that because of missing observations, an independent sample could not be formed. In similar tests using a dependent sample of weekly observations, all χ^2 statistics were significant at the 5% level.

It should be noted that the use of the word "bias" in this section is not in exact agreement with the usual statistical definition. For example, if the spot rate increases for 10 periods and then decreases for 10 periods, the underestimates in the first 10 periods may cancel the overestimates in the second 10 periods. Overall, the forward rate may appear unbiased while in each sub-period, an apparent bias develops.

[22] For a discussion of the theory and an application, see Nelson (1972).

According to one view, when information is costly, prices will never fully reflect information (Grossman and Stiglitz, 1976). In this case, composite forecasting may be helpful since an analysis of more markets may exploit more information. The composite model provides a framework for analyzing a prospective forecasting technique. If the new forecast reflects information that is not reflected in the existing models, the new forecast will lead to a significant reduction in MSE in the composite model.

Alternatively, information may be costless and all markets efficient and *still* composite forecasting may improve on simple forecasting. The reason is that there may be several sources of uncertainty in the world. In this case, it may require several prices to completely summarize (i.e., provide a sufficient statistic for) the current state of the world, even though each individual price fully reflects available information.[23]

Regression analysis is used to construct the composite forecast $(\hat{S}_t)$ using the four forecasting models $(\hat{S}_{i,t})$ analyzed in this study.

$$\hat{S}_t = b_0 + b_1 \hat{S}_{1,t} + b_2 \hat{S}_{2,t} + b_3 \hat{S}_{3,t} + b_4 \hat{S}_{4,t}$$

This equation is estimated for every country-horizon episode in the sample. A dependent sample of observations is selected from two sub-periods—the 1967–1973 pre-floating period and the 1973–1975 floating period.

To examine the impact of the composite forecast, the ratio of the composite forecast MSE to the MSE from a single forecasting model is calculated. A ratio less than 1.0 implies that MSE has been reduced in the composite model. The results appear in Table 12 and Table 13.

Table 12

RATIO OF MEAN SQUARED FORECASTING ERROR:
COMPOSITE MODEL/FORWARD-RATE MODEL

	Horizon					
	1–month		3–month		6–month	
Country	Pre-float	Float	Pre-float	Float	Pre-float	Float
Canada	0.93	0.92 ·	0.81	0.93	0.75	1.00
United Kingdom	1.00	0.78	0.95	0.71	0.89	0.77
Belgium	0.95	0.88	0.84	0.77	0.80	0.66
France	0.96	0.83	0.92	0.74	0.78	0.49
Germany	0.96	0.97	0.78	0.96	0.77	0.94
Italy	–	0.88	–	0.88	–	0.77
Netherlands	0.63	0.71	0.94	0.86	0.83	0.87
Switzerland	0.98	0.92	0.92	0.69	0.88	0.48
Japan	–	0.81	–	0.60	–	0.31
Average	0.92	0.86	0.88	0.79	0.81	0.70

[23] I am indebted to Alan Stockman for raising this issue.

Table 13

RATIO OF MEAN SQUARED FORECASTING ERROR:
COMPOSITE MODEL/LAGGED-SPOT MODEL

	Horizon					
	1–month		3–month		6–month	
Country	Pre-float	Float	Pre-float	Float	Pre-float	Float
Canada	0.96	0.98	0.83	0.96	0.80	0.95
United Kingdom	0.98	0.88	0.95	0.82	0.92	0.89
Belgium	0.95	0.93	0.79	0.83	0.74	0.76
France	0.94	0.92	0.88	0.84	0.68	0.60
Germany	0.90	0.97	0.67	0.94	0.66	0.90
Italy	–	0.96	–	0.91	–	0.76
Netherlands	0.64	0.69	0.86	0.81	0.72	0.81
Switzerland	0.94	0.92	0.86	0.69	0.78	0.48
Japan	–	0.97	–	0.89	–	0.57
Average	0.90	0.91	0.83	0.85	0.76	0.75

Composite forecasting appears to have a greater impact during the floating period and when the forecasting horizon is longer. For some countries (Canada and Germany) the improvement is negligible. For others, Netherlands (at the one-month horizon) and France, Switzerland, and Japan (at the six-month horizon), the improvement is large and significant. The largest reduction in MSE is 69% for the six-month forecast of the Japanese yen. Most of the reductions are in the 10–30% range.

Composite forecasting does not appear to have a smaller impact on those spot series that move randomly over time. For example, although the Swiss franc and Italian lira appear to follow a random walk, a six-month composite forecast reduces the MSE by 52% and 24% respectively, during the floating period.

Generally, it appears that composite forecasting can lead to substantial reductions in MSE especially as the forecast horizon lengthens. One interpretation is that there are several sources of uncertainty in the world. Another interpretation is that exchange rate expectations are not reflected equally in all market sectors. This may be due to efforts by central banks to restrict price movements or to differential transaction costs or information costs across markets. When the markets are segmented and the forecast horizon is longer, the data indicate that a composite model can significantly reduce forecast errors.

IV. FORECASTS AND RISKY INVESTMENT OPPORTUNITIES

A. A Methodology for Testing the Profitability of Forecasting Models

In the previous section, the possibility of using data-based models to generate consistent and accurate forecasts of the future spot exchange rate was investigated. Having shown that there are models which can forecast the future spot rate within an error term that depends on transaction costs and a risk premium, our concern shifts to test hypothesis two: Can these models be used to make an unusual speculative profit?

A general profit opportunity that is available to all investors is forward specu-lation. By taking an open forward position, investors gain a profit that is proportional to the difference between the future spot rate, S_{t+n}, and today's n-period forward rate, $F_{t,n}$.[24] The purpose of this section is to examine if our forecasting models can lead to unusual profit in forward speculation.

A framework for testing for unusual profits in a domestic equity market was developed by Fama, Fisher, Jensen, and Roll (1969). This technique relies on an asset pricing model to estimate expected returns. Actual returns in excess of expected returns are "unusual." In the foreign exchange literature, no consensus exists on a model relating speculative returns with risk. Furthermore, data limitations preclude a thorough testing of alternative models. Therefore, an alternative methodology is developed.

Assume that the speculator has made a forecast, $\hat{S}_{t+n}$, of the future spot rate. Observing $\hat{S}_{t+n} > F_{t,n}$ is a signal to buy the foreign currency forward while observing $\hat{S}_{t+n} < F_{t,n}$ is a signal to sell the foreign currency. Assume that the speculator buys one unit of currency forward independent of the deviation between his forecast and the forward rate observed in the market. Our investor is therefore risk neutral—he gambles a fixed amount after comparing the expected value of his forecast with the forward rate. Assuming 100% margin, the mean profit rate from following this strategy for M periods can be calculated as

$$\sum_{i=1}^{M} d_i (S_{t+n,i} - F_{t,i}) / (MF_{t,i}) \tag{5}$$

where

$$d_i = +1 \text{ if } \hat{S}_{t+n} > F_{t,n}$$
$$-1 \text{ if } \hat{S}_{t+n} < F_{t,n}.$$

If the investor had "perfect information," he could gain a profit in every period with the proper selection of d_i. Profits assuming perfect information are calculated as

$$\sum_{i=1}^{M} |S_{t+n,i} - F_{t,i}| / (MF_{t,i}) \tag{6}$$

In Levich (1976) it is shown that the ratio

---

[24] Testing our forecasts or any other forecasts in this way does not imply that the firm does or should speculate in foreign exchange. The issues of the accuracy of the forecast and the firm's use of the forecast are separable. Assume that the firm uses the forward rate as its estimate of the future spot rate. A new forecast, which is more accurate than the forward rate and therefore leads to speculative forward profits should increase the profits of the firm.

$$H = \sum_{i=1}^{M} d_i(S_{t+n,i} - F_{t,i}) \bigg/ \sum_{i=1}^{M} |S_{t+n,i} - F_{t,i}| \tag{7}$$

has expected value $(2p - 1)$ and variance $4p(1-p)/m$, where p is the probability of choosing d_i correctly in any period and m is the number of independent sample observations. For example, a rule which is correct half of the time has $p = 0.5$ and $E(H) = 0.0$. "Unusual" profits correspond to the case where H is greater than zero or p is greater than one-half.

In this paper, five rules for selecting the d_i are considered:

1. Select d_i using a forecast based on traditional interest rates.
2. Select d_i using a forecast based on external interest rates.
3. Select d_i using a forecast based on the lagged-spot rate.
4. Select $d_i = +1$ for all i.
5. Select $d_i = -1$ for all i.

Each rule is compared to rule (6): select d_i assuming perfect information.

B. Empirical Results

Table 14 displays the mean percentage profit from three-month forward speculation for alternative rules. Note that the results describe a dependent sample of observations for the entire sample period. In other words, we assume our investor makes a

Table 14

MEAN PERCENTAGE PROFIT
FROM SPECULATION
FOLLOWING ALTERNATIVE RULES

Country	Alternative rules					
	(1)	(2)	(3)	(4)	(5)	(6)
Canada	−0.103	0.203[a]	0.175	0.178	−0.178	0.878
United Kingdom	0.676[a]	0.327	0.044	0.078	−0.078	2.438
Belgium	0.186	0.486	0.498	1.040[a]	−1.040	2.430
France	−0.869	1.126[a]	0.679	0.937	−0.937	2.912
Germany	−0.322	0.555	−0.312	1.060[a]	−1.060	3.042
Italy	0.371	0.721[a]	0.431	0.527	−0.527	1.669
Netherlands	−0.537	0.760	−0.531	0.899[a]	−0.899	2.277
Switzerland	−0.327	1.331[a]	0.500	1.096	−1.096	2.603
Japan	0.382	−0.457	0.601	1.015[a]	−1.015	3.295

Note: The entries are percentage profit per three-month period. The sample period is 1967–1975. For explanation of numbering, see text.
[a]Most profitable rule for this country.

three-month investment decision in every week of our sample period. The reported profits are per three-month period; they have not been annualized.[25]

The several rules lead to a substantial difference in mean profit for each currency. For example, there are six currencies where one rule results in negative profits while another rule results in statistically significant positive profits.[26] For the other three currencies, the difference between profits from following the worst rule and the best rule is at least a factor of two.

Of the three forecast-based rules (1, 2, and 3), rule (3) is consistently dominated by rule (2) or rule (4)—the "always buy foreign currency" rule. This is true even for countries (e.g., United Kingdom and Italy) whose currency generally declined in value over the sample period. Similarly, rule (1) generally leads to negative or near zero speculative profits.

Overall, there are four cases where rule (2) is the most profitable, four cases for rule (4), and one for rule (1). In each of these cases, the mean profit is significantly greater than zero. With the possible exception of Canada, these profits appear to be in excess of transaction costs. If the profits are annualized, the rates of return are in the range 0.8% to 5.3%. These profits are small relative to the risk-free yield on U.S. Treasury bills over this period.[27]

In Table 14, observe that perfect information profits (column 6) vary across currencies. These profits are greatest for Japan (which also has the highest mean squared forecast error) and lowest for Canada (which had the lowest mean squared forecast error). This observation only confirms a definition. Potential profits from forward speculation are greatest when the forward rate is a poor forecaster of the future spot rate.

Statistics for analyzing the unusualness of these speculative profits are presented in Table 15. For the most profitable rules, the H ratio ranges between 0.23 for Canada and 0.51 for Switzerland; the corresponding probabilities (p) range between 0.62 and 0.76. While these estimates of p are larger than 0.5, they are based on a sample of 32 independent observations. Therefore, no estimate of p is significantly larger than 0.5 at the 5% confidence level. These rules do not result in unusual profits and therefore we cannot reject hypothesis two.

---

[25] A similar set of calculations was made for one-month and six-month forward speculation. The results for the three-month horizon appear representative of the other two periods. Since the data base consists of bid prices for both spot and forward rates, profits from speculative purchases of foreign currency are overestimated while profits from speculative sales of foreign currency are underestimated. Mean speculative profits may be unbiased and variability overstated if long and short foreign currency positions balance out over time. However, if the investor has a consistent long position in one currency, the estimate of mean speculative profits will be biased.

[26] A rule which leads to a negative profit can be adapted to result in a positive profit just by reversing the speculative activity indicated by the rule (i.e., reverse the d_i). In other words, if the forecast indicates that S_{t+n} will be greater (less) than F_t, we sell (buy) the foreign currency forward. None of these "adapted" rules result in higher profits than an alternative rule in Table 14.

[27] The returns appear similar to those calculated by Grubel (1966). Over the period July 1955–May 1961 Grubel calculated average annual rates of return between 16% and 27% for sterling speculation assuming a 10% margin. Adjusting our figures for a 10% margin implies rates of return in the range 8% to 53%. The rate of return from sterling speculation is 27% (0.676 × 4 × 10). Grubel did not calculate any empirical measure of the riskiness of his speculative profits.

Table 15

A TEST FOR UNUSUAL SPECULATIVE RETURNS

	Alternative rules							
	(1)		(2)		(3)		(4)	
Country	H	p	H	p	H	p	H	p
Canada	− 0.12	0.44	0.23[a]	0.62	0.20	0.60	0.20	0.60
United Kingdom	0.28[a]	0.64	0.13	0.57	0.02	0.51	0.03	0.51
Belgium	0.08	0.54	0.20	0.60	0.02	0.51	0.43[a]	0.71
France	− 0.30	0.35	0.39[a]	0.69	0.23	0.62	0.32	0.66
Germany	− 0.11	0.45	0.18	0.59	− 0.10	0.45	0.35[a]	0.67
Italy	0.22	0.61	0.43[a]	0.72	0.26	0.63	0.32	0.66
Netherlands	− 0.24	0.38	0.33	0.67	− 0.23	0.38	0.39[a]	0.70
Switzerland	− 0.12	0.44	0.51[a]	0.76	0.19	0.60	0.42	0.71
Japan	0.12	0.56	− 0.14	0.43	0.18	0.59	0.31[a]	0.65

[a]Most profitable rule for this country.

V. SUMMARY AND CONCLUSIONS

In this paper, a number of relationships in the international money market have been investigated. A set of simple models for forecasting the future spot rate were proposed and tested on a uniform data base. The most important results are that (1) forecast errors appear to be serially uncorrelated, (2) forecasting bias or currency preference does not appear to be predictable, and (3) mean-squared forecasting error rises in proportion to forecasting horizon. These results are consistent with the view that the market efficiently reflects information concerning future exchange rates.

Another important finding is that a composite forecasting model can significantly reduce forecast errors. The gain from composite forecasting may be the result of information costs, search costs, or government intervention which tend to separate financial markets. More generally, the model provides a framework for analyzing prospective forecasting techniques.

A final test investigated the profit opportunities available to the user of a simple forecast. Profits from forward speculation appeared to be small relative to a risk-free yield and relative to perfect information profits. The finding that a forecast model, based on publicly available information, cannot be used to earn an unusual profit is consistent with efficient market theory.

REFERENCES

ALIBER, ROBERT Z. "The Interest Rate Parity Theorem: A Reinterpretation. *Journal of Political Economy* **81**, No. 6 (November/December 1973): 1451–1459.

BILSON, JOHN F. O., and RICHARD M. LEVICH. "A Test of the Efficiency of the For-
    Ph.D. dissertation, University of Chicago, 1976.
————. "Rational Expectations and the Exchange Rate." 1978. Reproduced as
    Chapter 5 in this volume.
BILSON, JOHN F. O., and RICHARD M. LEVICH. "A Test of the Efficiency of the For-
    ward Exchange Market." Mimeographed. International Monetary Fund, June
    1977.
BOX, G. E. P., and G. M. JENKINS. *Time Series Analysis.* San Francisco: Holden-Day,
    1970.
DORNBUSCH, RUDIGER. "The Theory of Flexible Exchange Rate Regimes and Macro-
    economic Policy." *Scandinavian Journal of Economics* **78**, No. 2 (May, 1976):
    255–275. Reprinted in this volume as Chapter 2.
FAMA, EUGENE F. "Efficient Capital Markets: A Review of Theory and Empirical
    Work." *Journal of Finance* **25**, No. 2 (May, 1970): 383–417.
————. *Foundations of Finance.* New York: Basic Books, 1976.
FAMA, EUGENE F., LAWRENCE FISHER, MICHAEL C. JENSEN, and RICHARD ROLL.
    "The Adjustment of Stock Prices to New Information." *International Economic
    Review* **10**, No. 1 (February, 1969): 1–21.
FISHER, IRVING. "Appreciation and Interest." *Publications of the American Economic
    Association* **11**, No. 4 (August, 1896): 331–442.
FRENKEL, JACOB A. "A Monetary Approach to the Exchange Rate: Doctrinal Aspects
    and Empirical Evidence." *Scandinavian Journal of Economics* **78**, No. 2 (May,
    1976): 200–224. Reprinted in this volume as Chapter 1.
————. "The Forward Exchange Rate, Expectations and the Demand for Money:
    The German Hyperinflation." *American Economic Review* **67**, No. 4 (September,
    1977): 653–670.
FRENKEL, JACOB A.,   and   RICHARD M. LEVICH.   "Covered   Interest   Arbitrage:
    Unexploited Profits?" *Journal of Political Economy* **83**, No. 2 (April, 1975):
    325–338.
————. "Transaction Costs and Interest Arbitrage: Tranquil Versus Turbulent
    Periods." *Journal of Political Economy* **85**, No. 6 (December, 1977): 1209–1226.
GOSCHEN, GEORGE J. *The Theory of the Foreign Exchange.* 3d ed. London, 1862.
    Reprinted 4th ed. London: Pitman House, 1932.
GROSSMAN, SANFORD J., and JOSEPH E. STIGLITZ. "Information and Competitive
    Price Systems." *American Economic Review* **66**, No. 2 (May, 1976): 246–53.
GRUBEL, HERBERT G. *Forward Exchange Speculation and the International Flow of
    Capital.* Stanford, Calif.: Stanford University Press, 1966.
HODRICK, ROBERT J. "An Empirical Analysis of the Monetary Approach to the
    Determination of the Exchange Rate." 1978. Reproduced as Chapter 6 in this
    volume.
KOHLHAGEN, STEVEN W. "The Forward Rate as an Unbiased Estimator of the Future
    Spot Rate." Mimeographed. University of California, Berkeley, 1975.
————. "The Foreign Exchange Markets–Models, Tests and Empirical Evidence."
    Presented at the U.S. Treasury Workshop on Technical Studies on Economic
    Interdependence and Exchange Rate Flexibility, Washington, D.C., February
    26–27, 1976.
LEVICH, RICHARD M. "A Note on Testing for Unusual Returns in Speculative Markets."
    Mimeographed. New York University, 1976.

————. "The International Money Market: Tests of Forecasting Models and Market Efficiency." Unpublished Ph.D. dissertation, University of Chicago, 1977.

————. "The Efficiency of Markets for Foreign Exchange: A Survey." In R. Dornbusch and J. A. Frenkel (eds.) *International Economic Policy: An Assessment of Theory and Evidence*. 1978 (forthcoming).

MOSES, RONALD. *Anticipation of Exchange Rate Changes*. Unpublished Ph.D. dissertation, University of Chicago, 1969.

MUSSA, MICHAEL. "The Exchange Rate, the Balance of Payments, and Monetary and Fiscal Policy under a Regime of Controlled Floating." *Scandinavian Journal of Economics* 78, No. 2 (May, 1976): 229–248. Reprinted in this volume as Chapter 3.

NELSON, CHARLES R. "The Prediction Performance of the FRB-MIT-Penn Model of the U.S. Economy." *American Economic Review* 62, No. 5 (December, 1972): 902–917.

————. *Applied Time Series Analysis*. San Francisco: Holden-Day, 1973.

RICARDO, DAVID. *Reply to Mr. Bosanquet's Practical Observations on the Report of the Bullion Committee*. London, 1811.

SOLNIK, BRUNO H. *European Capital Markets*. Boston: D.C. Heath-Lexington, 1973.

STOCKMAN, ALAN C. "Risk, Information and Forward Exchange Rates." 1978. Reproduced as Chapter 9 in this volume.

TSIANG, S. C. "The Theory of Forward Exchange and the Effects of Government Intervention on the Forward Market." *Staff Papers* 7, No. 1 (April, 1959): 75–106.

WALRAS, LEON. *Elements of Pure Economics*. 1st ed. 1874. Translated by W. Jaffe. New York: Kelly, 1969.

WESTERFIELD, JANICE M. "Empirical Properties of Foreign Exchange Rates Under Fixed and Floating Rate Regimes." Department of Research, Federal Reserve Bank of Philadelphia. December, 1975.

WORKING, HOLBROOK. "New Concepts Concerning Futures Markets and Prices." *American Economic Review* 51 (May, 1961): 160–163.

CHAPTER 9

RISK, INFORMATION, AND FORWARD EXCHANGE RATES

ALAN C. STOCKMAN
University of California, Los Angeles

INTRODUCTION

Foreign exchange risk plays an important role in international monetary economics, yet it is rarely defined in a precise manner so that its consequences can be analyzed and empirically investigated. This paper shows that the risk of holding assets denominated in foreign exchange can be related to the stochastic properties of the rates of return on foreign and domestic currencies and on alternative investments. These stochastic properties combine with people's tastes for risk to determine the magnitudes of risk premiums on foreign exchange. These risk premiums can be studied empirically by examining forward exchange rates.

Nonzero risk premiums cause forward exchange rates to be biased predictors of future spot exchange rates. An expected future exchange rate may exceed the forward exchange rate if assets that are denominated in foreign currency are riskier in terms of utility. When an individual purchases foreign exchange on the forward market he therefore exchanges a less risky asset (domestic money) for a more risky asset (foreign exchange). The fact that payment for and delivery of the asset are deferred until a later date does not alter the risk of the asset because the forward price is set today. The individual will purchase the foreign exchange only if he is compensated, at the market price of risk, for the risk he is purchasing. This compensation takes the form of a discount on forward foreign exchange: a forward exchange rate that is lower than the expected future spot rate. I call this a negative risk premium on foreign exchange. A negative risk premium on pounds in terms of dollars is obviously a positive risk premium on dollars in terms of pounds.

There are two other determinants of forward exchange rates. One is a convexity term which is nonzero due to Jensen's inequality and has appeared before in the

This paper developed from a term paper at the University of Chicago, where Richard Karplus, Steve Magee, Merton Miller, and Myron Scholes provided useful comments on an earlier draft. Jacob Frenkel and Arnold Zellner provided very helpful and detailed comments on a subsequent draft.

exchange rate literature.[1] The other determinant of the forward exchange rate is the expected future spot exchange rate. This expected exchange rate is a function of the information available to the market about future values of variables that affect the exchange rate. As individuals acquire new information over time they are better able to guess the exchange rate that will prevail in the future. Both the forward exchange rate and the current spot rate (and, in fact, current prices of goods) are revised as these expectations change.[2] The speed at which the market acquires new information that affects expectations and thereby spot exchange rates is an important issue in the economics of exchange rates. This paper uses statistics from the forward foreign exchange market to empirically investigate the speed at which the market acquires new information. This topic is examined jointly with the size of the risk premiums on six currencies against the dollar for the period from early 1973 through mid-1977. A series of expected changes in exchange rates can be constructed from this estimation procedure without the arbitrariness involved in selecting a particular information set: the series reflects all information used in foreign exchange markets.[3] The speed at which new information becomes available is a key parameter in theoretical models such as Mussa's (1977), and empirical estimates of this parameter are therefore likely to be useful for improving our understanding of the role of information and expectations and for testing alternative hypotheses about the behavior and determination of exchange rates.

I. THEORETICAL ANALYSIS

Consider a world with one consumption good and two moneys. Individuals live for two periods; each enters period one with an endowment of the consumption good and each money. The consumption good need not be consumed this period: it may be planted in the ground (invested) to yield an uncertain return in period two. The probability distribution of this return is assumed to be known in period one. Individuals value the consumption good because it gives them direct utility. If each money is to be held (and at least two moneys are required for an analysis of exchange rates), these moneys must provide some services. Suppose that these services can be summarized in an indirect utility function for the representative individual:

$$U\left(c, \frac{M}{P}, \frac{M^*}{P^*}\right) \tag{1}$$

where c is consumption, M and M^* are holdings of moneys one and two, and P and P^* are the prices of the consumption good in terms of moneys one and two. Individuals may trade with each other in a variety of ways: they may exchange either money for goods, or one money for the other; they may borrow or lend either money (issue or

---

[1] Siegel (1972), (1975); McCulloch (1975); Roper (1975).

[2] This may be regarded as the central insight of the "asset approach" to exchange rate theory reflected in such papers as Frenkel (1976), Mussa (1976) and (1977), and Dornbusch (1976).

[3] Frenkel (1977) uses a series of this kind in conjunction with a purchasing power parity assumption to construct a measure of expected inflation in Germany, 1921–23.

purchase bonds denominated in either currency), or they may buy or sell either money on a forward market.[4] Finally, the quantity of each money may change at the beginning of period two through equal transfer payments to everyone. The money supply changes are uncertain during period one but may be described by known probability distributions.

This setup is simple but includes features that are important for an analysis of forward exchange rates. There are two moneys and hence an exchange rate; there is an uncertain rate of return on real investment; and there is uncertainty about the future price of goods in terms of each money (because future money supplies and future incomes are random). The uncertain rate of return on real investment is important because the risk involved in holding foreign exchange is properly measured in a portfolio context: the risk of an asset is the change in the risk of one's total wealth when more of that asset is held. The uncertainty about future price levels is important because the rates of return on domestic money and foreign exchange depend upon their future purchasing powers. The indirect utility function (1) seems restrictive, but in fact it captures in a simple manner the important issues involved. While in the real world most people specialize in holding only one money because foreign moneys provide no important services for them, the very notion of an equilibrium exchange rate implies that at some other price the supply and demand for foreign exchange would be unequal, so there must be foreign exchange market participants who are on the margin of substitution. This is the important feature captured in (1). Because there is only one good in this model, purchasing power parity is guaranteed in equilibrium by arbitrage conditions. But this feature of the model is not crucial to the results. The basic propositions about the forward exchange rate that follow from this simple framework can also be shown to hold in a model in which the demand for money is derived from a transactions technology rather than from its presence in a utility function and in which relative goods prices may change so that purchasing power parity does not always hold.[5,6]

This formulation is useful for analyzing the concept of exchange risk, a concept that has been loosely used in the international finance literature to refer to the risks of holding assets denominated in foreign moneys. This risk has two sources: there may be risk of changes in an asset price due to changes in the value of foreign money in terms of goods, and there may be risk due to political intervention such as exchange controls.[7] This paper concentrates on the first source of exchange risk.

Suppose that there are n possible states of the world in period two, and index them by $i = 1, \ldots, n$. Let r_i be the real rate of return on real investment if state of the world i occurs, and let M_i^s and M_i^{*s} be the supplies of the two moneys in state i. Each state i is therefore associated with particular values of r_2, M_2^s, and M_2^{*s}, namely r_i, M_i^s,

---

[4] In fact these identical individuals would not trade, but at equilibrium prices each individual would be indifferent between (infinitesimal) trades and no trades.

[5] Stockman (1977).

[6] The results reached by this simple two-period model can also be derived (with somewhat more work) in a continuous time model—see Kouri (1977) or Stockman (1976)—but no new economic issues are involved.

[7] Aliber (1975) and (1975a).

and M_i^{*s}. Note that this setup encompasses uncertainty about both real (r_2) and nominal (M_2^s, M_2^{*s}) variables. Each state of the world i has probability q_i, with $\Sigma_{i=1}^n q_i = 1$, and these probabilities are assumed to be known.

Each individual enters period one with an endowment of goods, y_1^s, and a stock of each money, M_1^s and M_1^{*s}. Each chooses first-period consumption, c, money holdings, M_1 and M_1^*, real investment, I, and loans of moneys one and two (bond purchases), B and B^*. These loans occur at nominal interest rates R and R^*, which are endogenously determined by the equilibrium conditions in the bond markets (negative values of B and B^* denote borrowings or bond sales). Each individual also chooses F, his purchases of money two with money one on the forward foreign exchange market at the price f. Finally, each individual chooses period-two consumption c_2 and money holdings, M_2 and M_2^*, for each possible state of the world in period two. Let c_i, M_i, and M_i^* denote these choices if state i occurs.

The individual chooses these variables to maximize discounted expected utility:

$$\text{maximize } U\left(c_1, \frac{M_1}{P_1}, \frac{M_1^*}{P_1^*}\right) + \rho \sum_{i=1}^n q_i U\left(c_i, \frac{M_i}{P_i}, \frac{M_i^*}{P_i^*}\right) \tag{2}$$

where $\rho < 1$ is a discount factor. This maximization is subject to

and

$$y_1^s + \left(\frac{M_1^s}{P_1} + \frac{M_1^{*s}}{P_1^*}\right) = c_1 + \frac{M_1}{P_1} + \frac{M_1^*}{P_1^*} + I + \frac{B}{P_1} + \frac{B^*}{P_1^*}$$

$$\frac{M_i^s}{P_i} + \frac{M_i^{*s}}{P_i^*} + (1 + r_i)I + (1 + R)\frac{B}{P_i} + (1 + R^*)\frac{B^*}{P_i^*}$$

$$= c_i + \frac{M_i}{P_i} + \frac{M_i^*}{P_i^*} - \frac{F}{P_i^*} + \frac{f}{P_i}F.$$

These are budget constraints in periods one and two. The individual ends period one with money holdings of M_1 and M_1^*; changes in either money supply take the form of transfer payments or taxes between periods. These transfers or taxes depend upon the state of the world. Each individual therefore begins period two with money holdings M_i^s and M_i^{*s}, the period two money supplies if state of the world i occurs, which are equal to M_1 and M_1^* plus transfer payments or minus taxes.

Let λ_1 be the Lagrange multiplier for the first budget constraint and λ_2 the random Lagrange multiplier for the second constraint. The multiplier λ_2 takes on a value λ_i in state of the world i. Then the first order conditions obtained by maximizing (2) with respect to c_1, B, B^*, c_i and F are

$$U_c(c_1, m_1, m_1^*) = \lambda_1 \tag{3}$$

$$\lambda_1 = \sum_{i=1}^n q_i(1 + R)\frac{P_1}{P_i}\lambda_i \tag{4}$$

$$\lambda_1 = \sum_{i=1}^n q_i(1 + R^*)\frac{P_1^*}{P_i^*}\lambda_i \tag{5}$$

$$\rho U_c(c_i, m_i, m_i^*) = \lambda_i \tag{6}$$

$$f \sum_{i=1}^{n} q_i \frac{\lambda_i}{P_i} = \sum_{i=1}^{n} q_i \frac{\lambda_i}{P_i^*} \tag{7}$$

where

$$m_1 \equiv \frac{M_1}{P_1}, m_1^* \equiv \frac{M_1^*}{P_1^*}, m_i \equiv \frac{M_i}{P_i},$$

and

$$m_i^* \equiv \frac{M_i^*}{P_i^*}.$$

The other first-order conditions are the budget constraints and

$$U_m(c_1, m_1, m_1^*) = \lambda_1 - \sum_{i=1}^{n} q_i \lambda_i \frac{P_1}{P_i}$$

$$U_{m^*}(c_1, m_1, m_1^*) = \lambda_1 - \sum_{i=1}^{n} q_i \lambda_i \frac{P_1^*}{P_i^*}$$

$$\lambda_1 = \sum_{i=1}^{n} q_i(1 + r_i)\lambda_i$$

$$\rho U_m(c_i, m_i, m_i^*) = \lambda_i$$

$$\rho U_{m^*}(c_i, m_i, m_i^*) = \lambda_i.$$

Arbitrage ensures that the current spot exchange rate is[8]

$$e_1 = \frac{P_1}{P_1^*} \qquad \text{or} \qquad e_1^* = \frac{P_1^*}{P_1}. \tag{8}$$

The exchange rate expected in period one to prevail in period two is[9]

$$E(e_2) = E\left(\frac{P_2}{P_2^*}\right) \qquad \text{or} \qquad E(e_2^*) = E\left(\frac{P_2^*}{P_2}\right). \tag{9}$$

The forward exchange rate can be derived in three equivalent ways. It can be deduced directly from (7) and (3), or the forward exchange purchase can be duplicated in the bond market. Or one can note that the purchase of any asset in a forward market is equivalent to purchasing that asset on the spot market, paying on credit, and renting the asset back to the seller during the interim.[10] Any one of these three methods of solving for the forward exchange rate will lead to the same conclusion:

$$f = \frac{E[U_c(c_2, m_2, m_2^*)/P_2^*]}{E[U_c(c_2, m_2, m_2^*)/P_2]}$$

$$= E(e_2) + \left(\frac{E(U_c/P_2^*)}{E(U_c/P_2)} - \frac{E(1/P_2^*)}{E(1/P_2)}\right) + \left(\frac{E(1/P_2^*)}{E(1/P_2)} - E\left(\frac{P_2}{P_2^*}\right)\right). \tag{10}$$

---

[8] Magee (1978) shows that many apparent deviations from purchasing power parity are really spurious.

[9] Hodrick (1978) and Bilson (1978) use similar purchasing power parity relations in different contexts.

[10] Dusak (1973).

The second line of (10) is obtained by simply adding and subtracting terms, and using (9).

The forward exchange rate thus can be expressed as the sum of the expected future spot rate and two other terms. The second term on the right-hand side of (10) may be termed a risk premium; it is analogous to the risk premiums studied in the finance literature. The size of the risk premium depends upon the concavity of the utility function (as usual) and upon the probability distributions on the real rate of return r and on the period two money supplies m_2^s and m_2^{*s}.

Consider an example. Suppose the utility function is

$$U(c, m, m^*) = \alpha_0 + \alpha_1 c - \tfrac{1}{2}\beta c^2 + \mu(m, m^*).$$

Then $U_c = \alpha_1 - \beta c$ so that

$$E\left(\frac{U_c}{P_2^*}\right) = E\left(\frac{\alpha_1}{P_2^*} - \beta \frac{c}{P_2^*}\right).$$

Now use the budget constraint for period two and the equilibrium conditions

$$M_2^s = M_2 \qquad \text{and} \qquad M_2^{*s} = M_2^* \tag{11}$$

to obtain

$$c_i = (1 + r_i)I + \frac{1}{P_i}[(1+R)B - fF] + \frac{1}{P_i^*}[(1+R^*)B^* + F]$$

so that

$$E\left(\frac{U_c}{P_2^*}\right) = (\alpha_1 - \beta I)E\left(\frac{1}{P_2^*}\right) - \beta I E\left(r\frac{1}{P_2^*}\right) - [\beta(1+R)B - \beta fF]E\left(\frac{1}{P_2}\frac{1}{P_2^*}\right)$$

$$- [\beta(1+R^*)B^* + \beta F]E\left(\frac{1}{P_2^*}\right)^2$$

$$\equiv g\left[E\left(\frac{1}{P_2^*}\right)^2, E\left(r\frac{1}{P_2^*}\right), E\left(\frac{1}{P_2^*}\frac{1}{P_2}\right)\right]$$

and similarly

$$E\left(\frac{U_c}{P_2}\right) \equiv g\left[E\left(\frac{1}{P_2}\right)^2, E\left(r\frac{1}{P_2}\right), E\left(\frac{1}{P_2^*}\frac{1}{P_2}\right)\right].$$

Therefore the risk premium in this special case of a strongly separable quadratic utility function can be written as

$$\frac{g\left[E\left(\frac{1}{P_2^*}\right)^2, E\left(r\frac{1}{P_2^*}\right), E\left(\frac{1}{P_2}\frac{1}{P_2^*}\right)\right]}{g\left[E\left(\frac{1}{P_2}\right)^2, E\left(r\frac{1}{P_2}\right), E\left(\frac{1}{P_2^*}\frac{1}{P_2}\right)\right]} \; \frac{E\left(\frac{1}{P_2^*}\right)}{E\left(\frac{1}{P_2}\right)}. \tag{12}$$

The risk premium therefore involves characteristics of the probability distributions of r, $1/P_2$, and $1/P_2^*$. One could further use the equilibrium conditions (11) to solve for $1/P_2$ and $1/P_2^*$ as functions of the exogenous random variables M_2^s, M_2^{*s}, and r:

$$\frac{1}{P_2} = h(M_2^s, M_2^{*s}, r),$$

$$\frac{1}{P_2^*} = h^*(M_2^s, M_2^{*s}, r).$$

(13)

By solving explicitly for the functions in (13) and substituting them into (12), one can write the risk premium as an explicit function of the moments of the probability distributions of M_2^s, M_2^{*s}, and r, that is, of their means, variances, covariances, and so on. Note that the risk premium involves some terms describing the interaction of uncertainty about real variables (the real rate of return on real investment) and nominal variables (the two nominal money supplies).

The risk premium also depends upon the representative individual's attitudes toward risk. In the example, $\beta > 0$ means that the individual is risk-averse in consumption. If, however, $\beta = 0$ then the individual is risk-neutral in consumption and the risk premium (12) equals zero. The risk premium would also collapse to zero if individual tastes and the probability distribution on the money supplies were such that $P_2 = \gamma P_2^*$ for some constant γ. More generally, uncertainty about both real and nominal variables will result in a nonzero risk premium on forward foreign exchange.

The existence of this risk premium does not upset arbitrage conditions such as interest parity.[11] Equations (3), (4), and (5) imply

$$1 + R = (1 + R^*) \frac{E\left(U_c \frac{P_1^*}{P_2^*}\right)}{E\left(U_c \frac{P_1}{P_2}\right)}$$

which, with Eqs. (9) and (10), becomes the interest parity condition

$$1 + R = (1 + R^*) \frac{f}{e_1}.$$

The third term on the right of (10) is a convexity term which is nonzero due to Jensen's inequality. Unlike the risk premium term, the convexity term does not depend directly on people's attitudes toward risk. The convexity term depends only on the probability distributions of P_2 and P_2^*, or, by (13) on the probability distributions of the money supplies and the real rate of return on real investment. The presence of this convexity term in (10) does not imply that profitable arbitrage opportunities exist—(10) was *derived* from utility maximization— yet even if the risk premium were zero, the forward exchange rate would not equal the expected future spot

---

[11] Frenkel and Levich (1975) and (1977) present evidence for interest parity.

rate until after this correction. Quantitatively, the convexity term is very small; one may therefore ignore it for empirical purposes.[12]

II. EMPIRICAL RESULTS

Equation (10) can be estimated empirically by imposing an operational form of rational expectations. This section presents estimates of the risk premium on forward foreign exchange for six currencies against the United States dollar from February 1973 through early May 1977. The data consist of weekly observations on 30-day forward exchange rates and spot rates. Forward rates are generally observed on Tuesdays; spot rates are observed on Thursdays four weeks later. All data are bid prices on the New York foreign exchange market at 1:00 P.M. as reported in the *International Monetary Market Yearbooks* and *Daily Reports*. A few Tuesday-Thursday pairs were not available because of holidays; these were replaced by Wednesday-Friday or Monday-Wednesday pairs.

Weekly data can be used to estimate (10) with a 30-day forward exchange rate by noting that the forecast errors will have a moving-average representation.[13] The difference between the actual spot rate at time $t + 30$ and the spot rate at time t can be written as the sum of shocks which affect the exchange rate on each intervening day:

$$e_{t+30} = e_t + \sum_{i=t+1}^{t+30} u_i$$

where each u_i may consist of both permanent and transitory shocks. Taking expected values conditional on information at time t and subtracting,

$$e_{t+30} - E_t(e_{t+30}) = \sum_{i=t+1}^{t+30} [u_i - E_t(u_i)]$$

$$\equiv \sum_{i=t+1}^{t+30} a_{it}$$

where the second line defines a_{it}. Each a_{it} is therefore the change in the exchange rate on day i that was unexpected as of day t. Now write

$$e_{t+30} = E_t(e_{t+30}) + \sum_{i=t+1}^{t+2} a_{it} + \sum_{i=t+3}^{t+9} a_{it} + \sum_{i=t+10}^{t+16} a_{it} + \sum_{i=t+17}^{t+23} a_{it} + \sum_{i=t+24}^{t+30} a_{it}$$

$$\equiv E_t(e_{t+30}) + v(t+1, t+2; t) + v(t+3, t+9; t) + v(t+10, t+16; t)$$

$$+ v(t+17, t+23; t) + v(t+24, t+30; t)$$

$$= E_t(e_{t+30}) + v(t+24, t+30; t) + K_1 v(t+17, t+23; t-7)$$

$$+ K_2 v(t+10, t+16; t-14) + K_3 v(t+3, t+10; t-21)$$

$$+ K_4 v(t-4, t+2; t-28) \tag{14}$$

---

[12] McCulloch (1975).

[13] Bilson and Levich (1977) also use this fact.

where

$$K_1 = \frac{v(t + 17, t + 23; t)}{v(t + 17, t + 23; t - 7)}$$

$$K_2 = \frac{v(t + 10, t + 16; t)}{v(t + 17, t + 23; t - 7)}$$

$$K_3 = \frac{v(t + 3, t + 10; t)}{v(t + 3, t + 10; t - 21)}$$

$$K_4 = \frac{v(t + 1, t + 2; t)}{v(t + 1, t + 2; t - 28)} \frac{v(t + 1, t + 2; t - 28)}{v(t - 4, t + 2; t - 28)}.$$

Equation (14) says that $e_{t+30} - E_t(e_{t+30})$ follows a fourth-order moving-average process.[14] The coefficients of this process will be given an economic interpretation in the next section. Now Eq. (10) says that the forward exchange rate set at day t for day $t + 30$ equals (approximately, because I ignore the convexity term) $E_t(e_{t+30})$ plus a risk premium. This risk premium depends upon people's taste for risk and upon the moments of various probability distributions. The justification for rational expectations is that the moments of these probability distributions are relatively stable so that people can implicitly learn about them. It may therefore be a reasonable first approximation to treat the risk premium as a constant.[15] Subtracting (14) from (10), one therefore obtains

$$\begin{aligned} Z_{t+30} &\equiv {}_tf_{t+30} - e_{t+30} \\ &= c - v_t - K_1 v_{t-7} - K_2 v_{t-14} - K_3 v_{t-21} - K_4 v_{t-28} \end{aligned} \tag{15}$$

where

$$v_t \equiv v(t + 24, t + 30; t).$$

Equation (15) describes the difference between the 30-day forward exchange rate and the subsequent spot rate, observed weekly, as a fourth-order moving-average process. The constant term is an estimator of the risk premium on forward foreign exchange. The contemporaneous disturbance, $-v_t$, is the sum of seven random variables with zero means (the a_{it}) and will be normally distributed if the underlying shocks on the

---

[14] An alternative method of deriving the moving average process, which involves somewhat different assumptions, is to apply the procedure of Zellner and Montmarquette (1971). This involves premultiplying the daily model by a matrix that picks out the weekly observations, deriving the variance-covariance matrix of the new (weekly) disturbances, and verifying that it is of a form that implies a fourth-order moving average process. Each element of this matrix can be written as the sum of several covariances of the a_{it}.

[15] An alternative possibility is that the risk premium is not constant but is a stable function of other known variables. The risk premium may also change if individuals learn over time about the moments of the relevant probability distributions or the variables that predict these moments. If the risk premium can be described as a constant plus an integrated autoregressive moving average process, then the results of Rose (1977) can be applied to derive the time series process for Z, which will no longer be a fourth-order moving average process.

exchange rate (the u_i) are normally distributed.[16] Proceeding on the tentative assumptions that v_t is normally distributed, that $K_1, \ldots, K_4$ are constants, and that the risk premium is a constant, Table 1 displays maximum likelihood estimates of (15) for six countries opposite the United States, from February 1973 through May 1977.

The constant terms are all expressed in one-hundreths of a United States cent per foreign currency unit (pound sterling, Canadian dollar, deutschemark, guilder, franc) except for Japan in which the units are per 100 yen. These are the estimates of the risk premiums. The t-statistics in Table 1 are relevant for testing the null hypothesis that the risk premiums are zero; in no case can one reject the null hypothesis on the basis of these tests. Kolmogoroff-Smirnoff tests for goodness of fit and histograms of the residuals indicate that the normality assumption on the v_t cannot be rejected. However, the residuals of some of the estimated equations appear to be autocorrelated; in that case the reported t-statistics do not in fact have student-t distributions and the tests are not valid. The Box-Pierce chi-square statistics, $Q(12)$, $Q(24)$, and $Q(36)$, are relevant for testing the null hypothesis that the first 12, 24, or 36 autocorrelations of residuals are jointly zero. The $Q(12)$ statistic for Britain is significantly different from zero at the 0.05 significance level, as are the $Q(24)$ statistic for Canada and the $Q(12)$ and $Q(24)$ statistics for Japan. Moreover, several other Q-statistics are significantly different from zero at the 0.10 level: the critical values at this significance level are 12.0, 27.2, and 40.2. While tests at the 0.10 level provide some indications of autocorrelation in the residuals for all of the countries except the Netherlands and Switzerland, one may reasonably argue that the 0.05 or 0.01 significance levels are more appropriate for these tests because with samples as large as 200 observations per country the power of the tests is high. The results at the 0.05 level, indicating autocorrelation in the residuals for Britain and Japan, accord with the autocorrelations of the raw Z data for those countries: in both cases the autocorrelation of the raw data extends beyond the fourth lag, a result which is inconsistent with a fourth-order moving-average process with constant parameters.

This autocorrelation of residuals for three of the countries may be due to any of four sources. First, the market may not make effective use of past forecast errors in setting forward exchange rates. This is an unsatisfying hypothesis which I reject on a priori grounds and on the basis of our knowledge of the "efficiency" of other asset markets.[17] Second, the risk premiums may not have been constant over the entire period. Third, the moving average parameters may not have been constant. Fourth, the sample means of the exchange rates may not be good estimators of the mathematical expectations if there is extensive government intervention in foreign exchange markets. In other words, the number of true degrees of freedom in the sample may be much

---

[16] The common finding of nonnormal Pareto distributions for many asset price changes over short intervals may be spurious: if the price change per transaction is normally distributed and the number of transactions per day is random then one can show that the distribution of daily price changes will have fat tails. The fatness will vanish upon temporal aggregation: this may explain why weekly or monthly asset price changes can often be described by a normal distribution even when daily changes cannot.

[17] Levich (1978) examines some market efficiency issues for the foreign exchange market.

Table 1*

FEBRUARY, 1973–MAY, 1977

Currency/Period		Constant	K_1	K_2	K_3	K_4	$Q(12)$	$Q(24)$	$Q(36)$
Z Britain	$t = 0.3$	17.0	1.02 (0.06)	0.92 (0.08)	0.73 (0.08)	0.33 (0.06)	14.7^a	28.0	34.1
Autocorrelations of residuals	0.02	0.08 0.11	0.10 0.12 0.07	0.00 0.03	0.06		-0.08 -0.07 0.06		
$R^2 = 0.76$									
Z Canada	$t = -0.5$	-8.31	1.07 (0.06)	1.03 (0.06)	0.98 (0.06)	0.62 (0.05)	12.8	30.9^a	33.9
Autocorrelations of residuals	0.01	0.07 0.00	-0.10 0.05 0.02	-0.12 0.04	0.08		-0.11 0.04 0.01		
$R^2 = 0.79$									
Z Germany	$t = -1.0$	-19.0	0.96 (0.06)	0.89 (0.07)	0.76 (0.07)	0.36 (0.06)	6.9	27.8	42.7
Autocorrelations of residuals	0.03	0.09 0.09	0.07 0.05 -0.05	-0.03 -0.01	0.03		-0.02 -0.01 -0.04		
$R^2 = 0.76$									
Z Japan	$t = -0.1$	-1.13	0.91 (0.07)	0.73 (0.08)	0.67 (0.08)	0.23 (0.07)	17.1^a	38.9^b	42.5
Autocorrelations of residuals	0.02	0.11 0.04	0.11 0.12 -0.13	0.09 0.10	0.05		-0.01 -0.04 -0.03		
$R^2 = 0.71$									
Z Netherlands	$t = -1.1$	-17.3	0.97 (0.07)	0.97 (0.08)	0.74 (0.08)	0.33 (0.06)	8.6	23.4	36.9
Autocorrelations of residuals	0.03	0.07 0.10	0.07 0.03 -0.13	-0.04 -0.01	0.02 0.01		0.00 0.02		
$R^2 = 0.77$									
Z Switzerland	$t = -1.2$	-19.0	0.78 (0.07)	0.68 (0.07)	0.53 (0.07)	0.22 (0.06)	7.8	16.6	39.4
Autocorrelations of residuals	0.03	0.04 0.03	0.01 0.04 -0.13	0.07 -0.03	0.05		0.05 -0.01 -0.02		
$R^2 = 0.58$									

a = significant at 0.05 level
b = significant at 0.01 level

*Standard errors appear in parentheses. The approximate standard error of the first twelve autocorrelations of residuals is, by Bartlett's formula, 0.07. The $Q(n)$ statistics have chi-square distributions under the null hypothesis that the first n autocorrelations of residuals are jointly zero.

Table 2*

Currency/Period	Constant	K_1	K_2	K_3	K_4	$Q(12)$	$Q(24)$	$Q(36)$
Z Britain								
2/73–3/75 $t = -1.3$	−132.4	1.03 (0.09)	0.88 (0.11)	0.71 (0.11)	0.33 (0.09)	6.5	17.1	27.1
Autocorrelations of residuals	0.02 0.08	0.10	0.12	0.05 −0.00	0.05		−0.08 −0.06	−0.03
$R^2 = 0.72$								
4/75–5/77 $t = 1.8$	161.1	1.01 (0.09)	0.95 (0.11)	0.74 (0.11)	0.32 (0.09)	9.3	18.8	22.4
Autocorrelations of residuals	−0.00	0.05 0.10	0.07 0.07	0.13	−0.06 0.02	0.10	−0.06 −0.08	0.14
$R^2 = 0.74$								
Z Canada								
2/73–3/75 $t = -0.4$	−5.6	0.96 (0.08)	0.88 (0.10)	0.77 (0.10)	0.39 (0.09)	9.7	24.2	32.7
Autocorrelations of residuals	0.02 0.10	0.06	0.01 0.09	0.00	−0.16 0.08	0.02	−0.10 0.06	−0.13
$R^2 = 0.74$								
4/75–5/77 $t = -0.2$	−5.2	1.19 (0.07)	1.26 (0.06)	1.23 (0.04)	0.76 (0.06)	7.0	14.7	20.5
Autocorrelations of residuals	−0.04	0.05 0.01	−0.09	0.01 0.03	−0.13 0.05	0.11	−0.12 −0.02	0.05
$R^2 = 0.82$								
Z Germany								
2/73–3/75 $t = -1.3$	−43.0	0.94 (0.08)	0.83 (0.10)	0.73 (0.10)	0.37 (0.09)	3.7	19.9	29.6
Autocorrelations of residuals	0.03 0.09	0.09	0.06 0.07	−0.03	−0.05 0.01	−0.02	−0.05 −0.01	−0.05
$R^2 = 0.75$								
4/75–5/77 $t = 0.4$	6.37	1.00 (0.09)	1.00 (0.10)	0.87 (0.09)	0.40 (0.09)	5.0	10.6	14.6
Autocorrelations of residuals	0.05 0.10	0.06	−0.00	0.03 −0.07	−0.00	0.09	0.08 0.02	−0.09 0.03
$R^2 = 0.79$								

Table 2 (Continued)

Currency/Period	Constant	K_1	K_2	K_3	K_4	$Q(12)$	$Q(24)$	$Q(36)$
Z Japan								
4/73–4/75 $t=$ 0.3	5.18	0.96 (0.09)	0.73 (0.11)	0.71 (0.11)	0.21 (0.10)	11.3	24.2	27.1
Autocorrelations of residuals $R^2=$ 0.74	0.02	0.14 0.03	0.14 0.10	-0.16 0.10	0.12 0.10	0.07 -0.02	-0.04	-0.03
5/75–5/77 $t=$ -0.9	-7.10	0.80 (0.10)	0.66 (0.11)	0.58 (0.12)	0.26 (0.10)	6.5	15.3	20.7
Autocorrelations of residuals $R^2=$ 0.60	0.01	0.04 0.03	0.05 0.10	0.03 -0.02	0.15	-0.08 -0.04	0.04	-0.12
Z Netherlands								
5/73–5/75 $t=$ -1.2	-32.5	0.91 (0.09)	0.90 (0.11)	0.65 (0.11)	0.30 (0.09)	6.4	16.9	26.9
Autocorrelations of residuals $R^2=$ 0.72	0.03	0.06 0.08	0.06 0.03	-0.17 -0.08	-0.07 -0.08	-0.06 0.00	-0.01	0.03
5/75–5/77 $t=$ -0.4	-7.8	1.14 (0.06)	1.30 (0.06)	1.18 (0.04)	0.54 (0.06)	10.9	15.8	23.2
Autocorrelations of residuals $R^2=$ 0.84	-0.00	0.10 0.14	0.07	0.08 -0.05	0.03 0.13	0.20 0.04	-0.01	0.06
Z Switzerland								
2/73–3/75 $t=$ -1.7	-47.5	0.58 (0.09)	0.64 (0.09)	0.67 (0.09)	0.33 (0.09)	4.0	16.8	35.0
Autocorrelations of residuals $R^2=$ 0.56	0.05	0.04 -0.03	-0.05	0.06 -0.11	0.07 -0.04	0.06 0.01	-0.03	0.00
4/75–5/77 $t=$ 0.9	14.6	0.85 (0.09)	0.85 (0.12)	0.40 (0.12)	0.16 (0.09)	2.9	7.6	12.6
Autocorrelations of residuals $R^2=$ 0.63	-0.01	0.01 0.05	0.01 0.04	-0.08	-0.00 0.04	0.01 -0.02	-0.01	-0.11

* Standard errors appear in parentheses. The approximate standard error of the first twelve autocorrelations of residuals is 0.09.

smaller than the number of observations. For example, the forward exchange rate for the Mexican peso consistently reflected a discount below the spot rate before the 1976 devaluation of the peso: over a period dominated by the months before that devaluation, the sample mean of the spot exchange rate did not equal the expectation held in the market.

The sample period was split in half in order to examine the temporal stability of the constant term and the moving average parameters. Table 2 displays estimates of (15) for the subperiods.

The residual autocorrelation in the British case disappears when the two half-samples are estimated separately. The risk premium was apparently not constant over the whole sample period: the point estimates of the risk premium change signs and are increased by a factor of nearly ten, and the t-statistics are higher (though still below the 0.05 level critical values). With the assumption that the two sample periods are independent,[18] the difference between the two constant terms, divided by the sum of the variances of each, follows a standardized normal distribution under the null hypothesis that the two constant terms are equal. I refer to this henceforth as the normal test.[19] The difference between the constant terms in Table 2 in the British case is 293.5, with a standard error of 135.3. So the normal statistic takes a value of 2.17, which is above the 0.05 critical value (all statistical tests hereafter are conducted at the 0.05 level). Therefore one can reject the null hypothesis that the constant term is the same in the two subperiods; that is, while one cannot reject the hypotheses that either constant term alone is zero, one can reject the hypothesis that they are both zero. So the risk premium on forward pounds sterling changed from negative to positive from the first period to the second.

Note that a negative risk premium corresponds to a situation in which pounds sterling are riskier than dollars: owners of pound sterling must therefore be compensated at the market price of risk. When pounds are purchased on the forward market with dollars, the buyer is exchanging a less risky asset (dollars) for a more risky asset (pounds), and this circumstance is not altered by the fact that payment for and delivery of the pounds is delayed until the future. The buyer of forward pounds is therefore compensated for bearing this risk by being able to purchase forward pounds at a price that is lower than the expected price in the future. So the results in Table 2 indicate that pounds were more risky than dollars in the first subperiod, and less risky in the second subperiod.

The moving-average parameters for the British case are stable over time. This conclusion applies whether the normal test is applied separately to each moving average parameter or whether an F-test is applied to the null hypothesis that they are jointly stable. The conclusion for the British case is therefore that the K_i are stable over time but that the risk premium changed around 1975.

---

[18] Think of the second period extending forward in time and the first period extending backward; then asymptotic properties of the test statistics still apply.

[19] This is simply a large sample t-test and should not be confused with the asymptotic normality assumption on the v_t, which again could not be rejected by a Kolmogoroff-Smirnoff goodness-of-fit test.

An exactly opposite conclusion applies to the Canadian case. The autocorrelation of residuals in Table 1 vanishes when the sample is split in two, but now the risk premium is stable over time while each K_i changes. The normal statistics for testing the stability of $K_1, \ldots, K_4$ take values 2, 3.2, 4.1, and 3.3, indicating that those parameters were not equal in the two subperiods. The risk premium, on the other hand, remained stable at a value not significantly different from zero.

The estimates in Table 1 for the deutschemark survive the results of splitting the sample in two. The normal statistics for testing equality of $K_1, \ldots, K_4$ are 0.5, 1.2, 1.0, and 0.3, while the normal statistic for testing stability of the risk premium is 1.3. The F-statistic for the null hypothesis that the constant and the K_i are jointly unchanged is 0.71. These results indicate that all the parameters in the German case remained stable over time; and while the point estimate of the risk premium changes signs from the first subperiod to the second, one cannot reject the hypothesis that it is zero.

The autocorrelation of residuals again vanished in the Japanese case when the sample is split in two. Neither the risk premium nor the moving-average parameters are estimated precisely enough to reject the hypotheses that these parameters are stable over time, individually and jointly. The risk premium is insignificantly different from zero.

The residuals in Table 1 were not autocorrelated in the cases of the Netherlands and Switzerland. Nevertheless, there is some evidence that the moving-average parameters, but not the constant term, changed in the Dutch case, while both may have changed in the Swiss case. The normal statistics for the K_i in the Dutch case are 2.1, 3.2, 4.5, and 2.2, indicating that these parameters did change, while the normal statistic for the constant term is less than one, indicating that the constant term was stable at a value insignificantly different from zero. In the Swiss case, the normal statistics for the K_i are 2.0, 1.4, 1.8, and 1.2 and the normal statistic for the constant term is 1.9. The F-statistic for the null hypothesis that all five parameters are stable is 3.0. There is, therefore, some weak evidence that the risk premium on Swiss francs changed from negative to positive from one period to the other.

III. NEW INFORMATION IN THE FOREIGN EXCHANGE MARKET

Tables 1 and 2 provide estimates of the risk premiums on foreign exchange; they also provide estimates of the rate at which new information about future exchange-rate changes becomes available to the foreign exchange market. Moreover, the residuals from the estimated equations provide estimates of unexpected exchange-rate changes and can be used to construct a series of expected changes.

The residuals from the estimated equations are estimates of $v(t + 24, t + 30; t)$, which is the sum of the shocks affecting the exchange rate during the week $(t + 24, t + 30)$ that were unexpected as of day t. By subtracting this sum of unexpected shocks from the actual change in the exchange rate during the week $(t + 24, t + 30)$, one can obtain the change in the exchange rate that was expected on day t to occur during that week. An entire time series of expected exchange rate changes can thereby be constructed without ever making assumptions about the information available to market participants. Furthermore, this procedure is valid regardless of the size of risk premiums on forward foreign exchange.

The moving-average parameters are estimates of K_1, K_2, K_3, and K_4. Note that each of these parameters has an economic interpretation: K_1 is the ratio of the sum of shocks affecting the exchange rate between days $t + 17$ and $t + 23$ that were unexpected on day t to the sum of shocks affecting the exchange rate (on these same days) that were unexpected on day $t - 7$. Thus the estimated value of $1 - K_1$ is an estimate of the amount learned between days $t - 7$ and t about the sum of shocks affecting the exchange rate during the week from $t + 17$ to $t + 23$, as a percentage of the sum of shocks that were unexpected on day $t - 7$. Similarly, the estimated value of $1 - K_2$ is an estimate of the percentage reduction in uncertainty that occurs between days $t - 7$ and $t + 7$ about the sum of shocks affecting the exchange rate during the week $(t + 17, t + 23)$. Formally,

$$
1 - K_1 = \frac{\sum_{i=17}^{23} [E_t(u_i) - E_{t-7}(u_i)]}{\sum_{i=17}^{23} [u_i - E_{t-7}(u_i)]}
$$

$$
= \frac{E_t(e_{t+23} - e_{t+16}) - E_{t-7}(e_{t+23} - e_{t+16})}{e_{t+23} - e_{t+16} - E_{t-7}(e_{t+23} - e_{t+16})},
$$

with similar expressions for $1 - K_2$, $1 - K_3$, and $1 - K_4$. These theoretical parameters bear a close resemblance to some key parameters in Mussa (1977), and the estimated parameters are estimates of the rate at which uncertainty about future exchange rate changes is reduced over time by the acquisition of new information.

The estimates in Tables 1 and 2 suggest that the rate at which new information was obtained over time about future exchange-rate changes was fairly stable from early 1973 to mid-1977 for the pound sterling, the deutschmark, and the yen. Uncertainty on day zero about the exchange rate change during the week (23, 30) was reduced less than 10% by day 7, reduced a total of 10% (or 27% in the Japanese case) by day 14, reduced by approximately 30% by day 21, and reduced by two-thrids (three-quarters in the Japanese case) by day 28. Therefore one-third to one-half of the uncertainty at day 21 (about the exchange-rate change during the week beginning on day 23) still remains by day 28. This is consistent with the well-known large magnitudes of transitory changes in exchange rates.

In contrast to the results for Britain, Germany, and Japan, the rate at which new information was obtained about future changes in the Canadian dollar and Dutch guilder exchange rates was greater in the first half of the sample period than in the second half. Before early 1975, the flow of new information about these exchange rates resembled the flow of new information about the pound or deutschemark. But after mid-1975, the flow of information about guilder and Canadian dollar exchange rates was different: virtually no new information about changes in these exchange rates was acquired during the three or four weeks prior to actual changes. The rate at

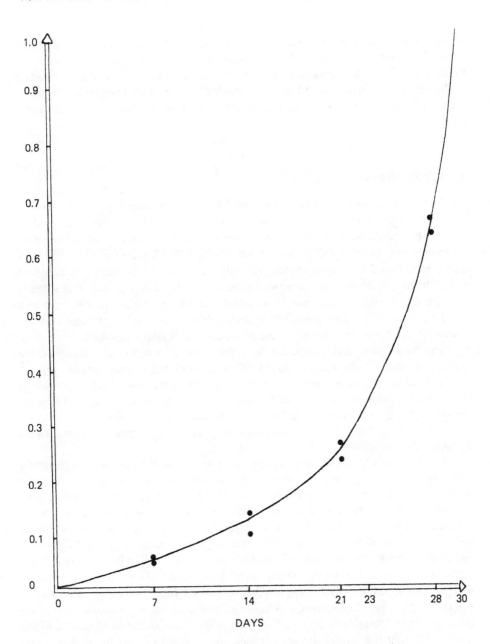

Fig. 1. New information about future exchange rates is obtained over time.

which new information was obtained about the future value of the Swiss franc also changed from the first half of the sample to the second.

Figure 1 sketches roughly the average rate at which new information about exchange-rate changes during a week (23, 30) is obtained in the foreign exchange markets beginning at day zero. The curve is constructed to begin at zero on day zero

and end at unity on day 30 when 100% of the uncertainty at day zero has been eliminated. The points were obtained from simple averages of the parameter estimates in
Tables 1 and 2. Further work along these lines is certain to improve our understanding
of the role of expectations and new information in foreign exchange markets and is
likely to be useful for testing alternative hypotheses about exchange-rate determination.

IV. CONCLUSIONS

The forward exchange rate can be expressed as a sum of three terms: the expected
future spot rate, a risk premium, and a convexity term. This paper attempted to
estimate the magnitudes of risk premiums for six currencies against the dollar under
the assumption that the risk premiums are constant. Evidence of nonzero risk premiums were found for two countries, but only after dividing the sample in halves so
that each risk premium could take two values during the sample period. This suggests
that the risk premiums may not be constant and an appropriate procedure would
therefore be to model these premiums as stochastic processes and apply Rose's results.
One might also try to link the risk premiums directly to financial variables.

The assumption that individuals have the same information and therefore the
same expectations could also be relaxed. While differing information sets can provide
one justification for the existence of many futures markets, forward foreign exchange
market transactions can be duplicated in bond markets. So the existence of a forward
market in foreign exchange is still linked to transactions costs. But different information sets for different market participants may have other implications for forward
foreign exchange markets.

One approach to discovering expected exchange rates is to postulate a particular
information set for individuals and assume that these individuals use optimal linear
predictions conditional on this information. That was not the approach taken here.
This paper used assumptions about the constancy of the risk premium and some learning parameters to impose a rational expectations hypothesis conditional on whatever
information is used by the market. The same procedure could be applied if the risk
premium were a known function of other variables. The learning parameters and risk
premium are estimated jointly under these assumptions. The learning parameters
measure the speed at which new information about future exchange rate changes
enters the foreign exchange market. A useful extension of this work would be to relate
these results to the price of information. One might examine the market value of the
information that the market obtains between days 7 and 14 about the exchange rate
change that will occur between days 23 and 30. This price will be related to a theoretical parameter in Rockafellar and Wets (1975), who formulate the solution to an intertemporal optimization problem in terms of a shadow price of nonanticipativity, that
is, of having to make decisions today before the information about tomorrow is available.

The source of this new information about (the probability distribution of) the
future exchange-rate change has not been examined in this paper. Whether this new

information is mainly related to money supplies, real incomes, interest rates, or relative prices is an important issue for understanding the observed behavior of flexible exchange rates. Finally, this work could be extended by examining statistics on foreign exchange futures prices (as opposed to forward prices) and examining forward exchange rates with different maturities.

REFERENCES

ALIBER, R. Z. "The Short Guide to International Finance." Unpublished manuscript, University of Chicago, 1975.

————. "Exchange Risk, Political Risk, and Investor Demand for External Currency Deposits." *Journal of Money, Credit, and Banking* 7, No. 2 (May, 1975): 161–180 (1975a).

BILSON, J. F. O. "Rational Expectations and the Exchange Rate." 1978. Reproduced in this volume as Chapter 5.

———— and R. M. LEVICH. "A Test of the Forecasting Efficiency of the Forward Exchange Rate." Unpublished manuscript, New York University, June, 1977.

BOX, G. E. P., and G. JENKINS. *Time Series Analysis.* San Francisco: Holden-Day, 1970.

DORNBUSCH, R. "The Theory of Flexible Exchange Rate Regimes and Macroeconomic Policy." *Scandinavian Journal of Economics* 78, No. 2 (May, 1976): 255–275. Reprinted in this volume as Chapter 2.

DUSAK, K. "Futures Trading and Investor Returns: An Investigation of Commodity Market Risk Premiums." *Journal of Political Economy* 81, No. 6 (December, 1973): 1387–1406.

FRENKEL, J. A. "A Monetary Approach to the Exchange Rate: Doctrinal Aspects and Empirical Evidence." *Scandinavian Journal of Economics* 78, No. 2 (May, 1976): 200–224. Reprinted in this volume as Chapter 1.

————. "The Forward Exchange Rate, Expectations, and the Demand for Money during the German Hyperinflation." *American Economic Review* 67, No. 4 (September, 1977): 653–670.

FRENKEL, J. A., and R. M. LEVICH. "Covered Interest Arbitrage: Unexploited Profits?" *Journal of Political Economy* 83, No. 2 (April, 1975): 325–339.

————. "Transaction Costs and Interest Arbitrage: Tranquil versus Turbulent Periods." *Journal of Political Economy* 85, No. 6 (December, 1977): 1209–1226.

HODRICK, R. J. "An Empirical Analysis of the Monetary Approach to the Exchange Rate." 1978. Reproduced in this volume as Chapter 6.

International Monetary Market, *Yearbook,* 1972–73, 1973–74, 1974–75, 1975–76, 1976–77.

KOURI, P. J. K. "International Investment and Interest Rate Linkages under Flexible Exchange Rates." In Aliber, R. Z. (ed.), *The Political Economy of Monetary Reform.* New York: Allan Held, Osmun, 1977.

LEVICH, R. M. "Tests of Forecasting Models and Market Efficiency in the International Money Market." 1978. Reproduced in this volume as Chapter 8.

MAGEE, S. "Contracting and Spurious Deviations from Purchasing-Power Parity." 1978. Reproduced in this volume as Chapter 4.

McCULLOCH, J. H. "Operational Aspects of the Siegel Paradox." *Quarterly Journal of Economics* 89, No. 1 (February, 1975): 170–172.

MUSSA, M. "The Exchange Rate, The Balance of Payments, and Monetary and Fiscal Policy under a Regime of Controlled Floating." *Scandinavian Journal of Economics* **78**, No. 2 (May, 1976): 229–248. Reprinted in this volume as Chapter 3.

———. "Real and Monetary Factors in a Dynamic Theory of Foreign Exchange." Unpublished manuscript, University of Chicago, 1977.

ROCKAFELLAR, R. T., and R. J. B. WETS. "Stochastic Convex Programming: Kuhn-Tucker Conditions." *Journal of Mathematical Economics* **2**, No. 2 (June, 1975): 349–370.

ROPER, D. "The Role of Expected Value Analysis for Speculative Decisions in the Forward Currency Market." *Quarterly Journal of Economics* 89, No. 1 (February, 1975): 157–169.

ROSE, D. E. "Forecasting Aggregates of Independent ARIMA Processes." *Journal of Econometrics* **5**, (1977): 323–345.

SIEGEL, J. "Risk, Interest Rates, and the Forward Exchange." *Quarterly Journal of Economics* **86**, No. 2 (May, 1972): 303–309.

———. "Reply." *Quarterly Journal of Economics* **89**, No. 1 (February, 1975): 173–175.

STOCKMAN, A. C. "Risk and Forward Exchange Rates." Unpublished manuscript, University of Chicago, March, 1976.

———. "A Theory of Exchange Rate Determination." Unpublished doctoral dissertation, University of Chicago, 1978.

ZELLNER, A., and C. MONTMARQUETTE. "A Study of Some Aspects of Temporal Aggregation Problems in Econometric Analysis." *Review of Economics and Statistics* **53**, No. 4 (November, 1971): 335–342.

CHAPTER 10

A STOCK ADJUSTMENT APPROACH TO MONETARY POLICY AND THE BALANCE OF PAYMENTS

JUNICHI UJIIE

The Normua Securities Co., Ltd.
Institutional Research and Advisory Department

I. INTRODUCTION

"Equilibrium" in the balance of payments (defined as a zero reserve money flow without restriction on external transactions) has been widely accepted as an appropriate objective of monetary policy in economies under the fixed exchange-rate system. Eminent examples can be found in the Keynesian (or Meade-Tinbergen-Mundellian) policy mix literature, in which balance-of-payments equilibrium is usually chosen as one of the prime policy objectives.[1] Also in empirical studies of reaction functions of monetary authorities (endogenous monetary policy), a balance-of-payments target is often included as a policy aim representing an external goal, even without firm evidence of a correlation between various indicators of the thrust of monetary policy and the balance of payments.[2]

It is clear that an economy under the fixed exchange-rate system, even of a key-currency country, cannot keep on recording deficits; nor would the country want to continuously record surpluses in its balance of payments—but it does not follow that payment-balance equilibrium is always an appropriate policy goal. Only when foreign reserves are at a properly defined desired level can balance-of-payments equilibrium be considered an appropriate policy objective.

More importantly, the notion of balance-of-payments equilibrium as an objective of monetary policy tends to conflict, first, with the classical understanding of the demand for money, and second, with the modern approach to the adjustment mechanism of the balance of payments. Concerning the demand for money, it is well known

---

This paper originates from a part of the author's dissertation submitted to the University of Chicago. The author is grateful to Professors Robert Z. Aliber, Jacob A. Frenkel and Harry G. Johnson. The author is also indebted to Professors Rudiger Dornbusch, Stephen Magee and other participants of the Chicago seminar on international economics. Alan Stockman's editorial help is also gratefully acknowledged.

[1] Much of the literature follows the works of J. E. Meade (1951) and R. A. Mundell (1968). See also J. M. Fleming (1962). For a comprehensive survey, see M. Whitman (1970).

[2] See, for example, W. G. Dewald and H. G. Johnson (1963), G. Reuber (1964), and R. Froyen (1974).

that the demand for money is a demand for stocks; i.e., flows of "money services" come from stocks of money rather than from their changes. It is also stocks of foreign reserves (money acceptable to the rest of the world) from which comforts arise, and it is a low level of stocks of foreign reserves from which discomforts arise. Hence it is the level of foreign reserves, not its change, to which external stabilization policy is applied under the fixed exchange-rate system.[3] Concerning the adjustment mechanism, recent studies stress the fact that the balance of payments is a stock adjustment rather than flow equilibrium phenomenon, and it attains an equilibrium value of zero when adjustments of the composition of portfolios and/or changes in the total size of portfolios are completed.[4] Hence, by itself, a balance-of-payments equilibrium cannot be considered a proper objective of stabilization policy, although the duration and size of payment imbalances are of central importance to the authorities. This implies that a proper target variable of external policy is the stock of foreign reserves rather than its change.

The purpose of this paper is to specify and to estimate equations for the balance of payments and for the reaction function of the monetary authorities, both of which follow from the stock disequilibrium nature of the adjustment process. The balance-of-payments equations are developed by explicitly taking account of portfolio adjustments by the private sector, and the authority's reaction function focuses on the stock disequilibrium of foreign reserves held by the monetary authority. These equations are then estimated using data on the postwar Japanese economy, which can be considered one of the best examples of monetary policy that is tightly geared to external objectives.

II. THE THEORETICAL FRAMEWORK

The Balance-of-Payments Adjustment
The economy is assumed to have three fiat assets which are gross substitutes in private portfolios: domestic bonds, B; foreign bonds, B'; and money, M.

Foreign bonds are internationally traded and in infinitely elastic supply at the world rate of interest. Domestic bonds exist as a result of past deficits in the government budget and are assumed not to be traded internationally, implying that the authorities cannot finance a balance-of-trade deficit by printing and selling bonds. The government budget is assumed to be kept in balance during the period in question. It is assumed for simplicity that bonds are of a fixed-price-variable-coupon type and that the private sector does not discount or capitalize future taxes or transfers. Hence changes in interest rates do not affect prices of bonds, and both types of bonds are part of the private sector's net wealth. These simplifying assumptions can be dropped without materially changing the conclusions.

---

[3] The analogy between private demand for domestic money and the official demand for international reserves has already been pointed out by R. A. Mundell (1968, Ch. 14), J. Niehans (1968), J. H. G. Olivera (1971), R. H. Heller (1966), J. A. Frenkel (1974a) and others.

[4] The stock adjustment process was emphasized by H. G. Johnson in the 1950's (1958, Ch. 6) and R. A. Mundell (1968, Ch. 18), and it is one of the cornerstones of the monetary approach to the balance of payments; see, for example, J. A. Frenkel and H. G. Johnson (1976).

Assuming the money multiplier to be unity, the total money supply can be written as,

$$M = R + Ba, \tag{1}$$

where R is the stock of foreign exchange reserves and Ba represents domestic bonds in the hands of the monetary authority. For simplicity, it is assumed that foreign bonds are not used as reserves. Although the private sector is indifferent as to whether M is backed by R or Ba, the monetary authority is not, since R is the only money acceptable to the rest of the world.

The private sector's total net wealth, then, can be written as,

$$W = R + Ba + (B - Ba) + B' = M + Bp + B', \tag{2}$$

where Bp represents domestic bonds held in the private sector.

Short-run portfolio equilibrium in the private sector, given W, can be written as follows:

$$Bp = B^d = n(i, i^*, y)W, \qquad n_1 > 0, n_2 < 0, n_3 < 0, \tag{3}$$

$$B' = B'^d = q(i, i^*, y)W, \qquad q_1 < 0, q_2 > 0, q_3 < 0, \tag{4}$$

$$M = M^d = l(i, i^*, y)W, \qquad l_1 < 0, l_2 < 0, l_3 > 0, \tag{5}$$

$$l + n + q = 1, \tag{6}$$

$$l_j + n_j + q_j = 0, \qquad \text{where } j = 1, 2, 3. \tag{7}$$

Superscript d denotes demand and subscript j denotes a partial derivative with respect to the jth argument. All asset demand functions are assumed to have unitary wealth elasticities. Equations (6) and (7) are "adding up properties" of the portfolio balance.[5] Assuming that the cost of rearranging the composition of total private wealth is negligible, there is always portfolio equilibrium at each point in time. Hence by differentiating the short-run portfolio equilibrium conditions with respect to time, we derive equilibrium time paths of R and B', i.e., "equilibrium" balance-of-payments and capital flows. Note that an "equilibrium" balance-of-payments or capital flow is not necessarily a zero payment balance or a zero capital flow. "Equilibrium" implies only that these magnitudes are determined along the portfolio equilibrium time path of the economy. By differentiating equations (3), (4), and (5) with respect to time and using an assumption of a balanced budget of the domestic government, we have,

$$\dot{R} = \frac{q_1}{n_1}\dot{Ba} + W\left(l_2 - n_2\frac{l_1}{n_1}\right)\dot{i}^* + W\left(l_3 - n_3\frac{l_1}{n_1}\right)\dot{y} + \left(l - n\frac{l_1}{n_1}\right)\dot{W}, \tag{8}$$

$$\dot{B}' = -\frac{q_1}{n_1}\dot{Ba} + W\left(q_2 - n_2\frac{q_1}{n_1}\right)\dot{i}^* + W\left(q_3 - n_3\frac{q_1}{n_1}\right)\dot{y} + \left(q - n\frac{q_1}{n_1}\right)\dot{W}, \tag{9}$$

where use is made of "adding up properties" and a domestic bond market equilibrium condition is used to eliminate the domestic interest rate. The first three terms on the

[5] For a specification of short-run asset demands along this line, see J. Tobin (1969), D. Foley and M. Sidrauski (1971), and M. Mussa (1976).

right-hand sides of both equations represent capital and reserve money flows caused by rearranging the composition of portfolios, while the fourth terms represent capital and reserve money flows caused by changes in the total size of portfolios. Note that there are simple relations between the coefficients of corresponding terms in equations (8) and (9). The coefficients of $\dot{B}a$, i^* and $\dot{y}$ in equations (8) and (9) all add up to zero and the coefficients of W in equations (8) and (9) add up to unity. Hence we can rewrite equations (8) and (9) as,

$$BP = (\dot{R}) = \beta_1 \dot{B}a + \beta_2 i^* + \beta_3 \dot{y} + (1 + \beta_4)\dot{W}, \tag{8'}$$

$$C = (-\dot{B}') = \beta_1 \dot{B}a + \beta_2 i^* + \beta_3 \dot{y} + \beta_4 \dot{W}, \tag{9'}$$

where BP is the balance of payments and C is capital inflow, and

$$\beta_1 = \frac{q_1}{n_1}; \qquad\qquad\qquad\qquad -1 < \beta_1 < 0,$$

$$\beta_2 = W\left(l_2 - n_2 \frac{l_1}{n_1}\right) = -W\left(q_2 - n_2 \frac{q_1}{n_1}\right); \qquad \beta_2 < 0,$$

$$\beta_3 = W\left(l_3 - n_3 \frac{l_1}{n_1}\right) = -W\left(q_3 - n_3 \frac{q_1}{n_1}\right); \qquad \beta_3 > 0,$$

$$\beta_4 = -\left(q - n \frac{q_1}{n_1}\right) = \left(l - n \frac{l_1}{n_1}\right) - 1; \qquad -1 < \beta_4 < 0.$$

Therefore, the balance-of-payments and capital-flow equations do not differ from each other except for the unity in the coefficient of $\dot{W}$. Subtracting both sides of equations (9') and (8'), we can see that $\dot{W}$ is equal to the current account, CA. This is because we assumed that the total amount of domestic bonds does not change and that total assets do not include physical capital. Hence the balance-of-payments equation which we estimate can be rewritten as,[6]

$$BP = \beta_1 \dot{B}a + \beta_2 i^* + \beta_3 \dot{y} + (1 + \beta_4)CA. \tag{10}$$

We need not estimate the capital-flow equation separately since it can be obtained merely by deducting unity from the estimated coefficient of CA in the balance-of-payments equation.

When B and B' are perfect substitutes, i.e., when capital is perfectly mobile internationally, we have,

$$BP = -\dot{B}a + \beta_2' i^* + \beta_3' \dot{y} + \beta_4' CA,$$

where $\beta_2' = Wl_2 < 0$, $\beta_3' = Wl_3 > 0$, and $0 < \beta_4' = l < 1$. That is, as capital becomes more mobile internationally, the coefficient of Ba approaches minus unity.

---

[6] P. Kouri and M. Porter (1974) derived a capital-flow equation which has a specification similar to that of equation (10). They derived their capital-flow equation only from stock-equilibrium conditions in the short run, treating flow variables as exogenous. This is the analytical device used by J. Tobin (1969).

Monetary Authority's Reaction

If the authorities react systematically to particular macroeconomic variables, then there are behavioral functions describing how monetary policy responds to these policy-goal variables. Assuming that the monetary authority follows a simple linear feedback rule of the Phillips' type (Phillips, 1954) we can write,

$$Z = \sum \alpha_j(X_j^* - X_j), \qquad j = 1, 2, \ldots, n, \tag{12}$$

where Z is a single quantifiable proxy indicator of a monetary policy measure, and X_j and X_j^* are the jth policy-goal variable and its desired level, respectively.[7]

While there is a wide range of arguments about which variables should be included as policy goals, we focus our discussion on a policy goal representing external transactions under the fixed exchange-rate system.

It is interesting that while most reaction functions describing the behavior of the monetary authorities have specified a target balance of payments as an objective of external policy, at the same time there has been much theoretical and empirical work on the demand for a stock of foreign reserves by monetary authorities.[8] Since flows of services from foreign reserves come not from a change in the stock but from the level of the stock, it is the level of reserves, not its change, to which stabilization is directed.

This lack of consensus seems to be a result of the overwhelming influence in the 1970's of the Keynesian (or Meade-Tinbergen-Mundellian) open-economy policy-mix literature. In the standard policy-mix framework, the balance of payments is assumed to remain at certain levels when income and interest rates are at their equilibrium levels and hence there are certain levels of policy variables—such as money supply and government expenditure—which equate the balance of payments, rather than foreign reserves, with the desired level.[9] However, this contains serious faults in the treatment of stocks and flows, in two senses. First, the level of domestic interest rates (or the interest-rate differential) is assumed to affect the balance of payments through capital flows, but a payments imbalance is assumed not to affect the level of domestic interest rates (or the interest-rate differential). Second, the balance of payments is considered

---

[7] This partial adjustment reaction function can be derived from a utility maximization under uncertainty; see D. Henderson and S. Turnovsky (1972).

[8] See the pioneering work by R. H. Heller (1966). Also see M. G. Kelly (1970) and J. A. Frenkel (1974a, 1974b).

[9] A standard framework of the policy mix model can be written as,

$$Y = E(Y, i) + T(Y, e) + \bar{G} \qquad 1 > E_y > 0, E_i < 0, T_y < 0, T_e > 0$$

$$\bar{M} = L(Y, i) \qquad L_y > 0, L_i < 0$$

$$B = T(Y, e) + K(i) \qquad K_i > 0$$

where Y is national income, E is private expenditure, i is interest rate, e is the exchange rate, $\bar{G}$ is government expenditure, T is the trade account, $\bar{M}$ is money supply, L is demand for money, B is the balance of payments, and K is capital flows. E_y, etc., denote partial derivatives of E with respect to Y and so forth. Endogenous variables of the system are Y, i, B, e. For a fixed-exchange-rate case, the system can be solved for Y, i, B, and for a flexible-exchange-rate case, the system can be solved for Y, i, and e.

as a flow equilibrium phenomenon rather than a stock adjustment process which goes to an equilibrium value of zero as adjustment processes are completed.

There are also disagreements about the choice of a single quantifiable proxy indicator of the overall thrust of monetary policy. Previous studies of reaction functions of monetary authorities used either levels of, or changes in, the stock of money, the monetary base, free reserves, or some interest rates. These proxy indicators, however, are subject to the criticism that they mix open and closed economy assumptions. This is because in a small open economy under a fixed exchange-rate system, the policy variable that the monetary authority can control is the domestic component of the monetary base. Neither the money supply, the monetary base, nor interest rates can be controlled by monetary policy in the long run. This is the well-known result of the monetary approach to the balance of payments.[10]

Based on the above arguments, the control part of our postulated reaction function of the monetary authority can be written as,

$$\dot{Ba} = \alpha(R^* - R), \qquad \alpha < 0, \tag{13}$$

where R^* is the desired level of foreign reserves. The exact channels through which monetary policy affects portfolio adjustment by the private sector and hence the level of foreign reserves can be heuristically described as follows. Suppose that actual reserves go below the desired level. Then the monetary authority reduces the domestic component of the monetary base (through, say, open market sales) and initially reduces the money supply.[11] This in turn raises the domestic interest rate so that the increased stock of privately available bonds is willingly held by the private sector. This higher domestic interest rate reduces the demand for money. However, it can be shown by manipulating the portfolio equilibrium conditions, (3), (4), and (5), that the reduction of the money supply exceeds the fall in the demand for money, and that the excess demand is filled by an inflow of foreign exchange reserves. Algebraically, we have,

$$\frac{dR}{dBa} = -1 - \frac{l_1}{n_1} = \frac{q_1}{n_1} < 0, \tag{14}$$

where we use the fact that $dBa + dBp = 0$ and the "adding up properties." This result derives from portfolio rearrangements by the private sector; that is, the higher domestic interest rate causes switching from foreign bonds to domestic bonds, and foreign bonds are promptly exported resulting in an inflow of reserves.

In the estimated reaction functions, we introduce some other conventional policy goal variables—inflation rate, unemployment, and real income—in addition to the desired level of foreign reserves, as follows,

$$\dot{Ba} = \alpha_1(R^* - R) + \alpha_2(\pi^* - \pi) + \alpha_3(U^* - U) + \alpha_4 \dot{y} + \alpha_5 BP, \tag{15}$$

$$\alpha_1 < 0, \alpha_2 > 0, \alpha_3 > 0, \alpha_4 > 0, -1 < \alpha_5 < 0,$$

---

[10] See J. A. Frenkel and H. G. Johnson (1976).

[11] The monetary authority may reduce Ba through reduction of loans and discounts to commercial banks, but there is no material change in the conclusion.

where π and π^* are the actual and the desired rate of inflation, U and U^* are the actual and the target level of unemployment rate, and $\dot{y}$ is the change in real income. If the monetary authority consistently sterilizes part or all of the reserve money flows, Ba has to be adjusted to take account of this operation by introducing the term, $\alpha_5 BP$.

III. EMPIRICAL RESULTS

Estimation Problems

In rewriting Eq. (15) in discrete time form, foreign reserves are entered with a one-period lag rather than contemporaneously. The reason is that without this lag the esti-mated coefficients may be dominated by the possible effect of sterilization operations (a rise in R implies a reduction of Ba) rather than the effect of reserve-level stabilization policy (increased R induces expansion of Ba). If, however, sterilization operations all occur within a quarter after an abrupt change in R, the introduction of this one-period lag will prevent the effect of the sterilization operations from dominating that of foreign reserve stabilization policies. Besides this a priori introduction of a one-period lag for R, we estimate (using Almon's polynomial distributed-lag method) lag struc-tures of the reaction function and the balance-of-payments equation in order to examine the speed of the authority's reaction to gaps between actual and desired levels of goal variables and the private sector's adjustment to portfolio disequilibrium.

One might ask whether the Japanese authority has conducted systematic steril-ization operations which imply a nonzero α_5 in Eq. (15). If they did, then ordinary least-squares estimators of the balance-of-payments and reaction-function equations may be subject to a simultaneous equations bias, since $\dot{Ba}$ and $\dot{R}$ are endogenous in Eqs. (10) and (15).[12]

It is true that there were large-scale sterilization operations in periods of furious speculative inflows of short-term capital in the second and third quarters of 1971. With the exception of these periods of speculation induced by the yen revaluation, however, the Japanese monetary authority seems not to have followed the rule of sterilization systematically, but to have let changes in foreign reserves affect directly the monetary base.[13] This conjecture is supported by negligible differences between respective estimates obtained by the ordinary least-squares and the two-stage least-squares methods.

Choice of Variables

All the data used in this analysis are seasonally unadjusted quarterly observations unless otherwise noted.

The term Ba, the domestic component of monetary base, is computed as reserve money minus foreign assets in the hands of the monetary authority. The major part of Ba has been loans and discounts of the Bank of Japan to commercial banks, rather than government securities held by the Bank of Japan.

---

[12] For a discussion of possible simultaneous equations bias see P. Kouri and M. Porter (1974).
[13] On this point see M. Michaely (1971) and M. Keran (1970).

The term R, foreign reserves, is taken from foreign assets held by the monetary authority. The term R^*, the desired level of foreign reserves, is computed as a moving average of the actual R over appropriate time spans. The use of the moving average of R as a proxy variable for R^* obviously contains restrictive assumptions. Among others, it assumes that on average the monetary authority has been successful in getting its desired level of foreign reserves. Although there is no a priori reason to choose a moving average over a particular time span, better results in terms of conventional standards such as t-ratio and R^2 were obtained by using a five-quarter moving average.

The term π, the rate of inflation, is taken from the rate of increase of the wholesale price index rather than that of the consumer price index since the Japanese monetary authority often expressed its interest in the movement of the wholesale price index. The term π^*, the target rate of inflation, is set equal to zero since, as long as π^* is constant over the period in question, a wrong choice of this parameter affects only the constant term.[14]

The unemployment rate is replaced by the index of the operation ratio of manufacturing, OR, because this is the index which seems to be considered a proxy measure of the level of economic activity by the Japanese economic policymakers. This is a production index divided by the production capacity index of manufacturing.

Quarterly data on the balance of payments, BP, published by the Bank of Japan, go back to 1961, but H. Ezekiel and C. Patal (1967) reported their estimated quarterly data for 1959 and 1960, which are used in this study.

The foreign interest rate, i^*, is approximated by the three-month U.S. Treasury bill rate.

The income variable in the balance-of-payments equation, y^*, should be the proxy for permanent income rather than current income. An eleven-quarter moving average of seasonally adjusted real GNP is used for this proxy variable.

Results of Estimations

The period covered in estimation is 1959 through 1972. The beginning period is determined by the availability of quarterly balance of payments data and the end period is determined by the breakdown of the fixed exchange-rate system. Two observations for 1971–II and 1971–III are dropped, due to large-scale sterilization operations caused by speculative capital inflows.

Results of estimation of the balance-of-payments equation are shown in Tables 1 and 2. Regression (1) is estimated by ordinary least squares and regression (2) is estimated by the Cochrane-Orcutt iterative method to take care of serial correlation of the residuals. In both equations the estimated coefficients of the domestic credit expansion terms, ΔBa, are found to be significant and have the expected negative signs, and this result is invariant with respect to different methods of estimation. This result suggests an expansion of domestic credit induced a larger deficit or a smaller

---

[14] Some readers may wonder why only R^* is generated by moving-average procedure, while π^* and U^* are assumed to be constant. There are good reasons to assume an increase in the desired level of money acceptable to the world as the size of economic activity of a country increases. Buy why should the desired rate of inflation and unemployment rise as an economy expands?

Table 1

BALANCE-OF-PAYMENTS EQUATION

Dependent Variable	Independent Variables	ΔBa	Δi^*	Δy^*	CA	C	R^2	SE	DW	ρ
(1) *BP* (1959–1972)		−.16 (−2.49)	.31 (.66)	3.26 (.85)	.70 (12.3)	−6.04 (.14)	.86	163	1.50	
(2) *BP* (1959–1972)		−.16 (−3.35)	−.56 (−1.24)	5.02 (1.68)	.80 (13.2)	−31.6 (−.73)	.91	131	1.96	.39

Notes: (1) Figures in parentheses are *t*-ratios.
(2) Regression (2) is estimated by Cochrane-Orcutt iterative method.
(3) Definitions of variables.

ΔBa –Change in domestic component of the monetary base.
Δi^* –Change in the foreign interest rate.
Δy^* –Change in permanent income.
CA –The current account.
C –Constant.

R^2 –The coefficient of determination.
SE –Standard error of regression.
DW –Durbin-Watson statistic.
ρ –Coefficient of first-order autocorrelation.
BP –The balance of payments.

LAG STRUCTURE OF THE BALANCE-OF-PAYMENTS EQUATION

Dependent Variables	Independent Variables	ΔBa	Δi^*	Δy^*	CA	C	R^2	SE	DW	ρ
(3) *BP* (1959–1972)		−.66	−.28	7.35	.73 (10.4)	−3.97 (−.05)	.92	136	1.60	.28

	t	$t-1$	$t-2$	$t-3$
Ba	−.17 (−2.11)	−.23 (−2.46)	−.19 (−2.06)	−.07 (−1.03)
i^*	−.91 (−2.05)	.66 (1.89)	.72 (1.98)	−.75 (−1.51)
y^*	6.33 (1.81)	1.43 (.52)	−.61 (−.23)	.20 (.10)

Notes: (1) Figures in parentheses are *t*-ratios.
(2) Estimates of coefficients of ΔBa, Δi^* and Δy^* are sum of lag coefficients.

surplus in the balance of payments. Estimated coefficients of changes in the foreign interest rate, Δi^*, and changes in permanent income, Δy^*, yield an ambiguous picture. One of the estimated coefficients of Δi^* is found to be negative, as expected, when serial correlation is corrected, but it is not significantly different from zero at the 5 percent level. One of the factors responsible for this result may have been the restrictions imposed by the Japanese authorities on capital flows until the end of the 1960's, and another may be our disregard of forward exchange rates. Estimated coefficients of Δy^* are found to be positive in both equations, but only one significant estimate at the 5 percent level is obtained when the serial correlation is corrected.

Lag structures of the balance-of-payments equation are also examined to analyze how soon the effects of changes in Ba, i^*, and y^* appear in the balance of payments through the stock adjustment mechanism of portfolio balance in the private sector. The results are shown as regression (3) in Table 2.

Estimates of the distributed lag coefficients of Ba are significant and have the expected negative sign up to a three-quarter lag. Estimates of lag coefficients of Δy^* indicate that its effect on the balance of payments tends to be completed within about one quarter. Estimates of lag coefficients of Δi^* were highly unstable, and no suggestive implication can be derived from those estimates.

Although results of estimation of regressions (1), (2), and (3) did not provide firm evidence on the effects of changes in permanent income and the foreign interest rate on the balance of payments, these results do indicate that there has been a stable effect of a change in domestic credit on the balance of payments despite various regulations imposed on international transactions.

Results of estimation of the reaction function are shown in Tables 3 and 4. We first estimate the function over the whole sample period, and then estimate it over two clearly different subperiods separately. The first subperiod, 1959 through 1967, was characterized by a cyclical movement of the balance of payments, with a relatively stable level of foreign reserves. The second subperiod, 1968 through 1972, was characterized by continuous surpluses in the balance of payments and hence a rapidly increasing level of foreign reserves.

Regressions (4) and (5) in Table 3 cover the whole sample period. Estimates of coefficients of the reserve level stabilization term are statistically significant. Estimated coefficients of changes in real income are found to be significantly different from zero with the expected positive sign, but estimated coefficients of all other goal variables are found to be insignificant at the 5 percent level. Regressions (6) and (7) in the table cover the earlier subperiod. Significant estimated coefficients are again found for the stabilization of the level of foreign reserves. Estimated coefficients of all other policy goal variables do not differ significantly from zero. These results suggest that at least through 1967, the Japanese monetary authority might have adhered to a single policy goal, stabilization of the level of foreign reserves.

The results in regressions (8) and (9) cover the later period and indicate a different picture from that obtained above. While estimates of the coefficients of operation ratios and rates of inflation are found to be significant, those of the stabilization term of the level of foreign reserves are insignificant. The sterilization term becomes mar-

Table 3

MONETARY AUTHORITY'S REACTION FUNCTION

Dependent Variables	Independent Variables $(R^* - R_{-1})$	π	OR	Δy	BP	D_1	D_2	D_3	C	R^2	SE	DW
(4) ΔBa (1959–1972)	−.70 (−3.43)	.07 (.02)	−.07 (−.14)	.11 (2.56)		315 (3.62)	261 (3.16)	915 (11.3)	−325 (−.67)	.79	212	2.46
(5) ΔBa (1959–1972)	−.85 (−3.85)	1.71 (.04)	.15 (.03)	.07 (1.50)	.17 (1.64)	312 (3.65)	220 (2.59)	863 (10.1)	−358 (−.77)	.80	208	2.45
(6) ΔBa (1959–1967)	−.97 (−2.70)	−11.3 (−.56)	.41 (1.48)	.02 (.62)		203 (5.43)	174 (4.82)	617 (17.3)	−600 (−2.26)	.93	75	1.67
(7) ΔBa (1959–1967)	.73 (−1.56)	−9.42 (−.46)	.32 (1.04)	.02 (.72)	.10 (−.82)	205 (5.44)	193 (4.50)	634 (15.5)	−517 (−1.81)	.93	75	1.67
(8) ΔBa (1968–1972)	−.35 (−1.37)	192 (1.78)	−3.58 (−1.85)	−.06 (−.66)		696 (3.86)	505 (3.31)	1,524 (10.3)	3,678 (1.62)	.94	217	2.01
(9) ΔBa (1968–1972)	−.11 (−.40)	303 (2.59)	−6.93 (−2.67)	−.06 (−.81)	−.37 (−1.75)	755 (4.50)	717 (3.89)	1,744 (9.49)	7,535 (2.50)	.95	198	1.98

Notes: (1) Figures in parentheses are t-ratios.
(2) Definitions of variables not defined before.
$\quad R$ - The level of foreign reserves held by the monetary authority.
$\quad R^*$ - The desired level of foreign reserves planned by the monetary authority.
$\quad \pi$ - The rate of inflation measured by percentage change of the wholesale price index.
$\quad OR$ - The operation ratio.
$\quad \Delta y$ - Change in real income.
$\quad D_1, D_2, D_3$ - Seasonal dummies.

Table 4

LAG STRUCTURES OF MONETARY AUTHORITY'S REACTION FUNCTION

Dependent Variables	$(R^* - R_{-1})$	π	OR	Δy	BP	D_1	D_2	D_3	C	R^2	SE	DW
(10) ΔBa (1959–1967)	-1.77	-27.6	.17	.03 (1.12)		194 (5.34)	167 (4.69)	623 (17.8)	-359 (-1.58)	.94	71	1.92
(11) ΔBa (1959–1967)	-1.60	-24.9	12	.03 (1.16)	-.06 (-.45)	197 (5.25)	180 (3.94)	633 (14.8)	-319 (-1.29)	.94	72	1.92
(12) ΔBa (1968–1972)	71	331	6.74	.12 (-1.36)		709 (3.18)	480 (2.69)	1,639 (10.4)	7,431 (2.07)	.95	229	3.28
(13) ΔBa (1968–1972)	30	383	-8.72	-.11 (-1.31)	-.33 (-1.66)	768 (3.79)	681 (3.39)	1,790 (10.6)	9,666 (2.78)	.97	205	2.91

Lag structure (figures in parentheses are t-ratios):

Eq.	Variable	t	$t-1$	$t-2$	$t-3$
(10)	$(R^* - R_{-1})$	-.87 (-2.75)	-.53 (-3.85)	-.27 (-1.45)	-.10 (-1.58)
	π	-10.9 (.53)	-8.27 (-.75)	-5.60 (-.49)	-2.85 (.32)
	OR	.24 (1.19)	.05 (.68)	-.06 (1.75)	.07 (-1.79)
(11)	$(R^* - R_{-1})$	-.76 (-1.83)	-.48 (-2.61)	-.26 (-1.35)	-.10 (-.61)
	π	-10.5 (-.50)	-7.48 (-.66)	-4.74 (-.41)	-2.25 (-.24)
	OR	.20 (.89)	.03 (.43)	-.06 (-1.72)	.07 (-1.57)
(12)	$(R^* - R_{-1})$	-.26 (-.69)	.21 (-.91)	-.16 (-.96)	.08 (-.85)
	π	215 (2.18)	99.3 (1.79)	24.9 (.37)	-8.14 (.15)
	OR	-6.41 (-1.53)	-2.02 (-2.20)	.51 (.25)	1.18 (.60)
(13)	$(R^* - R_{-1})$	-.04 (-.11)	-.09 (-.40)	-.10 (.67)	-.07 (-.78)
	π	276 (2.89)	115 (2.27)	15.2 (.25)	23.1 (-.47)
	OR	-7.52 (-1.97)	-2.62 (-2.92)	.27 (.15)	1.14 (.64)

Notes: (1) Figures in parentheses are t-ratios.
(3) Estimates of coefficients of $(R^* - R_{-1})$, π and OR are sum of lag coefficients.
(3) The coefficients for lagged series of $(R^* - R_{-1})$, π and OR are obtained from polynomial of second degree.

ginally significant and has the expected negative sign. These results suggest that emphasis among the alternative goals of monetary policy was switched from stabilization of the level of foreign reserves toward other internal goals.

We next turn to a study of lag structures of the reaction function. Since there might have been a shift in emphasis among several policy goals, as Table 3 indicates, lag structures are estimated for each subperiod separately. Results are shown in Table 4.

Regressions (10) and (11) cover the earlier subperiod. While lags in the stabilization of foreign reserves are found to be one to two quarters, lags in the stabilization of operation ratios are found to be longer than two quarters.

The above pattern seems to have been reversed in the later subperiod, as can be seen from regressions (12) and (13). Lags in the stabilization of operation ratios are found to be one to two quarters, but estimated lag coefficients of the stabilization of foreign reserves become statistically insignificant.

As mentioned before, the main conclusion we can derive from the previous works (in which the external goal is treated as equilibrium in the balance of payments) is at most ambiguous. Our results, however, indicate that at least through 1967 there was a systematic reaction by the monetary authority to the goal of external balance—when external balance is considered as an equality between actual and desired levels of foreign reserves, rather than as equilibrium in the balance of payments.

IV. CONCLUSIONS

This paper has stressed the stock adjustment nature of the equilibrium process of the balance of payments and the stock disequilibrium nature of monetary policy assigned to an external goal.

A balance-of-payments equation was derived from the time path of the short-run portfolio equilibrium of the private sector. A reaction function of the monetary authority was constructed in order to focus on the stock disequilibrium of the level of foreign reserves held by the monetary authority. These equations were estimated using data for the postwar Japanese economy. Basic findings are the following: First, the monetary authority seems to have adhered to stabilization of the level of foreign reserves until the late 1960's. It seems to have reduced (or increased) the domestic component of the monetary base as the actual level of foreign reserves went below (or above) the desired level. Second, expansion (or contraction) of domestic credit seems to have a strong impact on the balance of payments, as predicted by a stock adjustment model.

REFERENCES

DEWALD, W. G., and H. G. JOHNSON. "An Objective Analysis of the Objectives of American Monetary Policy, 1952–61." In D. Carson (ed.) *Banking and Monetary Studies.* Homewood, Ill.: Irwin, 1963.

EZEKIEL, H., and C. PATAL. "Fluctuations in Japan's Balance of Payments and the Role of Short-term Capital Flows: 1959–66." *IMF Staff Papers* **14** (November, 1967): 403–30.

FLEMING, J. M. "Domestic Financial Policies under Fixed and under Flexible Exchange Rates." *IMF Staff Papers* **9** (1962): 369–380.

FOLEY, D., and M. SIDRAUSKI. *Monetary and Fiscal Policy in a Growing Economy.* London: Macmillan, 1971.

FRENKEL, J. A. (1974a). "Openness and the Demand for International Reserves." In R. Z. Aliber (ed.) *National Monetary Policies and the International Financial System.* Chicago, Ill.: University of Chicago Press, 1974. pp. 289–98.

————. "The Demand for International Reserves by Developed and Less Developed Countries." *Economica* **41**, No. 161 (February, 1974b): 14–24.

FRENKEL, J. A., and H. G. JOHNSON. (eds.) *The Monetary Approach to the Balance of Payments.* London: Allen & Unwin; and Toronto: University of Toronto Press, 1976.

FROYEN, R. "A Test of the Endogeneity of Monetary Policy." *Journal of Econometrics* **2** (1974): 175–88.

HELLER, R. H. "Optimal International Reserves." *Economic Journal* **76** (June, 1966): 296–311.

HENDERSON, D., and S. TURNOVSKY. "Optimal Macro-economic Policy Adjustment under Conditions of Risk." *Journal of Economic Theory* **4**, No. 1 (February, 1972): 58–71.

JOHNSON, H. G. *International Trade and Economic Growth.* London: Allen & Unwin, 1958; and Cambridge, Mass.: Harvard University Press, 1967.

KELLY, M. G. "The Demand for International Reserves." *American Economic Review* **60**, No. 4 (September, 1970): 655–67.

KERAN, M. "Monetary Policy and the Business Cycle in Post-War Japan." In D. Meiselman (ed.) *Varieties of Monetary Experiences.* Chicago, Ill.: University of Chicago Press, 1970.

KOURI, P., and M. PORTER. "International Capital Flows and Portfolio Equilibrium." *Journal of Political Economy* **82**, No. 3 (May/June, 1974): 443–67.

MEADE, J. E. *The Theory of International Economic Policy. Vol. One: The Balance of Payments.* London: Oxford University Press, 1951.

MICHAELY, M. *The Responsiveness of Demand Policies to Balance of Payments.* New York: NBER, 1971.

MUNDELL, R. A. *International Economics.* New York: Macmillan, 1968.

MUSSA, M. *A Study in Macroeconomics.* New York: North Holland, 1976.

NIEHANS, J. "Monetary and Fiscal Policies in Open Economies under Fixed Exchange Rates: An Optimizing Approach." *Journal of Political Economy* **76**, No. 4 (July/August, 1968): 893–920.

OLIVERA, J. H. G. "The Square-Root Law of Precautionary Reserves." *Journal of Political Economy* **79** (September/October, 1971): 1095–1104.

PHILLIPS, A. W. "Stabilization Policy in a Closed Economy." *Economic Journal* **64** (June, 1954): 209–323.

REUBER, G. L. "The Objectives of Canadian Monetary Policy: 1949–61." *Journal of Political Economy* **72** (April, 1964): 109–32.

TOBIN, J. "A General Equilibrium Approach to Monetary Theory." *Journal of Money Credit and Banking* **1** (February, 1969): 15–29.

WHITMAN, M. v. N. "Policies for Internal and External Balance." *Special Papers in International Economics*, No. 9, Princeton University, 1970.

CHAPTER 11

DEVALUATION IN AN EMPIRICAL GENERAL EQUILIBRIUM MODEL

KENNETH W. CLEMENTS
University of Chicago

I. INTRODUCTION

This paper analyzes the effects of devaluation on trade flows and domestic prices. We do this by simulating a unilateral devaluation of the home country's currency within a multisector econometric model of the open economy. As a result, we are able to make statements about the actual numerical size of the effects of devaluation, rather than, say, just the sign.

At the outset, it must be emphasized that the model is very new, it has not yet been extensively analyzed, and that its properties have not been compared with those of other existing econometric models. Hence, the simulation results have to be treated with extreme caution by users wanting to make policy inferences. The simulations are probably best regarded as representing a numerical experiment with a model which empirically implements a new approach, an approach which seems to be potentially interesting and fruitful.

In Section II of the paper, we give an overview of the structure of the model and of its estimation. We discuss the effects of devaluation within the model in Section III. Section IV contains the simulation results, and some concluding comments are given in Section V. In the Appendix, the model is set out in detail, together with a description of the parameter estimates and the data base used in estimation.

This paper is based on part of the author's Ph.D. dissertation, and he would like to acknowledge the help of his thesis committee, Jacob Frenkel (Chairman), the late Harry G. Johnson, Stephen Magee, and Larry Sjaastad. The author would also like to acknowledge the generous help of Clifford Wymer, and the excellent research assistance provided by Izan Haji Yaakob. In addition, for their specific comments on a previous draft of this paper, the author thanks Jacob Frenkel and Stephen Magee. This research was supported by Lilly Honor and Morganthau Field Fellowships at the University of Chicago.

II. OVERVIEW OF THE MODEL AND ITS EMPIRICAL IMPLEMENTATION

In this section, we give a brief verbal description of the model and of its empirical implementation. Further details are given in the Appendix and in Clements (1977).

The model has its foundations in the general equilibrium models which are well-known from the pure theory of international trade (e.g., Johnson, 1971 and Jones, 1965). There are three key general equilibrium characteristics of the model. First, the economy's production point is constrained to lie on the transformation surface, the location and shape of which are determined by the economy's factor endowment and by technology. Second, the behavior of consumers satisfies the three general demand-theoretic restrictions of homogeneity of zero degree of the demand equations, symmetry of the substitution effects, and, finally, additivity–i.e., the consumption point must satisfy the budget constraint. The final general equilibrium characteristic of the model is the role of the budget constraint. As emphasized by the absorption approach to the balance of payments (Alexander, 1952), an excess of imports over exports, for example, means that, from the budget constraint, domestic expenditure exceeds income. The role of the budget constraint is, therefore, to link imports, exports, domestic expenditure, and income. This link is explicit in the model.

There are three individually distinguished commodities in the model–exportables, importables, and nontraded goods. That is, we partition the whole economy into three sectors. The output of the exportables sector is either exported or consumed domestically; exports and that part of the output of the exportables sector which is demanded domestically are taken to be perfect substitutes in production. Similarly, domestic demand for importables is satisfied by either the output of the importables sector or by imports, and commodities from the two sources of supply are taken to be perfect substitutes on the demand side. Domestic demand for the nontraded goods must, by definition, be satisfied in total by the output of the sector producing those commodities.

There are three fundamental building blocks of the model. The first is a system of demand equations which represent the domestic consumer demands for the three commodities. The specific functional form which we use here is Stone's (1954) linear expenditure system (LES), behind which lies the Klein–Rubin (1947) utility function. The reason for using LES is twofold. First, it has the advantage of simplicity: LES is relatively easy to estimate and interpret, and it is also very economical in terms of the number of parameters required to be estimated. The second reason for using LES is that it has been widely used in applied demand analysis with much success, and has proven to be a useful empirical tool (see, e.g., Brown and Deaton, 1972).[1]

We consolidate the government sector in with the private sector, so that the only other type of demand for commodities in the model, in addition to the consumer

---

[1] Although LES allows only a limited amount of substitution to take place (Powell, 1974) (and this is related to the direct additivity of the Klein–Rubin utility function), this system would tend to be more satisfactory when applied to broad commodity groups, such as in our application. This is because the substitution possibilities permitted in LES become more plausible the higher is the level of aggregation (i.e., the smaller is the number of individually distinguished commodities).

demands, is investment demand. For simplicity, all investment demands are taken as exogenous. The total domestic demand for a given commodity is the sum of the quantities demanded by consumers and investors.

The second building block of the model is a system of three domestic supply equations. This system is generated by solving a producer maximization problem: producers choose the composition of output to maximize its value subject to a transformation function. The transformation function characterizes both the technology and the factor endowment of the economy. One interpretation of this setup is as follows: the production behavior of the firms in the economy can be modeled as if they all produce some of each commodity, and the transformation function is a multiple-output production function of the representative firm. It is assumed that the transformation function is a quadratic form in the quantities produced of each commodity.[2] Diewert (1974) has extensively analyzed this functional form, and he shows that it is a flexible functional form in that it provides a second-order local approximation to an arbitrary transformation function, given some weak regularity conditions. The functional form of the supply equations is, then, determined by the form of the transformation function.

It should be noted that there is no compelling reason for using a quadratic form for the transformation function, other than that it yields tractable results, and that locally it possesses the required regularity properties. In contrast to applied demand analysis, there has been very little empirical work carried out with systems of supply equations,[3] so that it is not possible to draw on previous experience here.[4]

The final building block consists of the link between the demand and the production parts of the model. This is the income identity and the absorption equation. Nominal income is defined as the sum of the value of output, interest income on net holdings of foreign securities (the surplus on the debt service account), the increase in the domestic credit component of the monetary base, and, finally, the increase in the nominal value of wealth due to inflation. The money-supply term is included in income because it is assumed that this type of new money enters the economy via government spending.

The reason for the presence of the wealth term in the income expression is that wealth is taken to be denominated in real terms, so that its real value is invariant to changes in the price level. Hence, we include in the definition of nominal income $\hat{P}W$, where $\hat{P}$ is the percentage change in the price level, and W is nominal wealth.[5] Our

---

[2] Johnson (1965) uses a variant of this functional form in a two-sector model application.

[3] Indeed, the supply system used in this study has not been previously estimated.

[4] Some relevant applied studies are Christensen, Jorgenson, and Lau (1973), Hasenkamp(1976a, 1976b), and Powell and Gruen (1968).

[5] Including $\hat{P}W$ in income is really only an accounting convention; an alternative procedure would be to include this term directly in the wealth accumulation relationship, when expressed in nominal terms. The latter procedure, however, is in every way equivalent to including the term in income. The reason is that, as it turns out, an implication of the model is that $\hat{P}W$, if included in income, will be totally saved, and hence go indirectly into the wealth accumulation relationship. This is exactly as it should be since $\hat{P}W$ is not income available for consumption in the usual sense—it has to be totally saved in order to maintain the real value of wealth.

wealth variable consists of holdings of outside money, claims on real capital, and net holdings of foreign securities.

The absorption equation which we use states that total expenditure equals income plus a constant fraction of the gap between the actual stock of wealth and the long-run desired stock.[6] If, for example, the actual stock of wealth is less than that desired in the long run, absorption will be less than income or, in other words, saving will exceed investment, and the economy will accumulate wealth by purchasing foreign assets (securities and money), and run a current account surplus. In the long run, when desired and actual wealth are equal, income is totally spent, and the current account balance will be zero.

It should be pointed out that we have no portfolio theory and that wealth is a scalar. In turn, this means that we have no theory of the determination of the balance of either the capital or the money accounts; we model only the determination of their sum, which is the negative of the current account balance. The reason for using scalar wealth, and hence ruling out compositional effects, is one of focus: we are interested in the determination of trade flows and the current account, and not in the division between the capital and money accounts.[7]

In this model, it turns out that wealth is the buffer stock to consumption so that if, for example, income falls, then, in the short run, consumers decumulate wealth by spending more than their income in order to smooth consumption. This decumulation does not represent a position of long-run equilibrium, and it ceases once actual wealth falls to the now lower desired stock; the desired stock falls because income has fallen.[8]

Another property of our model of saving is that desired wealth and, hence, also saving in the short run are functions of relative prices.[9] This property generates a dynamic response to a parametric change in the traded goods prices and this has important implications for the effects of devaluation, which are discussed in the next section.

The trade flows in each commodity are determined as follows. We take the traded goods prices as exogenous and, given these, the nontraded goods price adjusts to equate the domestic demand for and supply of nontraded goods. The resulting equilibrium relative price of traded to nontraded goods is associated with the equilibrium excess supplies of the traded commodities. The negative excess domestic supply of importables is the quantity imported, while the positive excess supply of exportables represents exports.

---

[6] Since investment in real capital is taken to be exogenous, the absorption equation can be translated into a consumption function. This type of consumption function, only with wealth replaced by real cash balances, has been used by Dornbusch and Mussa (1975), Mundell (1968, Chapter VIII), and Prais (1961), among others, in analyzing the real balance effect. The general notion of the wealth-consumption relationship comes from Metzler (1951).

[7] For studies which do explicitly model the determination of the individual accounts of the balance of payments, see Dornbusch (1975) and Frenkel and Rodriguez (1975).

[8] Rodriguez (1976) develops an interesting related model which possesses similar dynamic properties.

[9] The effect of relative prices on saving behavior has been previously analyzed by Harberger (1950). For a summary of subsequent developments along these lines, see Johnson (1956). It is of interest to note that other more recent work in applied demand analysis also contains a similar effect: see Lluch (1973).

With this three-sector setup, the model is reasonably small, being made up of 18 simultaneous equations, 7 of which are stochastic and the remainder, identities. The model has been estimated with annual postwar U.S. data by full information maximum likelihood, and the parameter estimates are given in the Appendix. Also in the Appendix, we give some key characteristics of the data base.

III. DEVALUATION MECHANISMS

In this section, we discuss the ways in which devaluation affects trade flows and domestic prices within this framework.

In the model, devaluation is represented by an increase in the domestic price of the traded goods which is equiproportional to the devaluation. This is because we take the world prices of these goods as parametric, unaffected by the devaluation. We thus abstract from short-run deviations from the purchasing-power parity for traded goods.[10]

Devaluation has two effects in the model. First, there is an initial change in the prices of the traded goods relative to the nontraded goods, and this causes long-run desired wealth to increase. This results in a gap between actual and desired wealth, which is closed gradually by spending being less than income. From the budget constraint, this means that, in the transition period, the current account will improve by exports increasing relative to imports. Over time, actual wealth is brought into line with the desired stock, and, in full equilibrium, they are equal; here, spending again equals income, the balance of the current account is zero, and there will be no change in the trade balance.[11]

The second effect of devaluation is a transient change in both the production and consumption pattern caused by the relative price change. The rise in the relative price of traded goods induces an increase in their production and a decrease in the quantity demanded domestically, while the supply of nontraded goods falls and their demand rises. The devaluation-induced relative price change will, however, tend to be reversed over time. The mechanism by which this takes place is that the initial change in relative prices generates an excess demand for nontraded goods, and this pushes up their price. If the full equilibrium position of the economy is unique, we would expect the devaluation to have no permanent effect on relative prices. This follows from the

---

[10] For an analysis of purchasing-power parity (PPP) in the short run, see Dornbusch (1976), and for a discussion of alternative interpretations of PPP, see Frenkel (1976). Magee (1978) provides an interesting reconciliation of apparent deviations from PPP in the short run by interpreting the deviations in terms of a distinction between the actual transaction and contract prices of traded goods.

[11] Recent monetary models of devaluation (e.g., Blejer, 1975; Connolly and Taylor, 1976; Dornbusch. 1973a, 1973b, 1974; Frenkel and Rodriguez, 1975; and Johnson, 1976a, 1976b) emphasize the following mechanism by which spending is less than income over the adjustment period. Devaluation raises the domestic price level, causing real cash balances to fall. Holdings of real balances are gradually restored to their previous level by hoarding part of income, and running a trade balance surplus (in the simplest versions of these models). Such a real balance effect is not present in our model because we specify that all wealth is denominated in *real* terms.

property of the model of homogeneity of degree zero in all nominal variables. Hence, in the long run, devaluation has no real effects.[12] The reason why there are real short-run effects of devaluation, or, in other words, the reason why relative price changes at all, is that initially spending differs from income.

These two effects of devaluation might be termed an expenditure-reducing effect and an expenditure-switching effect (cf. Johnson, 1958).

IV. SIMULATION RESULTS

In this section, the estimated model is used to simulate a hypothetical devaluation of the U.S. dollar. The effects of this shock on U.S. trade and prices are isolated by comparing the new solution to the model with the control solution. The former is obtained by solving the model each period using the previous period's simulated values of the endogenous variables for this period's lagged endogenous variables, the new values of the exogenous variables associated with the hypothetical policy change, and the actual values of the remaining exogenous variables. The control solution is obtained by solving the model dynamically with the actual values of *all* the exogenous variables.

Comparing the two solutions in this way means that we are not comparing the new solution with the actually observed paths of the endogenous variables over the sample period, but with the paths predicted by the model when all the exogenous variables take their actual values. This means that we are abstracting from the simulation errors—the difference between simulated and actual values. This procedure also means that the experiment is essentially *ceteris paribus* in the following sense. Changes in the other exogenous variables of the model have a common effect on both solutions, and, hence, the difference between the two solutions solely reflects the effects of the policy change.

The devaluation is assumed to take place in 1959, and we give the new time paths of the endogenous variables of interest for the period 1959 to 1971 (the last year of the sample period). The simulation program we use is PREDIC, written by Wymer (1974).

We simulate a 10 percent unilateral devaluation by increasing the domestic prices of both exportables and importables by 10 percent for the period 1959 to 1971.[13] Also, since interest income on net holdings of foreign securities is expressed in terms of domestic currency units, we increase the debt-service surplus by 10 percent for the same period. This amounts to specifying that all domestic holdings of foreign securities are denominated in terms of foreign currency. Following this procedure means that we

---

[12] For other studies which also emphasize the role of changes in the relative price of traded to non-traded goods over the adjustment period following a devaluation, see, e.g., Blejer (1975), who analyzes these changes empirically, Dornbusch (1973a, 1974), and Mundell (1968, Chapter VIII). The homogeneity property of all the models employed in these studies results in the long-run neutrality of devaluation.

[13] That is, we take the world prices of the two traded goods as unaffected by the devaluation, so that the domestic currency prices of exportables and importables rise by exactly the percentage devaluation, as was discussed in the previous section. The price of nontraded goods is endogenous to the model.

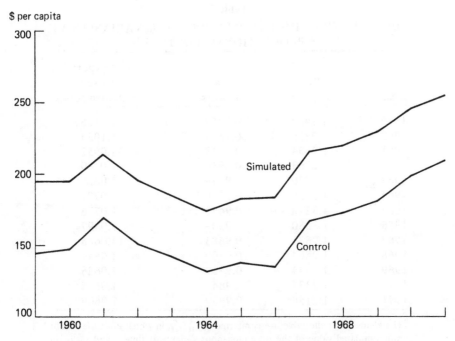

Fig. 1. Real exports: Devaluation simulated and control.

are partly abstracting from the associated capital gain on domestic holdings of foreign securities. That is, the value of foreign security holdings in terms of the domestic currency increases by the same percentage as the devaluation (if these securities are denominated in terms of foreign currency, as we assume they are).[14]

In Figs. 1 through 3, we plot the devaluation simulated and the control values of the endogenous variables of interest. Also, in Table 1, for these variables we give the simulated value as a proportion of the control value.

From Fig. 1, it can be seen that real exports[15] increase substantially during the year of the devaluation; from Table 1, real exports increase by about 35 percent in

---

[14] We do, however, take account of these capital gains to the extent that the domestic price level rises as a result of the devaluation. This is because we specify that real wealth is invariant to changes in the price level, and, as was previously discussed, in the income definition we have the term PW, the increase in the nominal value of wealth due to a rise in the price level. and included in W are holdings of foreign securities. It is unlikely that the domestic price level would rise by the full amount of the devaluation contemporaneously; it is more likely that only after some time will the price level rise by the full amount. The reason why we cannot be more specific about the behavior of P following the devaluation is that it is an endogenous variable, being (approximately) a weighted average of the domestic prices of the traded and nontraded goods (see Table A1 of the Appendix).

Hence, the error involved in using this procedure is likely to be one of timing of the capital gain on the foreign securities: our procedure shows the full capital gain some time after the devaluation.

[15] Real exports are defined as the value of exports divided by the domestic price of exportables. Similarly, real imports are computed as the value of imports deflated by the domestic price of importables.

Table 1

DEVALUATION SIMULATED ENDOGENOUS VARIABLES AS
A PROPORTION OF CONTROL[a]

Year	Real exports	Real imports	Price of exportables relative to nontraded goods
1959	1.3467	0.7357	1.1126
1960	1.3236	0.7884	1.1034
1961	1.2634	0.8613	1.0951
1962	1.2963	0.8956	1.0880
1963	1.3030	0.9174	1.0825
1964	1.3229	0.9320	1.0779
1965	1.3228	0.9472	1.0736
1966	1.3580	0.9509	1.0697
1967	1.2831	0.9683	1.0666
1968	1.2684	0.9709	1.0644
1969	1.2644	0.9759	1.0625
1970	1.2337	0.9847	1.0615
1971	1.2158	0.9979	1.0609

[a]The elements of the table are computed as y_{it}^s/y_{it}^c, in which y_{it}^s is the devaluation simulated value of the ith endogenous variable at time t, and y_{it}^c is the control solution value of that variable.

1959 as a result of the devaluation. Although there is a tendency for this increase to die out over time, the rate of decay is low, and twelve years after the devaluation, in 1971, exports are still approximately 22 percent larger than they would otherwise be. Hence, the speed of adjustment of the system as a whole is slow.

There is some tendency for the devaluation-induced percentage increase in exports to display a cyclical pattern. This probably means that the system has a complex characteristic root.

To be contrasted with exports is the behavior of real imports. From Fig. 2, imports fall somewhat as a result of the devaluation. Over time, however, they rise back to what they would have otherwise been: by 1965, six years after the devaluation, they are about 95 percent of what imports would otherwise be, while by 1971 they are approximately the same as the control value.

As can be inferred from the behavior of exports and imports, devaluation improves the trade balance and the current account. This improvement, as it turns out, is most marked in the three years following the devaluation; after that period, the devaluation still has a beneficial effect and each year's improvement in dollar terms is about the same order of magnitude.[16]

---

[16] The improvement in the trade balance, for example, for the 13 years (1959–1971) is as follows (units are current dollars per capita): 90.02, 82.25, 72.90, 64.94, 57.95, 54.08, 54.85, 59.25, 57.04, 56.52, 59.13, 60.07, 57.69.

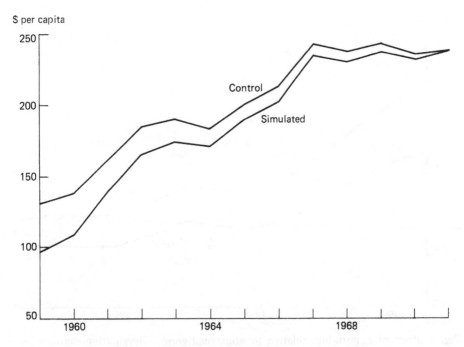

Fig. 2. Real imports: Devaluation simulated and control.

The long-run effect of devaluation on real-trade flows should be zero, as discussed above. Our simulation results do not either support or refute this prediction, since the system apparently takes longer than 13 years to reach its new steady-state position. We can, however, make the following summary statement. The beneficial effect of devaluation on trade flows does indeed fall over time, but the lags appear to be long.

The behavior of the time path of the domestic price of exportables relative to nontraded goods, plotted in Fig. 3, displays some interesting characteristics. In the year of the devaluation and the year following, there is some overshooting of this relative price: its percentage increase is more than the devaluation (see Table 1), indicating that the nontraded goods' nominal price actually falls relative to the control in the initial two years. The reason for this fall is that the expenditure-reducing effect of the devaluation, which tends to depress the price of nontraded goods, outweighs the expenditure-switching effect, which has the opposite effect on this price. It is of interest that Connolly and Taylor (1976, pp. 294–295), in their theoretical analysis of devaluation, explicitly consider this possibility. This overshooting is reversed two years after the devaluation. This relative price falls continuously following the devaluation, and twelve years later it is about 6 percent higher than otherwise. Again the speed of adjustment to long-run equilibrium which, in this case, is represented by no change in relative prices, as discussed above, seems to be slow.

In summary, the results indicate that devaluation does have substantial real effects, and that these effects tend to persist for a relatively long period. As a result, devaluation may be an attractive policy option to pursue in some circumstances. In

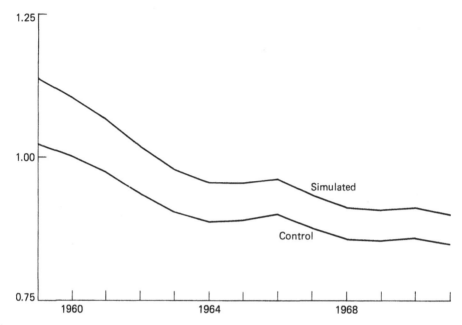

Fig. 3. Price of exportables relative to nontraded goods: Devaluation simulated and control.

evaluating the findings, however, the general qualifications relating to the newness of the model, discussed in Section I, together with the specific caveats of the next section, should be kept in mind.

V. CONCLUDING COMMENTS

In this paper, we have used a general equilibrium econometirc model to simulate the effects of devaluation on U.S. trade flows and domestic prices.

Several caveats are, however, required to preclude uncritical acceptance of the results.[17] First, the level of employment is exogenous to the model; hence, any net real-output effects of devaluation are ruled out. These effects may have some implications for trade flows in times of below normal output.

Second, the role of expectations is somewhat suppressed by the assumption of static expectations.[18] It seems clear that the real effects of exchange rate changes would tend to diminish as these changes become widely expected. For example, if the

---

[17] Some of these caveats refer to properties of the model which are not discussed in this paper; they are, however, important potential limitations. For a fuller appreciation of these points, see Clements (1977).

[18] See the papers by Bilson (1978), Hodrick (1978), and Mussa (1976) contained in this volume, for a somewhat related analysis of the role of expectations on the exchange rate.

home country has been inflating at a rate greater than the rest of the world for a considerable time, and is widely expected to continue to do so, then, in the long run, its exchange rate will depreciate at a rate equal to the inflation differential, in order to maintain purchasing-power parity. In such a situation, the continual devaluation of the exchange rate exactly offsets the rise in the nominal price of nontraded goods caused by the domestic inflation, so that relative prices do not change. Therefore, here devaluation would have no real effects.

The final caveat is that the U.S. is treated as a small open economy in this study, allowing us to take the prices of the traded goods as exogenous. Due to its large size, the U.S. may in fact, however, have some short-run monopoly power in international trade, causing the traded commodities prices to be endogenous. Hence, this may be a potential limitation of the results of this paper.[19] Although the application of the model to the U.S. may not fully satisfy the assumptions of the model, it may nevertheless be viewed as an illustrative application of a framework which is readily applicable to other countries, and this is the intended contribution of the paper.

APPENDIX

The Model, the Data Base, and Parameter Estimates

The theoretical model is nonlinear in the variables in four places: in the aggregate price index, the supply system, the income identity, and in the trade-flow expressions. To ease the computational burden associated with the estimation of this type of model, we linearize, in terms of the variables around sample means, these four parts of the model. We retain, however, all the restrictions on the parameters· there are nonlinear restrictions on the parameters within and across equations.

The linearized model is set out in Table A1. Here, we retain some generality by using an n-sector setup. We use the following notation in the table: Greek letters are used to denote parameters and Latin for variables; the subset of commodities which are traded is denoted by ψ; sample means are denoted by a bar and units are chosen such that each commodity price has a unit mean; finally, Δ is the first difference operator.

After substituting out the unobservable long-run desired wealth variable (W^*) from the system (which is the procedure used for the estimation and simulation of the model), the model is a system of $(6 + 4n)$ linear simultaneous equations. We give the $(6 + 4n)$ endogenous variables in Table A2, and the predetermined variables in Table A3.

The derivation of the model and further details are given in Clements (1977).

We estimate the model with $n = 3$ individually distinguished commodities, exportables, importables, and nontraded goods. The data base is made up of annual

---

[19] A related point is that, in addition to its overall size, the U.S. is also characterized by a large nontraded goods sector. Hence, there is a presumption that it is relatively easy to substitute against nontraded goods. This property of the U.S. may account for the observed slow speed of adjustment to devaluation, a conjecture which would be very interesting to check by estimating the same model with data from a smaller, more open economy. Research along these lines is planned.

Table A1
THE MODEL[a]

Absorption

$$A = Y + \alpha(W - W^*)$$

Long-run Desired Wealth

$$W^* = P\gamma_{n+1} + \frac{1}{\alpha}\left(Y - \sum_{i=1}^{n} p_i\gamma_i\right)$$

Consumption

$$C = A - I$$

Wealth

$$W = W_{-1} + Y - C$$

Expenditure System

$$v_i^c = p_i\gamma_i + \theta_i\left(C - \sum_{j=1}^{n} p_j\gamma_j\right) \quad i = 1, \ldots, n$$

$$\sum_{i=1}^{n} \theta_i = 1$$

Aggregate Price Index

$$P = \kappa_1 + \sum_{i=1}^{n} \theta_i p_i$$

Supply System

$$z_i = \kappa_{i+1} + [\bar{z}_i(\phi_{ii}/\phi_{i.} - \phi_{i.}/\phi_{..})]p_i + \sum_{j \neq i} [\bar{z}_i(\phi_{ij}/\phi_{i.} - \phi_{j.}/\phi_{..})]\, p_j + (\bar{z}_i/\bar{K})\, K$$

$$i = 1, \ldots, n$$

$$\Phi = \Phi', x'\Phi x > 0 \quad \text{for any} \quad x \neq 0,$$

in which

$$\phi_{i.} = \sum_{j=1}^{n} \phi_{ij},$$

$$\phi_{..} = \sum_{i=1}^{n} \phi_{i.},$$

and

$$\Phi = [\phi_{ij}]$$

Income

$$Y = \kappa_{n+2} + \sum_{i=1}^{n} (z_i + \bar{z}_i p_i) + \Delta D + DS + \bar{W}_{-1}(\Delta P) + (\Delta\bar{P})\, W_{-1}$$

Table A1 (continued)
THE MODEL[a]

Total Expenditures

$$v_i = v_i^i + v_i^c \quad i = 1, \ldots, n$$

Trade Flows

$$\kappa_{i+n+2} + z_i + \bar{z}_i p_i - v_i = \begin{cases} e_i & i \in \psi \\ 0 & i \notin \psi \end{cases}$$

Trade Balance

$$B = \sum_{i \in \psi} e_i$$

[a]See Tables A2 and A3 for meaning of notation.

Table A2
THE ENDOGENOUS VARIABLES

Variable	Description
A	Absorption
C	Consumption
W	Wealth
$v_i^c \ (i = 1, \ldots, n)$	Domestic consumption expenditure on commodity i
P	Aggregate price index
$z_i \ (i = 1, \ldots, n)$	Output of sector i
Y	Income
$v_i \ (i = 1, \ldots, n)$	Total domestic expenditure on commodity i
$e_i \ (i \in \psi)$	Value of trade flow in good i
$p_i \ (i \notin \psi)$	Price of nontraded good i
B	Trade balance

Table A3
THE PREDETERMINED VARIABLES

Variable	Description
I	Total domestic investment expenditure
W_{-1}	Lagged wealth
K	Aggregate resource endowment
ΔD	Change in domestic credit component of monetary base
DS	Debt service surplus
$v_i^i \ (i = 1, \ldots, n)$	Domestic investment expenditure on commodity i
$p_i \ (i \in \psi)$	Price of traded good i

U.S. data, expressed in per capita terms, for the period 1952–1971. A good deal of effort was devoted to constructing a data base which is both internally consistent, and consistent with the requirements of the model. The primary source for most of the data is the U.S. National Accounts.

Some key characteristics of the data base are given in Table A4. Here, exportables, importables, and nontraded goods are denoted by the subscripts 1, 2, and 3, respectively. Notice that, with this three-sector setup, nontraded goods dominate: for both investment and consumption, nontraded goods represent over one-half of the respective totals. Full details of the data are given in Clements (1977, Appendix).

The model has been estimated by full information maximum likelihood using RESIMUL, written by Wymer (1973). This program uses a Newton–Raphson search procedure to locate the maximum of the likelihood function.

To obtain the parameter estimates, the error vector of the model is assumed to be multivariate normal and to follow a first-order autoregressive process with a diagonal coefficient matrix. Transforming the model so that the new disturbances are white noise introduces a further nonlinearity in the parameters. This transformation also adds additional predetermined variables in the form of the lagged values of most of the variables contained in the untransformed model (i.e., the model as set out in Table A1). The contemporaneous disturbance covariance matrix is taken to be full (i.e., non-diagonal), allowing for correlation across equations of the error terms.

Since the supply equations are homogeneous of degree zero in the parameters ϕ_{ij}, it is not possible to identify them without a normalization.[20] The normalization rule which we use is that they sum to unity.

In obtaining the parameter estimates, the supply system parameter matrix $\Phi = [\phi_{ij}]$ was constrained to be diagonal. This was required because of the slow rate of convergence of the unconstrained parameter estimates. This means that the fitted transformation function is no longer a flexible functional form. In fact, the associated supply system is quite rigid (Clements 1977, p. 47).

In Table A5, we give the maximum likelihood parameter estimates and their asymptotic standard errors, derived from the information matrix. For all the parameters except the fourth and the last in the first column of the table, we use the subscripting convention adopted previously: exportables, importables, and nontraded goods are denoted by the subscripts 1, 2, and 3, respectively. The other notation is as follows. The parameter γ_4 corresponds to γ_{n+1} in the long-run desired wealth equation of Table A1; the ϕ_i ($i = 1, 2, 3$) are the diagonal elements of Φ, the supply system parameter matrix; ρ_1 is the first-order autoregressive parameter of the expenditure system disturbances,[21] ρ_2 is the corresponding parameter in the absorption equation, and the remaining ρ_i ($i = 3, 4, 5$) are the supply equation autocorrelation coefficients;

---

[20] More generally, identification requires non-singularity of the information matrix [Rothenberg (1971)]. Since the Newton–Raphson procedure uses the inverse of this matrix, convergence of the algorithm means that the model is identified (at least locally). Convenient analytical checks of the identification of nonlinear systems are not in general available.

[21] The reason for imposing the restriction that the autocorrelation coefficients in each equation of LES take the same value is given in Clements (1977, p. 47).

Table A4

CHARACTERISTICS OF THE DATA BASE[a]

	Absorption and investment					Consumption				Prices			
	A	v_1^i	v_2^i	v_3^i	I	v_1^c	v_2^c	v_3^c	C	p_1	p_2	p_3	P
1952	2186.47	124.11	24.63	251.54	400.28	250.14	571.80	964.25	1786.19	0.9505	0.9934	0.6992	0.7913
1961	2799.10	146.57	20.29	320.36	487.22	289.65	679.59	1342.64	2311.88	0.9804	0.9598	0.9789	0.9735
1971	5070.67	304.19	38.94	540.92	884.05	428.90	1207.91	2549.81	4186.62	1.2102	1.1938	1.3893	1.3165
Sample mean	3206.79	196.42	31.95	356.81	585.18	310.45	785.55	1525.61	2621.61	1.0000	1.0000	1.0000	0.9976

	Production				Income, change in domestic credit, debt service, wealth and factor endowment				Trade flows		
	z_1	z_2	z_3	Y	ΔD	DS	W	K	e_1	$-e_2$	B
1952	502.07	501.98	1738.81	2878.61	5.73	8.96	14696.3	0.3465	102.96	97.74	5.22
1961	581.66	604.81	1698.80	3009.36	4.35	15.96	19889.9	0.3098	134.02	119.40	14.62
1971	831.76	799.24	2224.71	6516.82	43.00	22.72	32418.0	0.3438	273.53	292.73	−19.20
Sample mean	655.95	659.54	1849.81	3834.21	13.32	15.63	21250.5	0.3307	157.79	153.69	4.10

[a]See Tables A2 and A3 for meaning of notation. Data sources are given in Clements (1977, Appendix). The subscript 1 refers to exportables, 2 to importables, and 3 to nontraded goods. All variables (except prices) are expressed in per capita terms and the units of all values are current dollars per capita.

Table A5

MAXIMUM LIKELIHOOD PARAMETER ESTIMATES[a]

Parameter	Estimate	Parameter	Estimate
γ_1^b	289.15 (15.02)	ρ_2	1.01118 (0.00531)
γ_2^b	697.88 (65.02)	ρ_3	0.98301 (0.03989)
γ_3^b	1271.47 (122.80)	ρ_4	0.94912 (0.03480)
γ_4^b	31463.51 (1767.31)	ρ_5	0.76243 (0.10648)
θ_1	0.06591 (0.01037)	κ_1	-18.56 (5.84)
θ_2	0.29778 (0.02024)	κ_2	-40.82 (7.94)
θ_3	0.63631 (0.02152)	κ_3	143.74 (51.33)
α	0.50746 (0.10396)	κ_4	-12.45
ϕ_1	0.06598 (0.10657)	κ_5	0.00243
ϕ_2	0.53186 (0.09667)	κ_6	3668.47
ϕ_3	0.40216 (0.04724)	κ_7	1817.21
ρ_1	0.78696 (0.04505)	—	—

[a] Asymptotic standard errors in parentheses. See text for meaning of notation.
[b] Units of the γ's are dollars per capita at sample mean prices.

finally, the κ_i $(i = 1, \ldots, 7)$ are the constant terms in the three supply equations, the wealth equation, the aggregate price index expression, the income equation, and the nontraded goods market clearing requirement, respectively.[22] The constant terms in the "identities," the κ_i $(i = 4, \ldots, 7)$, are set at values such that the residuals of each have a zero mean,[23] and this is the reason they have no standard errors.

For a discussion of the parameter estimates, see Clements (1977, Ch. III).

REFERENCES

ALEXANDER, SIDNEY S. "The Effects of a Devaluation on a Trade Balance." IMF *Staff Papers* 2 (April, 1952): 263–278.

BILSON, JOHN F. O. "Rational Expectations and the Exchange Rate." 1978. Reproduced as Chapter 5 of this volume.

BLEJER, MARIO I. "Money, Prices and the Balance of Payments–The Case of Mexico 1950–1973." Ph.D. dissertation, Department of Economics, University of Chicago, 1975.

BROWN, ALAN, and ANGUS DEATON. "Surveys in Applied Economics: Models of Consumer Behavior." *Economic Journal* 82 (September, 1972): 1145–1236.

CHRISTENSEN, LAURITS R., DALE W. JORGENSON, and LAWRENCE J. LAU. "Transcendental Logarithmic Production Frontiers." *Review of Economics and Statistics* 55 (1973): 28–45.

CLEMENTS, KENNETH W. "The Trade Balance in Monetary General Equilibrium." Ph.D. dissertation, Department of Economics, University of Chicago, June 1977.

CONNOLLY, MICHAEL, and DEAN TAYLOR. "Adjustment to Devaluation with Money and Nontraded Goods." *Journal of International Economics* 6 (1976): 289–298.

DIEWERT, W. E. "Functional Forms for Revenue and Factor Requirements Functions." *International Economic Review* 15, No. 1 (February, 1974): 119–130.

DORNBUSCH, RUDIGER. "Currency Depreciation, Hoarding, and Relative Prices." *Journal of Political Economy* 81, No. 4 (July/August, 1973a): 893–915.

———. "Devaluation, Money, and Non-traded Goods." *American Economic Review* 63 (December, 1973b): 871–883.

———. "Real and Monetary Aspects of the Effects of Exchange Rate Changes." In R. Z. Aliber (ed.), *National Monetary Policies and the International Financial System*. Chicago: University of Chicago Press, 1974, pp. 64–81.

———. "A Portfolio Balance Model of the Open Economy." *Journal of Monetary Economics* 1 (January, 1975): 3–20.

---

[22] Note that our subscripting convention here for the κ's departs from that used in Table A1. We have also added a constant term to the wealth "identity" because it is only an approximation when the model is estimated with data deflated by population (Clements 1977, p. 44).

Observe that estimates of the constants for the exports and imports equations are not given in Table A5. The reason is that these two equations can be dropped in estimation since these serve only to define two variables (the value of exports and the value of imports) which appear nowhere else in the system, i.e., the model is recursive in these two variables. In the simulation, estimates of these constants are not required because we use the true nonlinear excess supply relations to generate exports and imports; for simulating the other endogenous variables, we use the linearized model, as set out in Table A1.

[23] These "identities" have residuals merely because of the linearization.

————. "The Theory of Flexible Exchange Rate Regimes and Macroeconomic Policy." *Scandinavian Journal of Economics* **78**, No. 2 (1976): 225–275. Reprinted as Chapter 2 of this volume.

DORNBUSCH, RUDIGER, and MICHAEL MUSSA. "Consumption, Real Balances and the Hoarding Function." *International Economic Review* **16**, No. 2 (June, 1975): 415–421.

FRENKEL, JACOB A. "A Monetary Approach to the Exchange Rate: Doctrinal Aspects and Empirical Evidence." *Scandinavian Journal of Economics* **78**, No. 2 (1976): 200–224. Reprinted as Chapter 1 of this volume.

FRENKEL, JACOB A., and CARLOS A. RODRIGUEZ. "Portfolio Equilibrium and the Balance of Payments: A Monetary Approach." *American Economic Review* **65**, No. 4 (September, 1975): 674–688.

HARBERGER, A. C. "Currency Depreciation, Income, and the Balance of Trade." *Journal of Political Economy* **58**, No. 1 (February, 1950): 47–60.

HASENKAMP, GEORG. *Specification and Estimation of Multiple-Output Production Functions.* New York: Springer-Verlag, 1976a.

————. "A Study of Multiple-Output Production Functions: Klein's Railroad Study Revisited." *Journal of Econometrics* **4**, No. 3 (August, 1976b): 253–262.

HODRICK, ROBERT J. "An Empirical Analysis of the Monetary Approach to the Determination of the Exchange Rate." 1978. Reproduced as Chapter 6 of this volume.

JOHNSON, HARRY G. "The Transfer Problem and Exchange Stability." *Journal of Political Economy* **64**, No. 3 (June, 1956): 212–225.

————. "Towards a General Theory of the Balance of Payments." In *International Trade and Economic Growth.* London: Allen and Unwin, 1958, pp. 153–168.

————. "The Costs of Protection and Self-Sufficiency." *Quarterly Journal of Economics* **72**, No. 3 (August, 1965): 356–372.

————. *The Two-Sector Model of General Equilibrium.* Chicago: Aldine Atherton, 1971.

————. "The Monetary Theory of Balance of Payments Policies." In Jacob A. Frenkel and Harry G. Johnson (eds.), *The Monetary Approach to the Balance of Payments.* Toronto: University of Toronto Press, 1976a, pp. 262–284.

————. "Elasticity, Absorption, Keynesian Multiplier, Keynesian Policy, and Monetary Approaches to Devaluation Theory: A Simple Geometric Exposition." *American Economic Review* **66**, No. 3 (June, 1976b): 448–452.

JONES, R. W. "The Structure of Simple General Equilibrium Models." *Journal of Political Economy* **73** (December, 1965): 557–572.

KLEIN, L. R., and H. RUBIN. "A Constant Utility Index of the Cost of Living." *Review of Economic Studies* **15**, No. 2 (1947–1948): 84–87.

LLUCH, CONSTANTINO. "The Extended Linear Expenditure System." *European Economic Review* **4**, No. 1 (April, 1973): 21–32.

MAGEE, STEPHEN P. "Contracting and Spurious Deviations from Purchasing-Power Parity." 1978. Reproduced as Chapter 4 of this volume.

METZLER, LLOYD A. "Wealth, Saving, and the Rate of Interest." *Journal of Political Economy* **59** (April, 1951): 93–116.

MUNDELL, ROBERT A. *International Economics.* New York: Macmillan, 1968.

MUSSA, MICHAEL. "The Exchange Rate, The Balance of Payments and Monetary and Fiscal Policy under a Regime of Controlled Floating." *Scandinavian Journal of Economics* **78**, No. 2 (1976): 229–248. Reprinted as Chapter 3 of this volume.

POWELL, ALAN A. *Empirical Analytics of Demand Systems.* Lexington, Mass.: D. C. Heath, 1974.

POWELL, ALAN A., and F. H. G. GRUEN. "The Constant Elasticity of Transformation Production Frontier and Linear Supply Systems." *International Economic Review* 9, No. 3 (October, 1968): 315–328.

PRAIS, S. J. "Some Mathematical Notes on the Quantity Theory of Money in an Open Economy." IMF *Staff Papers* 8, No. 2 (May, 1961): 212–226.

RODRIGUEZ, CARLOS A. "The Terms of Trade and the Balance of Payments in the Short Run." *American Economic Review* 66, No. 4 (September, 1976): 710–716.

ROTHENBERG, THOMAS J. "Identification in Parametric Models." *Econometrica* 39 (May, 1971): 577–592.

STONE, RICHARD. "Linear Expenditure Systems and Demand Analysis: An Application to the Pattern of British Demand." *Economic Journal* 64, No. 255 (September, 1954): 511–527.

WYMER, C. R. "Computer Programs: RESIMUL Manual." London School of Economics, July 1973. (Mimeographed.)

————. "Computer Programs: PREDIC Manual." London School of Economics, May 1974. (Mimeographed.)

AUTHOR INDEX

AUTHOR INDEX

Alexander, S. S., 194, 209
Aliber, R. Z., 11, 17n, 22, 67n, 74, 75n, 85n, 94, 102, 114, 129n, 132, 156, 161n, 177, 179n
Allen, W., 44n, 45
Almon, S., 185
Angell, J. W., 3, 22
Argy, V., 27, 45

Balassa, B., 20, 22
Banz, R. W., 1n
Barro, R. J., 75n, 76, 76n, 81n, 82, 94
Bilson, J. F. O., x, 1n, 8, 22, 68n, 74, 75-96, 75n, 85n, 94, 94n, 98n, 99n, 107n, 116, 117n, 121n, 127, 130n, 133n, 148n, 157, 163n, 166n, 177, 202n, 209
Black, S. W., 8, 22, 27, 27n, 31n, 45, 58n, 64
Blejer, M. I., x-xi, 94, 117-128, 118n, 120n, 127, 197n, 198n, 209
Boulding, K. E., 117, 127
Box, G. E. P., 99n, 105n, 106n, 114, 133n, 157, 177
Branson, W. H., 1n, 85n, 94
Bresciani-Turroni, C., 3-4, 8n, 22
Britton, A. J. C., 44n, 45
Bronfenbrenner, M., 117, 127
Brown, A., 194, 209
Bunting, F. H., 3, 22

Cagan, P., 11, 22, 99, 101n, 114
Calvo, G. A., 93n, 94

Cannan, E., 5, 22
Carr, J., 84n, 94
Cassel, G., 3, 4, 6, 22-23, 115
Caves, R. E., 51n, 64
Chow, G. C., 101n, 115
Christensen, L. R., 195n, 209
Clark, P. B., 84n, 94
Clements, K. W., xi-xii, 1n, 67n, 193-211, 194, 202n, 203, 206, 206n, 207n, 209, 209n
Collery, A., 29n, 45, 98n, 115
Connolly, M., 197n, 201, 209
Corden, M., 30n, 45
Culbertson, W. P., Jr., 117, 127

Deaton, A., 194, 209
Dewald, W. G., 179n, 191
Diewert, W. E., 195, 209
Dornbusch, R., viii-ix, x, 1n, 2n, 5, 8, 11, 23, 27-46, 30n, 31n, 45, 47n, 58n, 64, 67n, 74, 75n, 79n, 94, 97n, 98n, 105n, 115, 117n, 121n, 128, 129n, 130n, 157, 160n, 177, 179n, 196n, 197n, 198n, 209-210
Dufey, G., 68, 74
Dusak, K., 163n, 177

Einzig, P., 4, 5, 22, 23, 117, 128
Ellis, H. S., 3, 23
Ethier, W. E., 84n, 95
Ezekiel, H., 186, 191

216

Fama, E. F., 75n, 95, 129, 129n, 153, 157
Fischer, S., 1n, 27n
Fishelson, G., 118n, 128
Fisher, I., 131, 131n, 133n, 157
Fisher, L., 153, 157
Fleming, J. M., 27, 41n, 45, 179n, 192
Foley, D., 181n, 192
Frenkel, J. A., viii, x, 1–25, 2n, 11, 14n, 19n, 23, 27n, 32n, 45, 47n, 64, 67n, 68n, 74, 75n, 79n, 85n, 94n, 95, 97n, 98, 98n, 99n, 103, 115, 117n, 121n, 128, 129n, 130n, 133n, 138n, 142n, 157, 159n, 160n, 165n, 177, 179n, 180n, 183n, 184n, 192, 193n, 196n, 197n, 210
Friedman, M., 4, 23, 99, 101, 115
Froyen, R., 179n, 192

Giddy, I., 68, 74
Girton, L., 93n, 95
Glassman, J. E., 99n, 114
Goldberger, A. S., 91n, 96
Goldfeld, S. M., 89, 89n, 95, 101n, 115
Gordon, R. J., 1n
Goschen, G. J., 23, 130, 157
Graham, F., 4, 8n, 22, 23
Gregory, T. E., 2, 5, 23
Grossman, S. J., 151, 157
Grubel, H. G., 155n, 157
Gruen, F. H. G., 195n, 211

Haache, G., 101n, 115
Haberler, G., 2, 3, 15, 23
Hansen, A. H., 4, 24
Harberger, A. C., 196n, 210
Hasenkamp, G., 195n, 210
Haugh, L. D., 106n, 115
Hawtrey, R. G., 3, 4, 24
Heckscher, E. F., 3, 24
Hekman, C. R., 20, 24
Heller, R. H., 180n, 183n, 192
Henderson, D., 183n, 192
Hodgson, J. S., 8n, 24, 95
Hodrick, R. J., x, 75n, 94n, 95, 97–116, 98n, 105n, 117n, 128, 130n, 133n, 157, 163n, 177, 202n, 210
Houthakker, H. S., 4, 24

Isard, P., 98n, 115

Jaffee, D., 27n
Jenkins, G. M., 99n, 105n, 114, 133n, 157, 177
Jensen, M. C., 153, 157
Johnson, H. G., xii, 1n, 2n, 3n, 6n, 24, 31n, 45, 47n, 64, 75n, 97n, 115, 119n, 128, 179n, 180n, 184n, 191, 192, 193n, 194, 195n, 196n, 197n, 210
Jones, R. W., 51n, 64, 194, 210
Jorgenson, D. W., 195n, 209

Karplus, R., 159n
Kelly, M. G., 183n, 192
Kemp, D. S., 47n, 64
Keran, M., 185n, 192
Keynes, J. M., 1, 3n, 5, 15, 24
Kindahl, J. K., 68, 74
Klein, L. R., 194, 194n, 210
Kohlhagen, S. W., 129n, 133n, 157
Kouri, P. J. K., 2n, 24, 58n, 64, 117n, 128, 161n, 177, 182n, 185n, 192
Kravis, I. B., 68n, 74

Laffer, A., 129n
Laidler, D., 101n, 116
Lau, L. J., 195n, 209
Laursen, S., 31n, 45
Levich, R. M., xi, 11, 32n, 45, 68n, 74, 75n, 85n, 95, 103, 107n, 115, 116, 129–158, 129n, 130n, 133n, 138n, 142n, 148, 148n, 153, 157, 158, 165n, 166n, 168n, 177
Lipsey, R. E., 68n, 74
Lluch, C., 196n, 210
Lucas, R. E., 57n, 63, 64–65, 76, 76n, 81n, 95
Lursen, K., 24

Magee, S., x, 32n, 45, 67–74, 71, 74, 75n, 95, 98n, 116, 159n, 163n, 177, 179n, 193n, 197n, 210
Marshall, A., 3n, 5, 24
McCulloch, J. H., 160n, 166n, 177
Meade, J. E., 179, 179n, 183, 192
Metzler, L. A., 2n, 24, 196n, 210
Michaely, M., 117, 128, 185n, 192

Mill, J. S., 5, 24
Miller, M., 44n, 45
Miller, M. H., 159n
Minford, P., 44n, 45
Montmarquette, C., 167n, 178
Moses, R., 142, 158
Mundell, R. A., 2n, 24, 27, 39, 46, 54,
   65, 119n, 128, 179, 179n, 180n, 183,
   192, 196n, 198n, 210
Mussa, M. L., ix–x, 2n, 24, 31, 46, 47–
   65, 47n, 58n, 59n, 62, 65, 75n, 95, 97n,
   116, 117n, 128, 158, 160, 160n, 174,
   178, 181n, 192, 196n, 202n, 210
Muth, J., 13
Myhrman, J., 2n, 24

Nelson, C. R., 129n, 133n, 135n, 150n,
   158, 160
Niehans, J., 27, 46, 180n, 192

Officer, L. H., 85n, 95
Ohlin, B., 3, 24
Olivera, J. H. G., 180n, 192

Palm, F., 113, 116
Parkin, M., 1n
Patal, C., 186, 191
Patinkin, D., 1n
Pearce, I. F., 51n, 65
Pedersen, J., 24
Phelps, P., 95
Phillips, A. W., 183, 192
Pick, F., 125, 128
Pierce, D., 106n, 114
Pigou, A. C., 3, 25
Plosser, C., 100n, 116
Polak, J. J., 31n, 46
Porter, M., 27, 45, 182n, 185n, 192
Powell, A. A., 194n, 195n, 211
Prais, S. J., 196n, 211

Reuber, G. L., 179n, 192
Ricardo, D., 2, 5, 25, 130, 158
Ringer, F. K., 25
Robinson, J., 5, 25, 31, 46
Rockafellar, R. T., 176, 178
Rodriguez, C., 2n, 23, 93n, 94, 97n, 115,
   196n, 197n, 210, 211

Roll, R., 153, 157
Roper, D., 93n, 95, 160n, 178
Rose, D. E., 167n, 176, 178
Rothenberg, T. J., 206n, 207n, 211
Rubin, H., 194, 194n, 210
Rueff, J., 4, 25

Samuelson, P. A., 3, 15, 25
Sargent, T. J., 13n, 25, 57n, 58n, 59n,
   65, 75n, 76, 76n, 95
Scholes, M., 129n, 159n
Schwartz, A., 4, 23, 101n, 114
Schwert, W., 99n
Sheen, J., 41n, 46
Sheikh, M. A., 117, 128
Shiller, R., 58n, 65
Sidrauski, M., 181n, 192
Siegel, J., 160n, 178
Sjaastad, L. S., 193n
Smith, L. B., 84n, 94
Solnik, B. H., 132n, 158
Stevens, G., 91n, 96
Stigler, G. J., 68, 74
Stiglitz, J. E., 151, 157
Stockman, A. C., xi, 68n, 74, 78n, 96,
   107n, 116, 121n, 128, 132n, 151n, 158,
   159–178, 161n, 178, 179n
Stoll, H., 102, 116
Stone, R., 194, 211
Swoboda, A. K., 41n, 46

Taussig, F. W., 25
Taylor, D., 197n, 201, 209
Telser, L. G., 1n
Theil, H., 86–87, 87n, 91n, 96, 110n, 116
Tinbergen, J., 15n, 25, 179, 183
Tobin, J., 181n, 182n, 192
Tsiang, S. C., 8n, 25, 131n, 158
Turnovsky, S., 183n, 192

Ujiie, J., xi–xii, 107n, 116, 123n, 179–192

Vargo, F., 67n
Viner, J., 2, 3, 3n, 25

Wallace, N., 13n, 25, 57n, 58n, 59n, 65,
   75n, 76, 76n, 95
Walras, L., 130, 158

Weinig, D., 67n
Westerfield, J. M., 140, 158, 160
Wets, R. J. B., 176, 178
Wheatley, J., 5, 25
Whitman, M. v. N., 75n, 96, 179n, 192
Wicksell, K., 2, 5, 25
Wonnacott, P., 39, 46
Working, H., 132n, 158
Wymer, C., 193n, 198, 206, 211

Yaakob, I. H., 193n

Zellner, A., 97n, 113, 116, 159n, 167n,
   178